the Sopranos

ON THE COUCH

the Sopranos
ON THE COUCH

ANALYZING TELEVISION'S
GREATEST SERIES

Maurice Yacowar

CONTINUUM · NEW YORK · LONDON

2002

The Continuum International Publishing Group Inc
370 Lexington Avenue, New York, NY 10017

The Continuum International Publishing Group Ltd
The Tower Building, 11 York Road, London SE1 7NX

www.continuumbooks.com

Printed in the United States of America

Library of Congress Cataloging-in-Publication Data

Yacowar, Maurice.
  The Sopranos on the couch : analyzing television's greatest series /
Maurice Yacowar.
      p. cm.
Includes bibliographical references and index.
  ISBN 0-8264-1410-9 — ISBN 0-8264-1401-X (pbk.)
  1. Sopranos (Television program) I. Title.
  PN1992.77.S66 Y33 2002
  791.45'72—dc21
                                                    2002000374

To my wife Anne,

with love and thanks

Contents

"This fantasy of yours has meaning."

(Dr. Jennifer Melfi, I, 12)

Introduction

THE PHENOMENON

The Sopranos rules. In fact, it could be the best TV series ever made.

The show certainly captured a large, avid, and discriminating audience—which must be one criterion. In American pop culture the series was probably the most addictive program since cinemas had to turn on the *Amos 'n' Andy* radio show to lure people to the flicks. Quickly the HBO series attracted 3.7 million viewers on Sunday nights, 10 million in its four weekly airings; that topped the cable audience ratings. Its Season Two opener scored the highest cable show rating in history—without the *Dallas* dangle of a major murder mystery from the previous season's end. That the HBO audience of 25 million is only a quarter of the network's audience makes the show's numbers and influence even more remarkable.

The Sunday telecast killed the restaurant business in some areas, as families preferred to stay in for the latest episode. Some ingenious restaurants—of the "If you can't lick 'em . . ." persuasion—offered a late special for appetites whetted by the Sopranos' cholestera-rollicking dinners.

You can see the difference between the first two seasons' preview parties. Season One premiered downstairs at the Virgin megastore on Broadway, with a party afterward at John's Pizzeria on West 44th. For the Season Two premiere at the Ziegfeld and the party afterward at Roseland, 1,000 were expected but 1,800 showed up. HBO had to bus the overflow to its headquarters (Stephen Holden, pp. 170, 167). The phenomenon was secure.

In Canada, we heard about the series long before we had the chance to see it. In a brilliant coup, the private CTV network ran a nightly marathon of Season One *Sopranos* against the public CBC coverage of the Olympics. (For such relief, much thanks.) The nation thus hooked, seasons two and three followed on a cable movie channel, drawing closer to the American telecast, and were repeated on CTV.

For its "mesmerizing television," the show won the Peabody Award each of its first two years. Otherwise, the industry awards were surprisingly slow. Its first season netted 16 Emmy nominations—but only two won:

Edie Falco for best lead actress and David Chase and James Manos Jr. for best dramatic script, for "College," I, 5. (By my code here, that means Season I, episode 5. *Kapeesh?*) As Ralph Blumenthal suggested in the *New York Times*, "Maybe the Emmy voters never heard what happens to people who rob the mob"—or was it "the networks' reluctance to accept cable television channels as full industry partners?" (Holden, pp. 142, 145)

The 1999 Golden Globes were more just, with awards to Falco, James Gandolfini, and Nancy Marchand, along with Best Drama Series. Gandolfini was nominated for an Emmy the first two years and won Best Actor the second, when he was the show's only winner from its 18 Emmy nominations. In its first season the show swept the Screen Actors Guild for Best Drama Ensemble performance and for leads Gandolfini and Falco, the Directors Guild Best Director award for David Chase's pilot, the Writers Guild Award for "Meadowlands," the Producers Guild Award (David Chase, Episodic TV Producer of the Year), and the TV Critics Association awards for outstanding drama, new program, and individual achievement (which Gandolfini repeated the next year). The second season won the International Radio and Television Society Foundation Award, the Banff Rockies Award, the Chicago International Television Competition, and the CIBE Golden Eagle Award (for the season opener).

The verdict on its 22 Emmy nominations in 2001 was postponed twice by the September 11 terrorist attack and the US-led military response against the terrorists in Afghanistan. When the showbiz smoke had cleared, *The Sopranos* had won the top acting awards (Gandolfini and Falco) and a writing award (for III, 4: "Employee of the Month"). It lost the Best Drama and best supporting actors' awards to *The West Wing*. The show's importance in the national psyche is suggested in one of the very first jokes made about that tragic event. An Internet site posted a Soprano gang photo with the caption: "Just tell us where bin Laden is and fuhgedaboudit."

The myriad fan-sites on the net prove *The Sopranos* quickly grew from program into cult. Each new episode fired watercooler conversations for the next week. The argot crept into conversational usage. "Whacked" came to mean something other than what you did to your carpets—or what doing that made you feel. Newspapers and magazines chronicled its addicts' fidelity and fervor.

The Internet flogged a cornucopia of *Sopranos* merchandise, from Satriale's Pork Shop and Beansie's Pizza T-shirts to the classic elegance of the Bada Bing Babe ashtray, shot glass, beer stein, tumbler, and enough different coffee cups to give new meaning to the term "mug's game." Even after Big Pussy Bonpensiero was ... whacked, actor Vincent Pastore "helped to develop" a cigar, hand-rolled in Dominica, for Don Diego. It zipped to the cover of *Cigar Afficianado*. You could harvest eBay for memorabilia—or relics?—of almost any actor/character on the show. Dominic Chianese (Uncle Junior) released a CD ambiguously titled *Hits*. CareerBuilder invited you to search for "jobs related to *The Sopranos*." But alas, they seemed legit, more like (lower case) family counseling than Tony's "waste management."

The actors became household faces and their characters household names. Paulie "Walnuts" Galtieri (Tony Sirico) feels like everyone's favorite business "uncle," not just Meadow's and AJ's. Sirico remained a lovable eccentric spirit even after *Harper's* magazine ("Method Acting," June 2001, pp. 22–25) quoted from the transcript of his real-life trial for gangsterism in 1971. He allegedly threatened a New York club owner for seeking police protection: "I have an arsenal of weapons and an army of men, and I'm going to use them, and after I take care of those guys I'm going to come back here and carve my initials on your forehead." The transcript was posted on *www.thesmokinggun.com*. Nonetheless, Sirico became a popular regular on *Hollywood Squares*.

The confusion between art and life continued when 16-year-old Robert Iler (Anthony Jr.) was arrested with two teenage friends and charged with robbing two other teenagers of $45 on Manhattan's Upper East Side. Pleading guilty to misdemeanor-petty larceny, Iler was sentenced to three years' probation. He reportedly swore at the arresting officer and bragged "Don't you worry about me—I'm a millionaire" (*New York Times*, August 30, 2001).

When London's *Independent* reported the Philadelphia trial of Joseph "Skinny Joey" Merlino, it reached to *The Sopranos* for its context—" 'Soprano' snitch brings down Mob," blared the headline (July 22, 2001)—and its credibility. The 50 witnesses reportedly told stories that "would have given years of material to scriptwriters of *The Sopranos*." Tony Soprano provided a realistic allusion—and the diction—in a Salman Rushdie short story in *The New Yorker*: "The gangster Tony Soprano might be going to a shrink, but fuck him, he was fictional" ("Summer of Solanka," July 16, 2001, pp. 66–75). We know a fiction has permeated the collective mind when it provides the reality base for another fiction.

The show was popular enough to become a public target. It was accused of defaming the Italian-American community by portraying them as gangsters. The American Italian Defense Association—*AIDA v. Sopranos* instead of by them?—sued the program's distributor, Time Warner Entertainment, under the Illinois Constitution's dignity clause, which condemns inciting hostility toward "persons by . . . reference to religious, racial, ethnic, national or religious affiliation." On September 19, 2001, Cook County Judge Richard A. Seibel delivered his 11-page judgment that "The aria may be offensive to Verdi, but the Sopranos have the constitutional right to sing." Does *The Sopranos* perpetuate the Italian-American stereotype as "greedy mobsters lacking virtue," as AIDA claimed? Stay tuned.

THE QUALITY

All that is popularity. What's so *good* about *The Sopranos*?

For openers: it's brilliantly written, performed, and filmed. Each episode has the polish of an excellent feature film—with a tighter yet more complex, resonant script than most. For example, in the Italian wedding that opens I, 8, the detail and variety of character and activity is what we expect of a big-budget film, not a weekly TV show. The image is even more impressive when viewed—as in DVD—in the widescreen format in which it was filmed, instead of the one shrunk to the TV screen's proportions.

Yet the first season episodes were budgeted at only around two million dollars each, with an eight-day shooting schedule. (True, the pilot was shot in sixteen.) In every episode the polish exceeds the budget and the conditions. Remarkably, these one hour films were produced on the schedule of the normal 42-minute drama that makes up a one hour program on commercial TV. As director Tim Van Patten points out (Season II DVD, disc one) "This show is like making a feature in nine to twelve days"—and 13 of them in a row!

The show is also relentlessly entertaining. The characters are engrossing, the plot twists astonishing but coherent, and the dialogue mined with ironies and poetic resonance quite beyond what we are used to hearing on the boob tube or even on the commercial cinema screen these days.

Unique for a television series, details connect not just across the hour but across a season and beyond. Creator David Chase calls this the show's "connective tissue" in his commentary on the Season One DVD (disc four): the phrases, devices and themes that flesh out the plot skeleton. That complexity requires—and rewards—"active viewing" (disc one). The viewer has to dig for links and meanings beyond what's spelled out on the surface and is often left with mysteries. That makes this show more like European cinema than American cinema—and a complete departure for

American television. At the same time, *The Sopranos* provocatively raises major questions about how and why we live.

The show also emulates European cinema in its narrative pace. Though each hour contains an astonishing range of incident and theme, it feels slow. It pauses for the long silences that realistically represent a marital scene or (other?) therapy session but it can erupt into frenzy. The show is this flexible because it is not scripted for commercial breaks. Its structure serves its material, without the false climaxes that hook us for the sponsors.

The show uses the television medium brilliantly. TV's essential strength lies in its domestic immediacy. That could also be its weakness, as we may pay it the attention we give our wallpaper. But watching a family saga in our own living/rec room can be intensely involving. As shows like *Coronation Street* have proved, viewers tend to "adopt" their continuing TV family as a virtual extension of their own. That is what makes the soap opera—and such relatives as game shows and TV wrestling—the most characteristic television genre. The "family" connection feeds on the medium's domestic register.

Hence the sitcom based on a continuing though loosely related "family": *I Love Lucy* begat *The Dick Van Dyke Show* who begat *The Mary Tyler Moore Show* who begat *Bob Newhart* who begat *Seinfeld* who begat *Ally McBeal* who. . . . TV seems to bring one virtual family, whether real, *Friends*ly or workplace, to another, as a marriage extends families by connecting them. The Soprano family/Family life fits this aspect perfectly.

As well, the rich dialogue, with its heavily flavored accent—salty and spicy both—exploits the fact that—even with its larger screens and better visual definition—television remains a primarily aural medium. We *hear* more of a television show than we *watch*, as we read the paper, knit, or count our bags of money in the comfort of our own home while "watching" TV. More often with this series, however, the performances, camerawork, and Bada Bing dancers compel us to watch.

The serial format enables viewers to get to know a show's characters much more fully—and with deeper emotional engagement—than a one-shot drama or even a mini-series allows. When characters this colorful are developed into such complex beings, then a television show provides a slice of life as textured, nuanced, and involving as—a Charles Dickens novel. Remember: Dickens published his massive sagas in periodic installments, too, just like our weekly television series. The *Sopranos*'s 13-episode season allows for plausible inconsistencies and psychological twists that a shorter drama has no time for and that the sitcom's need for reassuring familiarity precludes.

Reviewing the first season in the *New York Times*, Vincent Canby wisely proposed *The Sopranos* be considered a "megamovie," in the tradition of Rainer Werner Fassbinder's fifteen-and-a-half-hour *Berlin Alexanderplatz* (1980) and Dennis Potter's original six-hour *The Singing Detective* (1988): "It's a stunning original about a most particular slice of American life, a panoramic picture that is, by turns, wise, brutal, funny and hair-raising, and of significance to the society just beyond its immediate view" (Holden, pp. 177, 179). I'd go a step further. In *The Sopranos,* a television series achieves the heft of a classic novel.

Finally, *The Sopranos* is very much an expression of its time. For one thing, it anatomizes the Me-First Generation. As Chase remarks on his DVD interview (Season One, disc four), the show's original, absurd joke is that "life in America had gotten so selfish" that even a mobster, whose business invented Me First, can't stand it any more so he needs therapy. That's what this outlaw society represents, however charmingly tempered by its nostalgia, loyalty, and *omertà*—the protective silence of the gangster who refuses to "sing."

Furthermore, as Dr. Melfi observes (in I, 1), many Americans share Tony Soprano's feelings of having come in too late, at the end, when the best of The American Dream is over. Where Tony's ancestors built the beautiful church, now you can't find two guys who can properly grout a bathtub.

So, too, the show's unprecedented candor. It has set new limits in the vulgarity of its language, its unflinching probe of its criminal characters' private and business lives, the candid dramatization of family problems, and the hypocrisies in church, school, and government, and the complexity of its moral positions. The serious ambition of its themes enabled HBO to transcend the archaic decorum and moral simplicities that paralyze commercial television. After all, ABC, CBS, and the Fox network all passed on the pilot script before HBO shot and adopted it.

HBO luxuriated in the greater freedom it enjoys over network television. The cable liberty paid off handsomely. With *The Larry Sanders Show, Oz, Sex and the City, The Sopranos,* and *Six Feet Under,* HBO rewrote the conventions of TV—and in 2000 outgrossed—in both senses of the word—all the major American networks. More importantly for us non-shareholders: Here are shows for grownups, who want paradox in their characters, moral ambivalence in their plots, and a sense that we are seeing life as those fascinating people would live it. As *The Sopranos* brought adult drama to the boob tube, it was as liberating to that long-stifled medium as, fifty years earlier, *A Streetcar Named Desire* was to American film.

After the *Sopranos*'s gutteral accent, the networks could admit more realistic speech, albeit in more measured tones. *The West Wing* producer Aaron Sorkin was prepared to let a character use the Lord's name in vain and to let the president's secretary describe his father with a five-letter anatomical term. *Philly* producer Steven Bochco proposed admitting a banned scatological reference (*New York Times*, September 2, 2001). Though shock radio (e.g., Howard Stern) and the reported foibles of President Clinton helped to broaden this climate, clearly *The Sopranos* led the way. It justified colloquial realism. From its premiere on January 10, 1999, *The Sopranos* was an oasis of reflective, intensely moving popular fiction in the desert of consumerist fantasy. It needed that realistic language. This liberty was another step in the Aging Boomers' revolution.

In a sense, *The Sopranos* is another form of "Reality TV." But it is more artful and less manipulative than all those *Survivor* shows we had to survive—that other phenomenon of the day. After all, *The Sopranos* is about how realistic characters survive in the urbane jungle—about their wiliness, ingenuity, dishonesty, and courage. It is about how those people get and how they get to keep those gaudy estates. But where the Survivor shows were artificial situations posing as real life, *The Sopranos* was art, brilliantly conceived and scripted, with the honesty of declared fiction.

The cast of largely unknown performers teased the audience by blurring the line between fiction and reality. As Tony's "waste management" firm evoked the real Gambinos' business front, the series packs the thrill of dangerous exposure. But the show always retained the resonance of fiction. In the HBO's own book on the series, *The Sopranos: A Family History*, Allen Rucker cleverly pretended to provide the "real life" background on the show's characters. In addition to chatty background on the show's creators and performers, it extended its characters' reality, through testimony from other characters, putative memos, and correspondence, even lists of some characters' garbage. This fictional dossier playfully extended the pretense to reality.

The realism draws on the (mainly) New Jersey location shooting. Creator David Chase insisted on that, even though "These days, movies and television series shoot for less in Canada. In recent years, Toronto has been a generic stand-in for Chicago, New York, and all suburbs in between." Though Chase has shot in Toronto, "It isn't New Jersey. It looks different, and that's the end of the story. . . . There's no collision of Hispanic, Italian or black around an 1890s brownstone square in Toronto. These are small, unimportant details, perhaps, but not to me" (Holden, pp. 129–30). While the interiors are generally shot in a Queens studio, the exteriors are shot on fresh locations that evoke gangland.

It also sounds real, with the salty vernacular and often poetic color of the characters' speech. "The feds are so far up my ass I can taste Brylcream," quoth Uncle Junior, under house arrest (II, 3). The quip has period color, preciseness, anger, and imagination. Or "It hurts like the fucking 'Pit and Pendulum' just to wipe myself" (II, 4). As the Hollywood D-girl, Amy, would say, "Very imagistic" (II, 7). The talk is so brilliantly written it rings unscripted. The complexity of the characters and the moral dilemmas they make reflect our real life. David Chase says: "I was looking for the notion that life is so complex now that even a wiseguy needs help sorting it out" (Holden, p. 103).

UNDERSTANDING *THE SOPRANOS*

Perhaps the series' basic pun is the title. Sopranos "sing"—which is also the argot for ratting to the cops/Feds. That's the sense of the term in II, 12, when Janice—having just killed her fiancé—tells Tony on his tapped home phone, "I can't sing. . . . I can't sing now. Think a minute, OK?" Sopranos sing at the highest range, the most female. That is, it is unmanly to betray one's gang. Note that the first gang member to turn state's evidence is the softie named Pussy Bonpensiero. (Ironically, his surname more or less translates as "good thought.") Over the whole series hangs the threat of someone "singing" to the fuzz. More broadly, *The Sopranos* "sing" to the television audience about the secret lives, loves, and business ways of Gangland USA.

The series grew out of several established traditions in popular culture. From the American gangster films of the 1930s it drew the dynamic of gunfire, sexy music, and clubs, and the theme/value of individualism rampant against urban conformism. The hero climbs from the gutter to the top—and is brought down. The more Tony Soprano succeeds, the more riveting our wait for his doom. From the postwar American film noir, the series drew the awareness (not to mention the plot devices) of psychoanalysis. The wild, selfish Id escapes from the shadows of repression.

From postmodernism it drew its confidence that an audience will delight in irony, look for how this art draws from other art, and exult in transcending borders and conventions. So these gangsters deliberately style themselves after their favorite gangster films—especially Francis Ford Coppola's *Godfather* trilogy. (For a fuller discussion of this influence, see the appendix.)

From the Millennial turning point the show drew confidence that the times are ready for change, perhaps even something revolutionary, especially against censoring language and blinkering thought. The television audience was ready for a show about which it had to think and could argue. They would leave mush for meat. As James Gandolfini observed, "People are ready for a certain lack of political correctness. We do things with some respect" (Holden, p. 108)—especially (and this was radically new) respect for its audience's ability to deal with complexity.

The show's serious ambition was immediately recognized. As Stephen Holden introduced his anthology of *New York Times* coverage, "In forcing us to empathize with a thug whom we watch committing heinous acts, *The Sopranos* evokes a profound moral ambiguity" (p. xviii). For Peter Bogdanovich (Season One DVD, disc four), the interaction of the criminal and domestic worlds makes the family life more unusual, the gangster element more typical, and the resultant mix "strangely universal." Vincent Canby concluded, "*The Sopranos*, which plays as a dark comedy, possesses a tragic conscience" (Holden, p. 187).

J. Madison Davis, former president of The International Association of Crime Writers, North America, argued a Shakespearean dimension in *The Sopranos*. "The baseness of so many of the characters' acts and lives is contradicted by the nobility or the power of their emotions." Davis proposed that "the thrumming engine of the second season," Richie Aprile, is a New Jersey version of Shakespeare's Richard, duke of Gloucester, bent upon becoming Richard III—not to say just plain bent—with an outrageous marriage to help him along. "*The Sopranos* has always had a sense of high drama combined with a feel for the everyday, a sense of foolishness in the most serious situations, great dialogue, and, most important, a deep sense of humanity" (Holden, pp. 7–12).

How meaty can *The Sopranos* be? Let's consider the first shot of the first episode of the series. A suspicious Tony seems small between the foregrounded legs of a statue of a woman. He appears trapped by the woman he is looking up to, as if by scissors. The statue is not just a woman but the idea of Woman.

The male characters' sexual arrogance and insecurity form one of the series' primary themes. After all, Tony lives on Stag Trail Road and has named his boat *The Stugots* (that is, *cock* or, loosely, *balls,* connoting nerve and courage, gender-nonspecific). So the opening shot expresses the anxiety of a man insecure in his manhood, at once fascinated and frightened by Woman. The classical sculpture contrasts to the inflated dancers of the

Bada Bing, Tony's more natural habitat, over whom these men have such total control. In fact, the first shot inside the club foregrounds one stripper paralleling this bronze.

In Tony's unease before the nude sculpture we sense his vestigial Puritanism, his own twist on ethics, despite—or enabling—his corrupt profession. In his fear of Woman we get his fear of the womanly, specifically of being found to be weak, vulnerable, and—in particular—to break the code of silence. His female therapist, Dr. Melfi, will open his feminine side by making him talk and explore his feelings. Consistent with the towering Woman sculpture is the surprising strength of the women characters in this patriarchal clan. Carmela, Janice, Meadow, Livia, Melfi, even—briefly, fatally—Ralphie's whore, Tracee—all are strong, assertive women.

As the image stresses Tony's vulnerability, it sets off the series' most dangerous undertaking: It makes us sympathize with the Mafia killer. By immersing us in Tony's life, by rooting the fiction solidly in his perspective, the series challenges our moral judgment. It does an end-run around our usual morality. From Milton's Satan to Hitchcock's innocent criminals and criminal innocence, artists have known that evil has its own dangerous charm and that the best art will provide a moral test, not a polemic. Like the forbidden fruit in Eden, a moral work of art gives its viewer a challenge, not a confirmation.

As befits our percipient times, *The Sopranos* seems an exercise in moral relativism. Its hero hoods are not so bad—because we know them so well. They're not as bad as others who have not enjoyed the advantage of our identifying with them. That makes this series an exercise in moral judgment. As it betrays our knee-jerk responses, it tests us.

The complex dialectic of the opening shot—male vs. female, woman vs. idealized image of woman, strength vs. vulnerability, foreground vs. background—points to the series' central tension between the viewer's familiar morality and its violation by this criminal subculture. The viewer's rejection of the gang is itself complicated by their touching values of honor, family, and individualism. The result—from the first shot to the last—is an intense composition whose morality avoids the black and white in which we, confidently, naively, used to believe for the quicksands of reality grays.

AUTHOR! AUTHOR!

This guide will "read" each episode of *The Sopranos* across its first three seasons with the closeness we gave that opening shot. Rare among television series, *The Sopranos* bears the critical analysis routinely accorded good literature, drama, and films. As a thoughtful construction, here is a TV series as rich as our best feature films in all it manages to say through its dialogue, camerawork, plot development, music, characterization, and the design of its image. But who is its author?

In literary fiction and drama, the author—the person responsible for the work, what it says, how its meaning radiates from how its elements are organized—is obviously the author, the writer. (Got that? The author is the author. Good.)

In film, authorship is more complicated. Because so much always happens in the laborious passage from the page to the screen, the author of a film is almost never the original screenwriter. On rare occasions the authorial control may be the producer, when he is as savvy and intrusive as a Darryl Zanuck or a David Selznick. Sometimes the controlling force behind a film may be the star (for example, Barbra Streisand, Marlon Brando on some occasions, or Orson Welles in *Journey into Fear* and perhaps in Carol Reed's *The Third Man*).

But usually we assume that the organizing intelligence behind a film is the director. The director may have full control of the writing and realization of a work—for example, Antonioni, Bergman, Fellini, Godard, Woody Allen, Stephen Spielberg. Or s/he may work in (or as if in) the confines of a studio system, in tension with the assigned materials, for example, such *auteurs* as Dorothy Arzner, Ida Lupino, Fritz Lang, Vincent Minnelli, Douglas Sirk, Alfred Hitchcock, Howard Hawks, John Ford, Arthur Penn, Ang Lee, and others. Normally the director has the authority and responsibility for the vision and meaning delivered by the huge team of collaborators.

Television involves a different system of authorship. In a made for television movie, the author may well be the director, as in film. If the production system is similar, the difference may be only in the transmission. But a television series often deploys myriad writers and directors. In the first three seasons, *The Sopranos* credited 15 directors and 13 writers (who wrote sometimes alone, sometimes in twos or threes). This complicates the naming of one person as the source of the meaning and vision of the work. When that is possible in television it is usually the producer.

Except for the unique Alfred Hitchcock (who took his film persona to the small screen), Norman Lear was probably the first American television producer to stamp a series with his characteristic style and concerns. In fact, not just in one series but in a variety of them: *All in the Family, The Jeffersons,* and *Maude.* Network king Lear demonstrated that a producer can—and in a series normally would—provide the controlling impetus and cohesion for a continuing work. Similarly, James Brooks gave *Taxi* and the MTM range of sitcom series a characteristic stamp of values, tone, subject, and style. Today we can identify producer Aaron Spelling as the presiding author of his shows regardless of who else does the writing and directing. And it is clearly Steven Bochco's *NYPD Blue*.

The organizing intelligence behind *The Sopranos*, the person who "speaks" to us through each episode and their season collective, the "author" of the series, whoever may write or direct any component part, is David Chase. He conceived the idea, wrote and directed the pilot, and has been responsible for the work of his team—and for the meaning of their product—since. Chase continued to write some key episodes, including most season openers and closings: I, 1, 2 and 13; II, 4 and (with Todd Kessler) 13; and III, 1, 2 and (with Lawrence Konner) 13. He did "a lot of rewriting" on the early scripts before his writers absorbed his vision, he remarks on the Season One DVD (disc four) interview. And he insists on doing all the editing himself.

David Chase is the author—the creative source, voice, and vision—of *The Sopranos*. He knows the medium—having written for shows like *Kolchak: The Night Stalker, The Rockford Files*, and *Northern Exposure* since he was twenty-three. In 1988 he developed his first series, *Almost Grown*, another family drama with a popular music score. And given that his family name was DeCesare and he grew up in North Caldwell, New Jersey, he knows the cultural landscape. But "There was no cursing in my family," he assures us in his interview on the Season One DVD (disc four)—and he does not know anyone in the Mafia.

The series is full of Chase's personal touches. His daughter, Michelle Chase, plays Meadow's friend Hunter. Uncle Junior's name comes from one of Chase's cousins (He's the man in glasses who leaves the Vesuvio with Uncle Junior in I, 1). The key speeches—after allowance for the characters' spin and dramatic irony—convey Chase's opinions about life, morality, honor, the excessive excuse of bad behavior in therapy, the remarkable achievement of the Italian-American community, and the short-sightedness of the Italian Anti-Defamation League. Clearly, it is David Chase who propels this unique series with his values, ambition, and vision. Of course, no guide can be a substitute for the show itself.

Now, let's cut to the Chase country.

Season One

I, 1: The Pilot

Written and directed by David Chase.

Gangster Tony Soprano consults psychiatrist Dr. Jennifer Melfi about his anxiety attacks and blackouts but is skeptical about the therapeutic process. He misses the duck family that settled in, then vacated, his swimming pool. He and his protege Christopher assault Mahaffy, a medical administrator, over a gambling debt. Tony fails to dissuade his Uncle Junior from using the popular restaurant of friend Art Bucco to kill an errant hoodlum. Tony has the restaurant burned down to save Art's reputation. Christopher kills a rival's nephew, Emil Kolar, to discourage competition for a big garbage contract. In his personal life, Tony's bitter mother, Livia, rejects any seniors residence, his daughter Meadow flirts with delinquency, his son Anthony Jr. is an underachiever, and his wife Carmela (correctly) suspects Tony of having a mistress.

As we have noted, the first episode begins with Tony nervous about opening up to a woman. Our first surprise is that Tony is consulting a woman psychiatrist. Tony's unease continues in Dr. Melfi's office, as he explains his panic attack, blackouts, and depression. Out of his element, Tony's black shirt obtrudes against the harmonized browns of Melfi's suit and her office.

As he will throughout the series, Tony fights the therapy: "It's impossible for me to talk to a psychiatrist." Of the four appointments in the first episode, one Tony skips and from one he stomps out angry (when Melfi asks him to discuss his feelings about the ducks). At the last he asserts that the Prozac has helped him so much he does not have to come any more. Tony's suspicion of therapy includes how his salutary talking reflects on his manliness. He cries when he realizes that he fears losing his family as he lost his ducks.

The flashback structure demonstrates the effectiveness of exposing buried memories. The past materializes for us. Tony's weeping shows how far his therapy has already taken him. Self-consciously he anticipates his tears. Of course, he feels this treatment has brought him down rather than up, made him weaker not healthier. Is he no stronger than simple Artie, who weeps at the loss of his restaurant? Tony consoles him with what he learned from Melfi: "Hope takes many forms." Not to duck the metaphor, behind that counsel lurks poet Emily Dickenson's line, "Hope is the thing with feathers."

Though Tony resists the treatment, there are early signs he will be erotically drawn toward Melfi. After asking her about her family's roots, he concludes "My mother would have loved it if you and I got together." But she corrects his casual "Hon" to "Dr. Melfi." When they happen to meet at the restaurant, Melfi seems nervous, but her unclinical language suggests some kinship: "Shut the fuck up," she tells her surprised date, Nils.

The first episode establishes the male fear of talking—especially if he's a gangster. Melfi scrupulously defines the line between doctor-patient confidentiality and her responsibility to warn the police if she learns of anyone's imminent danger. But Tony sneers at psychoanalysis: "I had a semester and a half at college so I understand Freud. I understand therapy as a concept." He prefers the Gary Cooper model, "the strong, silent type. There was an American." As "Guys today have no room for the penal experience," they join the Witness Protection Program instead of manfully taking the rap. Tony knows that if his cronies knew of his therapy he could be killed. Hence his nervous "confession" to Carmela who, of course, is overjoyed that he is seeing a therapist.

Already nervous about the RICO law's admission of government wiretapping and surveillance, Tony fears himself—or Melfi—being considered a squealer. When Tony first mentions RICO Melfi asks, "Is he your brother?" No, but it is heavy: RICO is the Racketeer Influenced and Corrupt Organizations Act passed in 1970 to help the government investigate and prosecute organized crime. From the Sopranos' perspective make that "persecute."

The opening episode also establishes the spectrum of parent-child tensions. Tony's son, AJ, has his thirteenth-birthday party postponed when Tony collapses at the barbecue. He collapses again while showing his mother the seniors residence. When Dr. Melfi encourages Tony to "Stay on your mother," what she means is "Pull back for some perspective on her." Carmela agrees that Tony's mother is his major problem. His avoidance of Melfi's question about his father suggests another major memory is buried there (which is revealed in I, 7 and III, 3).

Livia rails against Tony's neglect, rejects his gift CD player, and resists his encouragement to move into a well-appointed seniors home (with adjacent nursing quarters). Tony charmingly dances with his mother (to Connie Francis's appropriate "Who's Sorry Now?"). But Livia insists that daughters take better care of their mothers than sons do (an illusion entirely exposed when Tony's sister Janice erupts in II, 1). As Tony tells Melfi, his mother's current adoration of her dead husband jars with her life-long abuse of him, when she wore him "down to a nub." But Tony still envies his father who, although he didn't achieve Tony's rank, lived in an age of honorable gangsters who would never sing to the feds. In Livia's and Uncle Junior's bitterness about the current generation, Livia does not react to Junior's suggestion that something may have to be done to her son. That feeds his later plot to kill him.

Meadow rejects her mother's discipline and pleasure (their annual shopping visit to New York) as she chafes under teenage rules. The set design catches the pivot in Meadow's emotional state. Her bedroom abounds with the toys and dolls of her childhood, but a large butterfly on her wall suggests an imminent emergence. As if to realize Meadow's sense of her mother, Carmela brandishes a major military gun when she catches Meadow trying to sneak back into her bedroom. The militant mother lightly anticipates Livia's plotting against her son's life. "Mothers and daughters," Tony assures Carmela, "she'll come back to you."

Meadow would rather appeal her mother's ban of the Aspen ski holiday than hear Tony's pride in their ancestors who did the masonry and carpentry on the magnificent church. But Meadow grows thoughtfully appreciative in the scene. Here Tony speaks directly for David Chase, who was surprised to learn late in life that his grandfather and his brothers were master craftsmen from Europe who built some classic New Jersey churches.

By trying to save the reputation of friend Artie Bucco's restaurant, Tony irks Uncle Junior, his father's younger brother and himself the victim of a sibling's insecurities. Tony remembers him taking him to Yankees games and Uncle Junior remembers playing catch with him. The macho identify with athletics. Uncle Junior shattered Tony's self-esteem by telling his nieces that Tony would never make the varsity sports teams (hence his brief college tenure). Now Tony exuberantly attends Meadow's volleyball game (and plots business in the stands) and he will later spur AJ into football.

More dramatic is the Sopranos' marital tension. Tony strides into the kitchen bare-chested and slaps his wife's butt in the presence of their children and Meadow's friend, Hunter. Though Carmela devotedly attends his 6:30 A.M. medical examination, when he romanticizes their good times she snaps at him about his *goomah* (the wiseguy's obligatory mistress) and predicts he will go to Hell. Right after telling Carmela that she's the only person with whom he is "completely honest," Tony confirms her reference to his therapist as a "him." Despite her attack, Carmela gives him a warm, concerned wave as he enters the machine.

But Tony moves in a man's world, which wants to keep betrayal and infidelity in marriage where it belongs. This is demonstrated by the restaurant owner's smoothness in successive scenes. Tony brings Irina, his Russian mistress, one night and Carmela the next. "Mr. Soprano, months we don't see you," the restaurateur exudes for Carmela's benefit, "Where you been? Signora Carmela!" *The Godfather* theme music in the background confirms this man's world. Understandably, Carmela is surprised—and relieved—when what Tony "confesses" is not adultery but his other therapy.

In this bent world even language can't be straight. Hence, the gangsters' professional euphemism. Tony tells Dr. Melfi he's "a waste management consultant," which is literally and metaphorically, but not exhaustively, true. He manages more kinds of waste—and wasting or whacking—than the term usually covers. At the restaurant, Tony tells Melfi that her "decorating tips" really worked. Insofar as his improvement is still superficial, the Prozac is a kind of decorating tip. When he tells Melfi that he and debtor Mahaffey "had coffee," we watch Tony gleefully run him down with Chris's new car in an office park in Paramus, N.J., then beat him into submission. But as Mahaffey drops his tray of coffees when he sees Tony coming, the euphemism is not untrue.

Situations can be as deceptively innocent as language. Mahaffey is persuaded to take Hesh as a partner, and to tap medical insurance for fictitious operations, when Hesh and Pussy take him to a bridge overlooking a deep chasm and a waterfall. Except for Pussy dropping his ice-cream cone down the deep gorge, the threat is unspoken. Mahaffey feels the most sinister pressure when he hears the ice-cream truck depart, leaving the men alone. The most innocent sound can carry a brutal subtext.

Tony's unsteady "nephew" (son of Carmela's cousin) Christopher is introduced as a weakling, late on his assignments, more concerned about his $60,000 Lexus than in kicking the loan-welcher, Mahaffey, at foot. Later, Chris almost blurts out the reason why Artie's restaurant, aptly named Vesuvio, was blown up. Christopher is of the yappy, indulgent generation that Tony rues. Open with his feelings, Chris objects that Tony did not congratulate him for killing Emil Kolar. When Chris mentions his autobiographical screenplay Tony explodes: "What you gonna do, a Harry

Hill on me now?" Hill was the hero who betrayed the mob in Martin Scorsese's *GoodFellas* (1990), the film David Chase calls his Koran (Season One DVD, disc one commentary).

In fact, Chase cites this scene as the precise point "we left network television behind." On the first day's shooting, this scene was the first shot. The script called for Tony to slap Chris, as if waking him out of his fantasy. But Gandolfini suggested his character would be much angrier at the danger of exposure. With his on-a-dime turns from concern about Chris, to rage at his threat, to warmth again, as he straightens Chris's clothing, Gandolfini made Tony both violent and cuddly. With that touch the show abandoned the usual sentimentalizing and excusing of the gangster hero.

Confirming his influence by films, Christopher kills Emil Kolar amid full-screen black and white stills—close-ups from the poster in the background—of Humphrey Bogart, Dean Martin, and Edward G. Robinson. To prepare for Emil's arrival Chris strikes Kung Fu movie poses. He sees himself as acting in those stars' gangster tradition. The song over the murder is Bob Diddley's swaggering, "I'm a Man." But Chris's heroic self-conception is undercut by the pig heads piled behind his left shoulder—not a flattering audience.

With the cocky insensitivity of the young and the shallow, Chris calls Emil E-mail. The image of Chris and Pussy swinging Emil's corpse *at* the dumpster wall instead of *up into* it is an emblem of Chris's frustrated aspiration. He will always want to swing higher than he can. The gangsters may model themselves after their film heroes, but Chris wants to enter that fantasy world.

Against all that artifice stands Tony's fascination with the wild ducks. They are a miraculous eruption of nature in his denatured life: "It was such a trip to have those wild creatures come into my pool and have their little babies." Mystifying his family, Tony wades into the pool to feed them. He offers to build them a better ramp. Tony's depression begins when the ducks leave. In his dream, his penis falls off. When he runs to get his Lincoln mechanic to restore it, a bird swoops it away. When Tony realizes "I'm afraid I'm gonna lose my family like I lost the ducks," his mood is caught by Sting's "I'm so Happy I Can't Stop Crying."

Perhaps the pastoral wistfulness of the duck family also lay behind his naming his daughter "Meadow." The name recalls an ideal lost and forgotten in the seamy New Jersey setting—especially the landscape surveyed in the show's title sequence (see our Conclusion) and especially distinguished from the "Meadowlands" where the gang beat and bury their enemies. Like the ducks, Meadow's name suggests a natural refuge from Tony's bleak world. But even nature can be deceptive and dangerous—as Mahaffey senses high above the waterfall.

In her first appearance, Artie's wife, Charmaine, resents the gangsters' patronage of the Vesuvio. Throughout the series she remains the one character of uncompromised conscience and values. Standing against a mountain of garbage, Artie has to give Tony back the "free" cruise tickets by which Tony hoped to get Artie to close his restaurant so Junior couldn't kill his gunsel there. Typical of Tony's poisoned life, he destroys his friend's prized restaurant to protect him. In this twisted ethos, Charmaine's ethics and Uncle Junior's stubbornness push Tony to arson. However irregular, it is generous.

Some witty editing enforces the sympathetic ambivalence. Right after Charmaine insists "someone donated his kneecaps for those tickets," Mahaffey hobbles into view in a knee-high cast and on crutches. After Mahaffy admits taking the tranquilizer Zolof, his tormentor Tony gulps Prozac as he practices his golf swing. The predator is as nervous as his prey. Just as Tony assures Chris, "Beautiful day—what could be bad?" we see the bitter Livia, being driven to AJ's party by Uncle Junior.

The episode closes on Tony's pool. Carmela pragmatically greets Livia and Uncle Junior: "OK, everyone, let's eat." As everyone heads off to dinner, Meadow's friend Hunter announces she won't eat. (Typical of the show's gathering ironies and coherence, in II, 2 Hunter is in the Eating Disorders ward at the hospital and in II, 3 she tells Meadow she uses bulimia as a strategic threat to control her parents.) Then three little boys run past laughing—and aiming a toy gun, like the men they may join their dads' business to become. The camera holds on the vacated pool, a benign shimmering blue, vacant of the partygoers, the divided families united within The Family, but vacant too of the glimpse of more natural family life that Tony found in his ducks. As the closing Nick Lowe song concludes, "God help the beast in me."

■ A poll on the HBO website—HBO.com/Sopranos—on the favorite line of dialogue in Season One chose AJ's response to Livia's refusal to come to his birthday party: "So what? No fuckin' ziti now?" In its unsentimental concern for the appetite the line may be an homage to Clemenza's classic line from *The Godfather:* "Leave the gun. Take the cannoli."

■ Because this pilot was filmed two years before airing, some of the characters look much younger than in episode two. The actors playing Irina and Father Phil were replaced. Carmela's priest enthuses over laser discs here, DVDs later. Drea de Matteo, who plays the restaurant hostess who couldn't seat Melfi and Nils, was so impressive that the role of Christopher's girlfriend, Adriana, was developed for her. And Satriale's Pork Store was built to replace the original Centanni's Meat Market. (In *The Godfather Part II*, we learn *cent' anni* is a toast: "We should all live happily for a hundred years.")

I, 2: 46 Long

Written and directed by David Chase.

Tony's relationship with Uncle Junior is shivered when Chris and his friend Brendan Filone steal a truckload of DVD players from a company protected by Uncle Junior. Meanwhile, Tony has his crew replace the stolen car of AJ's science teacher. Livia, after a kitchen fire and a driving accident, is moved into the Green Grove seniors' residence. Tony is infuriated by Dr. Melfi's suggestion that he hates his mother.

In the only pre-titles scene in the series, a television discussion in the background deals with the confusion and instability of the underworld, while in the fore Tony and his crew count their mountain of money. The staging emphasizes the speakers' remoteness from the Sopranos' life. U.S. Attorney Braun claims that because of drugs and squealers the gangsters have forever lost their heyday. This foreshadows Pussy's treachery and fall. But gangster-turned-author Vincent Rizzo argues that there will always be organized crime to serve such popular needs as gambling, drugs, and pornography. Twice in the first scene Silvio cheers Tony up with his Pacino imitation (from *The Godfather Part III*): "Just when I thought I was out they pulled me back in." The joke and all that money make the writer seem the wiser of the talking heads—even though Rizzo turned rat.

Perhaps the central metaphor of this episode derives from the newspaper item Pussy reads out in that prologue, a proposal to clone Princess Di. Silvio's impersonation of Pacino is a comic form of cloning. More broadly, Tony takes the traditional view: Only God can make life. But cloning is part of the new technology that, with its consequent compromised ideals, defines this episode. When Tony replaces Mr. Miller's stolen Saturn (implicitly to improve AJ's D+ in Science), it's with a different stolen car. The repainting makes it a bathetic kind of clone. The DVDs that Chris and Brendan steal and the new telephone equipment that befuddle Livia and Bing bartender Georgie point to the complexity of new technology that replicates image and voice.

This is also seen in Paulie's tirade against the ubiquitous gourmet coffee shops that exploit the superior Italian. "We invented this shit and all these cocksuckers are getting rich on it." In righteous indignation—"They ate *pootsie* until we gave them the gift of our cuisine"—he steals an espresso machine. Paulie feels swamped by the cloning of Italian food and coffee—from which only the "real" Italian, that is, he, should profit.

But even cloning can't replicate the family warmth Tony finds in the three photographs left in his mother's emptied house: the young woman, the mother with young Tony, his parents holding their baby boy. Tony falls, breathless, after seeing the pictures, because—like the lost blessing of his ducks—they represent a contentment he cannot recover. Worse, he never had it. The only loving experience he can recall for Dr. Melfi is the time Livia and her children all laughed when their father tripped and fell down the stairs. Even their one positive memory is based on cruelty.

Tony struggles to reconcile his mother as helpless little old lady and as psychological monster. Though his sisters have abandoned her, Tony feels guilty despite all his generous effort. Of course, for this mother nothing is ever enough. Even as Tony has gorged on her Virginia ham, she insists from her sick-couch, "You never let me feed you." To Carmela's offer, "You know you can come live with us," Livia replies: "I know when I'm not wanted." Yet Tony tells Melfi that Carmela won't let Livia live with them. His one specific praise—"She's a good woman. She puts food on the table every night"—better suits his *focaccio*-winner father.

The idea of "Mother" is so strong that it makes the Bada Bing dancers drop everything to come over to Tony when they hear Livia is in trouble. Later, they only pause vaguely when Tony beats up the phone-fumbling Georgie. The parallel connects violence and sentimentality. In the episode's last shot, the three pole-dancers personify the confused emotions of a valueless order.

Tony shares that confusion. Rather than acknowledge his anger at his mother, he stomps out of his last session with Melfi, insisting he won't talk to her again. Tony is ashamed and afraid of his emerging anger, despite Melfi's advice that "Sad is good; unconscious isn't." Clearly Livia has left Tony as "scathed" as the DVD truck driver asks his robbers to leave him. Like the over-dedicated son, the trucker provides the rope with which the robbers can—to save his job—leave him helpless.

The family betrayal spreads into Family betrayal when Chris robs the company paying Uncle Junior protection. Uncle Junior drags the cancer-stricken boss Jackie Aprile from his sickbed to award his tribute. Ironically, we will later learn that Uncle Junior had once hijacked Jackie's trucks, necessitating a "sit-down" to clear the air. Now Tony's loose cannon, Chris, has his own, looser cannon, Brendan, who again robs that company of a load of Italian suits. (Fancy dressing is one of the conventions of the gangster genre.) When the robber's inability to drive the truck leads to fatality, this Family conflict parallels Livia's accidentally running over her friend.

The dangerous disorder is pervasive. Tony is undermined by his mother's negativism in the one family and by his "nephew" Chris's unruly ambition and his own uncle's rigidity in the other. When Chris is denied admission into a popular club and gangster-film maestro Martin Scorsese (Anthony Caso) is welcomed in, Chris renews his resolve to parlay his life into a Hollywood film.

The narrative order confirms the duplicity and disintegration. Just after Tony tells Carmela how proud he is that Livia chauffeurs her less capable friends ("It gives me hope"), she drives into her passenger. When Tony insists Livia's black caregiver Perrilyn will stay, the camera holds on Livia's ambiguous close-up: Is she resigned or plotting? Carmela finds Perrilyn leaving in a rage, for reasons of which Livia pretends ignorance: "These blacks—who knows what they're gonna take the wrong way?" (Perhaps being referred to as "These blacks"?) Though Uncle Junior approves her hiring, as soon as Tony is gone Junior mutters: "A smoke he hires. For his own mother." The particular term works against Junior: Livia needs that "smoke" to prevent another kitchen fire. Tony is only slightly less preju-diced: "No ganji," he warns her at their first meeting.

In this show nothing positive goes undeflated. So Tony assures Livia that Carmela does not want her fine jewelry yet; they both want her to enjoy a long, healthy life. But when Livia says she gave all her jewelry to a cousin Tony explodes: "All I got was a vibrating chair?" Contrary to the nursing home director's reassuring Italian proverb, it will take more than time and patience to turn the mulberry leaf Livia into anything like silk. She's closer to the proverbial sow's ear—with a bullet.

In this world of imitation and copies, characters often project their weakness on others. When Livia claims Perrilyn stole "that beautiful plate that Aunt Septimia took from that restaurant in Rome," she projects her family's theft upon the innocent Trinidadian. So, too, Silvio wonders if the Royal Family had Diana whacked.

In one example of successful cloning, Pussy's car repair shop is named Bunuel Bros. The reference to Spanish film director Luis Buñuel declares the spiritual source of this series' black comedy and scathing anatomy of social hypocrisy and familial dysfunction. "I'm a big Buñuel fan," Chase remarks on the Season One DVD interview (disc four), with particular respect for his Surrealist dreams.

- When Pussy tracking the car thief jokes "I'm a fuckin' Rockford over here," he alludes to Producer David Chase's earlier career as a writer on *The Rockford Files.*
- The episode title, "46 Long," alludes to Silvio's intention to steal a suit from the thieves but is also a sum of money—$46,000.
- James Gandolfini (Tony) was born in Westwood, N.J., graduated from Rutgers, worked as a bouncer and nightclub manager, and broke into Broadway in 1992. He—along with Aida Turturro (Janice)—appeared in the 1992 Broadway revival of Tennessee Williams' *A Streetcar Named Desire,* starring Jessica Lange and Alex Baldwin. His pre-*Sopranos* films include *A Stranger among Us, A Civil Action, 8 mm, Get Shorty, The Juror, Crimson Tide,* and *True Romance.* In 2001, he played a gay hitman who becomes Julia Roberts's confidante in *The Mexican,* the prison warden who tyrannizes Robert Redford in *The Castle,* and the corrupt store-owner in the Coens' *The Man Who Wasn't There.* Even without the colorful Soprano language, he retained his expressiveness and remarkable physical presence.
- Edie Falco (Carmela) is the daughter of jazz drummer Frank Falco. She studied acting at SUNY, Purchase. Her films include *Bullets Over Broadway, The Funeral, Private Parts, Copland,* and the lead role in *Judy Berlin.*
- Jamie Lynn Sigler (Meadow) made her professional theatre debut at 12 in the musical version of *It's a Wonderful Life.* As she's quoted on the *Maxim* website, "I'm Cuban, Greek, Romanian and Sephardic Jew, so I couldn't get further from Italian." Robert Iler (AJ) began doing television commercials when he was six and has appeared on *Saturday Night Live* and the film *The Tic Code.*
- In his Season One DVD interview (disc four), Chase applauds his teenage actors for their direct, accurate portrayals. They contrast to all the unrealistically cute, bright, "empowered" children and youth on TV.

I, 3:   Denial, Anger, Acceptance

Written by Mark Saraceni, Directed by Nick Gomez.

Meadow and Hunter coax Christopher into getting them some speed to get them through their SATs. An elderly Hasidic Jew seeks Tony's help to get his daughter's divorce. Artie and Charmaine move into a cheaper home, still ruing the loss of their restaurant. At Livia's suggestion, Uncle Junior has Christopher roughed up and Brendan killed for their unruliness.

In this episode the collision between the gangster world and the religious takes two forms. The first contrasts the Hasidic Jewish and the Italian cultures. "Ah-seed-em but I don't believe 'em," quips Paulie, encapsulating their difference in belief and vision. The second ethical arena is domestic.

When they meet under the pig atop Satriale's Pork Store, the very location undercuts the orthodox Jews' venture. Clearly this partnership will not be kosher. Elderly Hasid Shlomo Teittleman offers Tony $25,000 to persuade Teittleman's son-in-law, Ariel, to grant his wife a divorce, without the half-share of the motel Ariel demands. For his help Tony demands a 25-percent share of the motel.

As the Jewish divorce is called a "get," it makes for some smooth wordplay: Tony will help Teittleman get the *get;* "Let's understand each other from the get-go;" "We got you your *get.*" But this harmony in language belies deeper differences. When Paulie suggests shooting Ariel instead, Silvio observes "It's taboo for his religion"—as if their Catholicism were not troubled by that nicety.

As usual in this series, the gangster world is reflected in the supposedly respectable one. Silvio reports that the DA put the "rabbi's goon squad" out of business. The deal runs against both Hesh's advice to Tony "not to get involved with these people"—by which he means not Jews but "fanatics"—and Teittleman's son Hillel's advice against dealing with gangsters. Both warnings prove prescient.

Ariel proves an indomitable adversary, a spirited Hasid who talks like the hoods. He's known Shlomo "since before I had hair on my *petzel*" (Yiddish, colloquialism: "little penis"). In that cocky quip lies the seed of his doom. Ariel draws from the Jews' heroic defense against the Romans at

Masada, where 900 Jews staved off 15,000 Romans for two years: "They chose death before enslavement. And the Romans: where are they now?" "You're looking at them, asshole," Tony replies. Silvio is impressed: "If we don't kill this prick we should put him to work."

Hesh advises Tony that castration is a more effective threat to a Jewish fanatic than death: "Finish his *bris*." Even a fanatic would rather die than live castrated. Hesh knows whereof he speaks: He is in bed with a beautiful young black woman. When Ariel settles with Teittleman for a 15-percent share in the motel, the old Hasid tries to renege on Tony's share, but Tony prevails.

In the family tension between ethics and expediency, Uncle Junior needs to rein in Christopher and Brendan, who are hiding behind Tony. He spurns Mikey's advice of violence: "Take it easy. We're not making a Western here." Livia capriciously shares Tony's love for Christopher because he once put up her storm windows. She suggests Junior have Christopher roughed up and Brendan shot: "Maybe Christopher could use a little talking to. You know. The other one? Filone? [pause] I don't know." Having planted her plot, she typically retreats, but reiterates her motive for revenge: "I'm a babbling idiot. That's why my son put me in a nursing home." In a parody of parental concern the unsuspecting Brendan remarks: "Kids. You think you can protect them. But you can't." Brendan takes a predator's pleasure from that conclusion.

In a double act of charity Carmela overrules Tony to host a fundraiser for the Pediatric Hospital. Hiring Charmaine and Artie to cater it adds expediency to her ethics. The good cause advances Carmela's social prospects and helps her friends. But the personal charity is not entirely successful. Charmaine is insulted when Carmela summons her with the same hand gesture she used for her Polish maid. Less to assuage Carmela's concern for her than to counter Carmela's condescension, Charmaine reveals that before they were married Charmaine dated and slept with Tony. Carmela is oddly unassured by this.

Their husbands' relationship also quivers when Tony attacks Artie for still bemoaning his restaurant. Tony is in close-up when Artie rhetorically asks: "Who would burn down a perfectly good restaurant? It's stupid. Insane." In Tony's "I'm sorry, Artie" an apology hides behind ritual sympathy. Feeling both guilty and justified, Tony explodes at Artie in the kitchen. After expletives the men playfully hurl food at each other. It starts when Artie's rhetoric unwittingly points to Tony's guilt: "What the fuck do you know about it?" Like the charge, the cold cut sticks to Tony's forehead.

As Carmela innocently smiles at the food fight, behind her we see almost lost in soft-focus the more suspicious Charmaine.

The Charmaine-Artie relationship gathers weight. In earlier episodes Charmaine criticized her husband's involvement with Tony, ostensibly because she rejects the mobster world. But Charmaine's resentment toward Tony may have some root in their old affair. Perhaps she needs to convince herself more than Carmela that she is happy with her marital choice (especially when she will leave Artie in III). In any case, the disclosure helps explain why Charmaine has distanced herself from her close friend Carmela. Certainly she is more aggressive and effective than Carmela in influencing the husband. But as Artie points out, Charmaine is inconsistent in agreeing to work the Sopranos' fundraiser but refusing Tony's help to restart their restaurant. She is more scrupulous than the other characters in defending her ethics against expediency. In an opposite virtue, Adriana persuades Chris to supply Meadow's speed to save her from the dangers of Jefferson Avenue.

Tony's meetings with Dr. Melfi dramatize the title's movement from denial through anger to acceptance, especially regarding his friend and Acting Boss Jackie Aprile's fatal cancer. Tony is disturbed when two pictures in Melfi's waiting room of a barn and a rotted tree remind him of mortality. In his Russian *goomah*'s bedroom, he is bothered by the image of a desert motel with an empty canvas chair in front of it, another image of departed humanity, though it reminds Irina simply of "David Hockey." As usual, the malapropism makes new sense: There is ice—or at least cold comfort—in that Hockney desert. Also as usual, Tony stomps out of the second session with Melfi. In the last visit he stays to wonder about our gift of knowing we will die.

Along with his quick anger, Tony shows stirring of a thoughtful nature. After all, he paused over those two pictures. Then he contemplates Ariel's willingness to die "if it's for something." In contrast, Jackie Aprile is helpless before his cancer. Tony's gift—a stripper busting out of her nurse's uniform checks Frankie's "vitals"—provides futile relief. His next visit dispels Tony's confidence that "Jackie's so fuckin' mean he'll scare that cancer away." Now Jackie is wasting away, too preoccupied to enjoy Ariel's conversion.

With Melfi, Tony considers Teittleman's charge that he's a Frankenstein monster, or its Jewish counterpart, the Golem—monstrous, inhuman, unfeeling. The dramatic montage that concludes the episode shows Tony is a man of feelings, but is operating in a world of savagery. Similarly, Ariel's beating is intercut with Carmela's civilized reception, especially her "schmoozing" with a Jewish woman.

In homage to the climaxes of all three *Godfather* films (not "a Western"), Uncle Junior's attack on Christopher and Brendan is intercut with Meadow's choir's performance of "All through the Night." This episode begins with the two bloods returning the hijacked truck as Tony's favor, not Uncle Junior's. It concludes with Junior's retribution for that act. Mikey brings the plot full circle when he greets Brendan with "Hijack, bye Jack." The interwoven chorale puts gangland justice in the context of spirituality and grace. The song over the violence lends a lyricism to the otherwise gratuitous shots of the last twitch of Brendan's toe and his last joint floating on the surface while blood swirls into his bath. In Chris's mock execution, he confesses he gave Meadow speed and befouls himself. He's left on the blood-red boards, his bravado exposed by the gun's blanks.

Within the choir scene, Meadow's and Hunter's choir and solo singing are intercut with close-ups of Tony watching, proud and obviously moved. His sentiment is genuine notwithstanding the violence in his business life. In this scene his family provides a blissful respite from the compromises of his Family. Tony's challenge is to sustain his family feelings against the callousness required in his Family role. His Family style encroaches upon his family bliss.

When Tony comes late to the recital he joins Carmela and takes her hand. She withdraws it quickly. In one of those resonant ambiguities that so distinguish this series, her particular motive is uncertain. Is she irked that he has—as usual—come late to an important family event? Does she suspect he is coming from his mistress? When Carmela brushes her nose, is she sniffing for that presence? Is she still disturbed by Charmaine's disclosure? Or does she want to indulge her pride in her daughter's performance without being reminded of Tony's compromising role in her life? Does she spurn his real hand to enjoy the idealized moment of her daughter?

Carmela's action suggests a complexity of emotional possibilities. This is the lot of a human nature whose impulses and activity range from the savage to the saintly. Ending on the choir's last note of "All through the Night" provides a counterpoise to the first episode's close on "God help the beast in me." But the end-credits' song returns to the gloomier theme of responsibility in the face of death. In "Complicated Shadows" Elvis Costello and the Attractions remind us, "Well, you know your time has come / And you're sorry for what you've done."

■ Lorraine Bracco (Dr. Jennifer Melfi) won an Oscar nomination as Henry Hill's wife in *GoodFellas*. Because she played that gangster's wife she declined the offer to play Carmela here and opted for the shrink. She also appeared in *Hackers, Getting Gotti, Even Cowgirls Get the Blues, Medicine Man, Radio Flyer*, and *Sea of Love*.

I, 4:   Meadowlands

Written by Jason Cahill. Directed by John Patterson.

Tony's alienation from Uncle Junior intensifies, as he avenges Christopher's beating. After Jackie Aprile dies at only 44—paradoxically for a gangster, of cancer—the captains support Tony as boss. But to make peace with Uncle Junior Tony submits to his leadership. Meanwhile, Meadow explains their father's gangster life to Anthony Junior.

In the opening shot Tony and Dr. Melfi present their faces in the same frame. Usually they are shot separately, as if they were speaking from separate worlds, or one is viewed beyond the other. This shot begins what turns out to be Tony's nightmare that his associates know about his secret therapy. The dream approaches reality when Paulie has a dental appointment up the hall. The nightmare presents scenes of increasing implausibility, from Tony openly admiring Melfi's legs, to Heshie having a therapy session with her, Silvio having sex, and Paulie and Pussy waiting outside. Melfi turns into Livia. Discovering AJ behind a door anticipates his learning about his father's real profession. The episode concludes on a wiser AJ leaning on a tombstone at Jackie Aprile's funeral. Finally aware of the family's Family life, he gazes stolidly back at his father's wink.

This episode deals with the shifting of power on both the personal and professional planes. When AJ fights his former friend Jeremy at school, the larger boy backs down after his father is frightened by Tony—innocently holding an ax—at a garden supply shop. But Tony is never simply innocent. He pressures the clerk to sell him some banned DDT. In the marriage, Carmela threatens divorce to keep Tony from ending his sessions with his therapist, whom he continues to let her assume is a man. ("He's got more degrees than a thermometer.")

In the most chilling show of strength Uncle Junior orders Tony out of his cafe and commands him to "come heavy" (that is, armed) if he ever returns. Their leadership rivalry feeds Junior's familial resentment: "A son who throws his mother in an asylum." Livia refuses to enjoy the $4,000-per-month retirement home Tony provides. After Jackie Aprile's death Tony returns to Junior's Sit Tite Loungenette, "heavy, like you said, but I don't want to use it." Contrary to Silvio's expectations ("Adios, Junior"), Tony makes peace by offering his uncle the leadership (for two prize territories, for Tony to "save face"). As he assures his aides and the other captains, though, Tony expects to be involved in his uncle's every decision. Tony applies to Uncle Junior the strategy Melfi proposed, to give Livia the illusion of being in control.

Another power shift involves Detective Vin Makazian, who covers his gambling debts and two alimonies on a $40K salary by doing odd investigations for Tony. Another loose cannon, Tony finds him urinating outside Livia's seniors residence. Hired to follow Melfi, Makazian stops her date's car and beats him up. The once confident tax lawyer Randall cowers in his house.

In their session Melfi reports this to Tony. "It's not your fault," she replies, when Tony says he's "sorry" about her friend's assault. As with Artie, Tony's formal sympathy allows him a safe "apology." As he set the cop on her tail, here the therapist is in ignorance and the client has the broader knowledge and counsel. The power has briefly shifted. Melfi is distracted when Tony recalls seeing his first corpse at the age of fifteen. She has lived "a sheltered existence," out of touch with "the climate of rage in American society" and "casual violence" that Vin Makazian has just shown her.

Christopher is the episode's primary loser of power. He's widely teased for having befouled himself during his beating. In a collision of language, after Adriana asks if he really "made number two in his pants," he proposes to go get some "shit" from Brendan. Adriana's decorum seems childish in Chris's world. Having been humbled in the (definitely non-pastoral) Meadowlands, he's afraid to step outside. The gangster is as traumatized as the tax lawyer. Assuming Tony ordered his assault, Chris screams at Meadow for tattling about her speed. When Tony does turn on Christopher, it's when the young man ignores Tony's sorrow at Jackie's death and urges war against Uncle Junior.

In the climactic power shift, Jackie Aprile's death shakes the society. Tony weeps at the news when he hears it on the television. In awe, one of the Bada Bing dancers stands under the set: "I'll never forget where I was this day." Her sad life seems briefly ennobled by the passing of this ostensible hero, the JFK, RFK, or Martin Luther King of the Bada Bing. The stripper's comment deflates her pathetic reverence and the gangster's false status.

At Jackie's funeral, Uncle Junior benignly receives the captains' respect, a small vainglory in the face of death. In surrendering the leadership to Uncle Junior, Tony seems to have created the monster that Teittleman called him in the previous episode. But, as he assures the wary *capos*, "I still love that man." The organ and the lyrics of Mazzy Star's "Looking down from the Bridge" give the end credits an elegiac wail.

■ In his delirium, the dying Jackie Aprile says two nonsensical things that assume ironic significance later. The first—"The fish is in my pocket"— anticipates the association of Pussy Bonpensiero's murder with fish. The second is unintended, a dramatic irony created by time (specifically, September 11, 2001), not the scriptwriter: "I'm at the World Trade Center." That line may be removed from future reruns. After all, in the fear of mailed-anthrax spores the networks withdrew the *Seinfeld* episode in which George's fiancée, Susan, dies from licking bad invitation envelopes.

■ Nancy Marchand (Livia) was already suffering from lung cancer and emphysema when the series began. She was on bottled oxygen between takes. Her character was supposed to die in the first season, but she proved so riveting that she continued into the second. Ms. Marchand died on June 18, 2000. Her acting career extended from the classic television show *Marty* in 1953, where she played Marty's (Rod Steiger) date, to her four-Emmy (1978–1982) career as the stately WASP publisher, Mrs. Margaret Pynchon, on *Lou Grant*. Her films included *Tell Me that You Love Me, Junie Moon; The Hospital; Regarding Henry;* and *Jefferson in Paris.*

■ Livia's character derives somewhat from creator David Chase's memories of his own mother: "The way she acted was very sad. As she got older, she started insulting more and more people, taking umbrage at things they said and cutting herself off from the world. . . . 'I don't cater to anyone,' she used to say. But there was a kind of self-awareness of what she was doing. . . . She was aware sometimes that she was being outrageous and provocative. . . . She would say 'I hate it' and later say 'I didn't say I hate it; I don't know where you got that from.' " She wielded "the tyranny of the weak" (Holden, pp. 18, 22–23). But of course Chase's "mother is not Livia. By any stretch of the imagination. In the first season, in the first few shows, in the pilot, some of Livia's dialogue is actual dialogue from my mother. My mother had a very Livia-like attitude. She was very unintentionally funny. Because she was so downbeat" (Rucker). As it happens, Mario Puzo said that he based his *Godfather* hero, Vito Corleone (Marlon Brando), on the strength and wisdom of his mother.

I, 5: College

Written by Jim Manos Jr. and David Chase. Directed by Allen Coulter.

When Tony drives Meadow to Maine to visit three prospective colleges, he spots a former associate who turned state witness then disappeared into the witness protection program. Tony and the frightened man stalk each other. While Meadow is at her second interview, Tony ducks out and kills him. Carmela is visited by Father Phil, who seems to have a romantic interest in her—and in her cooking—but his overnight stay ends up innocent.

The pre-visuals sound of church bells resumes from I, 3 the combination of religious music and secular violence. In a similar mix of culture and savagery here Tony kills the traitor while Meadow is at her Bowdoin College interview. The episode contrasts Tony's very warm and open scenes with his daughter to his strangulation of Fabian Petrullio, now "Fred Peters."

Two statements contend for the title of "central theme" here. The first is Father Phil's response to Carmela's questioning the "major contradictions" in Jesus's words. The priest's faith in love—"Hopefully, some day we'll learn to tolerate, accept and forgive those who are different"—seems vacuous amid the moral complexity in this series and especially in this episode. As the priest flirts with seducing Carmela, his "love" is rather ambivalent. Indeed, the predatory priest validates the second statement, the Nathaniel Hawthorne quotation that Tony reads on the wall of the classic writer's old college:

No man can wear one face to himself and another to the multitude without finally getting bewildered as to which may be true.

As Carmela suggests, we have to "face" the major contradictions in our own various faces, to discover our integrity and to understand others. So Hawthorne's statement trumps Father Phil's.

In a comic version of confusing faces, Peters has problems with lips on the busts he makes. Christopher mistook the Sinatra bust in Jackie Aprile's rec room to depict Shaquille O'Neal (not that common a confusion in life): "He fuckin' needs to practice a little on lips." Excessive lips are an apt weakness for someone who talked too much to the FBI. Tony confirms his identification of Peter when he spots the Ronald Reagan bust in the travel office—with Shaq's lips. Tony's "Hello Rat" could express a closet Democrat.

Though the squealer has gone to great lengths to put on a new face, he has not changed. Peters loses our sympathy when he aims to shoot Tony and when he tries to hire two drug buyers to kill him. The post-mob Peters remains shady. He threatens his druggies, "Want the cops to find out who burned down your historical house?" Petrullio/Peters gives a second meaning to Tony's unflagging purpose: "You know one thing about us wiseguys? The hustle never ends." As Petrullio "flipped" after he was busted for selling heroin, he foreshadows Pussy's predicament.

Tony's murder is shockingly interwoven with his squiring Meadow to university interviews and confronting her suspicions about his career. As Stephen Holden reflects on the first season, "As much as it banalizes its mobsters, it refuses to trivialize their viciousness. Tony's brutality is all the more disturbing because it erupts from within a social framework of apparent normalcy. That framework includes a devout young priest, who, like Dr. Melfi, skillfully sidesteps the deeper moral issues of Tony's life" (p. xviii).

The Hawthorne quotation applies to all the major characters in this episode. At its simplest, it shows when Christopher pushes his offer to fly to Maine to dispatch Peters. "I'm your soldier," he insists, so his duty requires that he do the job for Tony. But then he lets slip his true motive: Whacking Peters would ensure Chris's promotion. When Chris says he's "a cunt hair away from being made" and Tony kills Peters himself, Tony becomes that cunt hair. In III, 7, Junior declares himself to be the cunt hair separating Tony from owning all New Jersey. In both usages, womanizing men—immoral, insecure—denigrate woman. As both speakers are violent toward their lovers, the image expresses the insecurity behind their callous power.

The Hawthorne theme of faces is varied in Tony's scenes with Meadow. They leave the first campus in the familiar tension about what a daughter can safely tell her father. In this case, it involves the sexual liberty that undergraduates take at the respective colleges. Later, Meadow volunteers—"because you were honest with me today"—that she and her friends used speed. But Tony overreacts:

TONY: Right under my nose. You'd think you'd know.
MEADOW: No, Dad. You won't.

Meadow is reminded that a daughter has to balance the faces of Ostensible Innocence and Honest Experience. For his part, Tony prefers to see her positive faces: the college student, the Italian magazine model.

Meadow earlier put Tony to that test when she directly asked if he is in the Mafia. At first he is offended by the stereotyping of Italian waste managers as Mafiosi. After his reflex denial ("There is no Mafia"), under her steady stare Tony admits that some of his "money comes from illegal gambling and whatnot." Meadow is grateful for his candor: "At least you don't deny it, like Mom." Earlier Meadow beamed when he admitted (what she already knew) that he "got into a little trouble" as a kid. At their candlelit dinner Tony opens up even further: "My father was in it, my uncle was in it. There was a time there when the Italian people didn't have a lot of options." But Meadow challenges his rationalizing: "You mean like Mario Cuomo?"

Notwithstanding this candor Tony continues to deceive her, when he chases the "old friend" he spotted. Tony shows how good he is at proffering false faces when he smiles away his bloody interest in the man and later explains away both his dangerous chase and the murder evidence, his bleeding hand and muddy shoes. We approve his deception even as we appreciated his earlier honesty.

Of course, Tony's marriage is a dance of false faces. We are reminded of this when, before he phones Carmela, Tony phones his Russian mistress. Irina is upset that her one-legged cousin, Svetlana, has landed a husband after only two months in America. Tony's strategic excuse is that he has two children approaching college, not that he loves and would never leave Carmela. In another apt malapropism Irina tells Tony not to "throw up in my face" what he has bought her.

The Sopranos' domestic front is more dramatic at home, where Carmela has stayed behind with the flu. Sensitive to AJ's face, after he has brought her breakfast in bed, she sends him off to play video games with a friend. She is less prepared for Father Phil, whom this episode exposes as a negative paradox.

The priest is young, handsome, goateed, in a word, "cool." He drops Yiddish colloquialisms he learned growing up in the Yonkers melting pot. His first word in this episode is the ecumenical "*Oy.*" Aptly, he teaches her *schnorrer* and *schlep*. A rather catholic Catholic, in one breath he defends

Islam against its popular misrepresentation, then praises even more avidly the Chianti. For a celibate he seems excessively given to the appetites. On his entrance, he "confesses" to Carmela that he has "a jones for your baked ziti." The phrase seems a euphemism for "having a boner" for something, that is, an excited desire for it. Similarly, in I,1, he almost uses his Lord's name in vain: "Jeez, Louise!" Here it's "Aw, jeez."

Their conversation shifts between the religious and the secular. They discuss Willem Dafoe's Jesus in Martin Scorsese's *The Last Temptation of Christ* (1988), which was originally intended for Robert De Niro. "Bobby D.," quoth the priest, steeped in the text. Father Phil even impersonates Jesus *via* De Niro. When Father Phil offers that all Jesus' known speeches total only two hours, Carmela adds that all the Beatles's songs total 10. Behind this apparent non sequitur may lurk John Lennon's observation that the Beatles were more popular than Christ. In this priest's conversation, religion always fades into popular culture. His world serves up five times as much Beatles as Jesus. Eager to watch the DVD of *Remains of the Day,* Father Phil defends his appreciation of Emma Thompson: Observing a beautiful woman is the same as admiring a sunset, a Douglas fir, or any other example of God's handiwork. A flash of lightning behind him makes his explanation seem demonic.

The priest's intimacy with Carmela intensifies as they watch the film together on the couch. They touch each other as the Thompson and Anthony Hopkins characters do in the film—when the butler softly objects "You are invading my private time." Carmela is so moved by the film (and by Father Phil's physical contact) that she cries. The priest caresses her: "Carmela, if I can help, please." "How?" she turns on him abruptly. After a pause that should only be called pregnant, the priest retreats from the secular potential to propose to hear her Confession. Their exchange wavers between the religious and the carnal. "I'm a terrible person," she says. "No," the priest replies, with suspect gendering, "You're a wonderful woman."

Here Carmela lets several false faces drop. "I haven't truly confessed in 20 years," she begins. She admits that she has forsaken what is right for what is easy, she has admitted evil into her house, she has said or done nothing about her husband's "horrible acts." She has thus endangered her children's moral development, and all "because I wanted things for them." This recalls Meadow's silent skepticism in I, 1, when Carmela said "you can't just lie and cheat and break the rules you don't like." Meadow knows her parents' model.

As if to prove her point, the scene cuts to the motel, where Tony is carrying a drunk Meadow to her cabin and Peters has Tony in his gun sights, only to be distracted. We see Tony threatened right after Carmela says she expects God will compensate her "with outrage for my sins." At this point, Peters also embodies the danger that Carmela might betray Tony. But she still loves him: "I still believe he can be a good man."

Tony's bending over to kiss Meadow goodnight is intercut with Father Phil giving Carmela communion, with close-ups on her sensuous acceptance of Christ's body and blood. Carmela's reception of the wafer and wine is repeated, closer, to emphasize the physical sensation. The priest finishes the wine with secular aplomb. As he kneels to embrace her, we get a close-up of her blissful smile.

AJ's phone call, asking to sleep over at his friends, awakens Carmela from her sleep on Father Phil's shoulder. She has to crawl over the priest's lap to get to the phone. The priest remains visible in the background, reacting to their having the night alone. He caresses her back until they verge on a kiss. Then Father Phil quickly rises and runs to the bathroom to vomit (fulfilling Irina's earlier malapropism). In the priest's absence, Carmela phones Tony for reassurance but hangs up; his voice reassures her more than anything he might say.

Yes, the Lord moves in mysterious ways, all right.

The next morning, while Carmela drinks her coffee in the foreground, Father Phil awakens in his T-shirt on the sofa. He is uncertain whether they did "anything out of line?" "You have nothing to apologize for," Carmela assures him, but she keeps her back to him. When he admits he was tempted, she deflects him by reworking Bogart's line in *Casablanca*: "Of all the *fanook* [Americanized colloquial for 'gay, bent'] priests in the world, why did I have to get the one who's straight?. . . . It's a joke." The priest is obviously struggling with his faces as man of the cloth and as man of the flesh, while Carmela juggles her faces as faithful and betrayed wife, needy woman, and good Catholic.

Amid all these temptations, deceptions, and betrayals in deed or in intent, Tony strangles "Peters" because "You took an oath and you broke it." For Tony, betrayal of his friends justifies murder. Betraying his wife justifies carefulness.

At home Tony correctly infers from the vanished ziti that "Monsignor Jughead was in"(relating the priest to the always-hungry sidekick of the *Archie* comics). Tony's quip catches both the popular culture and the appetites that characterize Father Phil. Tony is skeptical when Carmela says the priest stayed overnight alone with her "but nothing happened." What did they do for twelve hours, play Name that Pope? "He spends the night here and all he does is slip you a wafer?" When Carmela says he's verging on sacrilege Tony apologizes: "I didn't mean to verge." He may loom but he would not verge. Ironically, given the range of his experience just in this episode, Tony is flummoxed at the idea that Father Phil stayed overnight innocently: "You know what? This is too fucked up for me even to think about."

But our Carmela trumps Tony again: "Your therapist called. [pause] . . . Jennifer?" She exits smartly, leaving Tony fumbling to recover his face as faithful husband. It's only therapy: they just talk.

The episode fades out on a shot of the vacated kitchen hallway. The empty space echoes the suspicions in the Sopranos' marriage. There are no song lyrics over this episode's conclusion, just music, because words have been broken or are false. When Carmela learned that Dr. Melfi is a woman she asked Father Phil rhetorically, "Why does he have to lie? What is he hiding?" The priest's assurance was as self-serving as Christopher's: Tony should supplement his therapy with work on his soul. In this episode no major character operates with a single, honest face.

▪ HBO executives argued against having Tony kill the traitor. "HBO said you can't do this. . . . You've built up the most interesting protagonist on television in the past 25 years, and now you're just going to lose it." Chase responded that that "we'd lose viewers" if Tony failed to kill the rat (Holden, pp. 155–56). The result was a story of powerful ambivalence and ironies that won the best dramatic series Emmy. In his interview on the Season One DVD (disc four), Chase calls this "the ultimate *Sopranos* episode" that could be "a film noir in and of itself."

I, 6: Pax Soprana

Written by Frank Renzulli. Directed by Alan Taylor.

Tony's cronies ask him to temper Uncle Junior's unilateral decisions, such as over-taxing Hesh, killing a drug dealer who sold his tailor's grandson drugs, and not sharing the spoils with his *capos*. Meanwhile, Tony has sexual dreams about Dr. Melfi and tells her he loves her. Father Phil discourages Carmela's thoughts of divorce.

This episode exposes varieties of male power, primarily through Tony's exchanges. His tension with Uncle Junior contrasts Tony's subtlety with Junior's direct force. Uncle Junior's power image is undermined when in his first appearance he is revealed to be pantless (he is being measured for a suit). In the last shot of the episode, the FBI promotes his picture from Capo to Boss. Beginning as a pantless preener, Junior ends as the image of authority, the FBI's target icon. But as the captains have accepted him only as a front man, his power is primarily image.

Tony is sensitive enough not to oppose his uncle openly. He solicits Livia's help, but she would rather manipulate Junior against Tony than for him. Then Tony works through Johnny Sack to get a sitdown on behalf of Tony's longtime friend, Hesh. There Tony plays ignorant of the issue and appears to side with his uncle. Similarly, before proposing his compromise, Johnny flatters Junior: "If there are any flies on you they're paying fuckin' rent."

Tony may have learned this style from Hesh whom, as Livia warns Junior, Tony regards highly. Hesh brings Tony his complaint in a soft tone, as they stroll along the street. Accepting the principle of the tax but questioning only the amount, Hesh appears far less agitated than Tony. After Uncle Junior reduces the tax without losing face, Tony persuades him to satisfy his five *capos* by sharing Hesh's back-tax among them (Tony returns his own share to Hesh). In a more sinister case of subtle power and image, a waiter at Uncle Junior's testimonial snaps photographs with a hidden camera for the FBI.

Tony is less successful in asserting his sexual power, especially when he targets Dr. Melfi. In one dream, accompanied by the black rhythm and blues tune, "What Time Is It?" (The Jive Five: "It's time for love"), Irina's blowjob turns out to be by Melfi. "Tony, I love your cannoli," Melfi says in Irina's voice. In another she appears naked to summon him into her shower.

In their real sessions, Tony sets out to seduce Melfi. To introduce their potential as lovers he cites Carmela's suspicion. He struggles to define her— "She didn't know you were a girl—you know, a woman—Excuse me, a doctor—a woman doctor."—outside his usual range of "woman."

He attributes to Carmela the burn wound that Irina jealously gave him and her anger at the suggestion she dress more like Melfi, to give his libido "a jump start." Here "jump" has a sexual undertone. After this seductive lie he compliments her "killer body under there." His sexual address begins when she charmingly laughs at his joke about prostate examinations: "Hey,

I don't even let anyone wag their finger *in my face!*" When she evades his kiss, he says he loves her. But it's his lies about Carmela that show he's trying for Melfi. This falseness coheres with his summary of psychoanalysis: "What you're feeling is not what you're feeling and what you're not feeling is your agenda."

Interestingly, Tony is so confident in his masculinity that he is unperturbed by Melfi's rejection and walks away tall. For her part, Melfi stands up to him, as unflinching as when she agreed to take him on as a client. Nor—for a man who so lives by his gun—is he as shaken by the drop in his libido as we might expect. When Carmela raises that issue, he blames his Prozac, citing Melfi. In Carmela's emphatic "*She* says that?" she remains more upset at his doctor's gender than by his diminished libido.

Carmela's current anger begins with Tony's neglect at their anniversary dinner, when he consults with Johnny Sack. In his sensitivity to Uncle Junior's feelings Tony insults Carmela's. As Tony erodes her self-respect her consoling spree at Roche-Bobois catches his attention.

Oddly, the new furniture does not change our impression of the house. If *The Godfather* displays the Corleones' respectability and Old World class—from Vito's first stolen carpet on—all the Sopranos' house "says" is that they have money. The house and its contents are bland, featureless, with neither the character of the antique nor the energy of the modern. "I don't have antiques. My house is traditional," Carmela says in III, 1 (after Martha Stewart). They might just as well, as Tony snaps, go live in the Roche-Bobois store, for all the hominess and personal character their home has.

In her materialism, however, as in her tolerance—even grateful appreciation—of Tony's *goomahs*, she is (as Father Phil points out) not sinless in complying with Tony's godless life. (The priest is right? As Tony reminds us, even a stopped clock is right twice a day.) Carmela is more worried about losing Tony than about her own soul.

Tony's sexual power is least effective with Irina, who—as his dream reveals—has been replaced in his lust by Melfi. In return, Irina ignores him when he calls her over. Paradoxically, the episode concludes on the peak of Tony's sexual power: his submission to his wife. As she joins him by the duck-less pool, he assures her that there is nothing to "this Melfi thing." To Carmela's dedication Tony replies "Carmela, you're not just in my life. You are my life."

As in love, so it is in management. The most effective power is that secured by other direction and by sharing. In that other macho arena, the parents' bleachers at the Little League baseball game, Tony tries to advise his uncle through a historical parallel: Augustus Caesar enjoyed a long, peaceful reign because he shared with his captains his power and its rewards. Junior proves impervious to history. But he responds to Tony's recalling Junior's old story about a bull teaching his son. The young bull suggests running down to a herd to screw a cow; the older sage prefers walking down and screwing them all. Power inheres in its measured use, not flash.

The male's sexual and political powers are again connected when Junior accepts Hesh's compromise on his tax: "What did I say? Hold on to your cock when you negotiate with these desert people." His joke extends the Jews' distinguishing circumcision to castration (and recalls Hesh's advice re: Ariel). It also coheres with the episode's theme of impotence, the threat to the "cannoli." Junior's joke about "the desert people" is undercut when Tony visits Hesh's plush, green horse farm. So much for ethnic stereotypy, whether of the desert Jews or of the Mafia Italians.

The horse farm scene also rebukes Livia's prejudice: "Just don't let certain people take advantage of you. . . . How's your Jewish friend? . . . Who ever heard of a Jew riding horses?" Junior imperils both himself and Tony by following her suggestions. Though Junior realizes Livia wants to punish Tony for putting her in a home, he acts on her advice anyway. With Tony, Livia also feigns innocence: "I don't know that world. . . . I don't want to get involved." But she continues to feed Junior malevolent ideas.

Livia will play her games: "Who is it?" "It's me, Ma." "Who?" At home in I, 1, she similarly pretended not to recognize her son. In I, 8, she immediately recognizes Carmela's voice at her door. She fakes not recognizing AJ's voice in II, 7 (maybe it's a male thing). Here Livia walks brusquely out of Tony's dance, as if she doesn't want to feel affectionate or close to her son. In the next episode—and even more in III, 3—we will learn that Tony's traumatic memory of his father, murder, sex, and meat also includes Johnny Boy's frisky dancing with Livia—and her evasion of him.

Melfi suggests that Tony chose an Italian-American woman as his therapist, over two Jewish males, because he thought that "by coming clean" with her he would be "dialoging with" the key Italian women in his life—Livia, Carmela, Meadow. She attributes Tony's love to their analytic progress: "You've made me out to be everything you're missing in your life—and in your mother."

As Livia's advice to Junior demonstrates, an ostensible gift can be an imposition of power. Because Melfi knows gifts can be used to control the recipient, she refuses even Tony's small gift, the decaf coffee. When he has her car stolen to replace its starter, she is frightened and outraged at his "violation of my privacy." But he didn't want to see her robbed, he explains. Replacing her car's "starter" relates his good deed to his wanting her "jump start" on his own sexuality. In a non-sexual context, he uses the term "kick start" instead (I, 12). Nor is there any generosity in the gifts Uncle Junior exacts, like his new tax on all poker games or his new tax on Hesh with a $500,000 back penalty. Gifts, whether volunteered or exacted, show the boss's power.

The episode's title derives from Tony's Roman model for popular rule—with the implicit danger of betrayal—the Caesars from Octavius to Julius. Ironically, in the BBC production of *I, Claudius*, Augustus's scheming, evil wife (played by Sian Phillips) is also named Livia, an irony that undercuts Tony's parable for Junior. Still, the *Pax Romana* model—augmented by Tony's bull—brings the *Pax Soprana* to both the business and home fronts, for the while.

- Dominic Chianese (Uncle Junior) toured in Gilbert and Sullivan's *The Mikado* and *Patience* in 1952. His television work includes *Kojak, East Side West Side*, and *Law and Order*. He also appeared in *Gotti, Dog Day Afternoon, All the President's Men, Fort Apache: The Bronx, Cradle Will Rock*, and the remake of *The Thomas Crowne Affair*. In *The Godfather Part II* he played Johnny Ola, the Corleones' Miami connection who "turned" Fredo and is killed with a coat hanger. Chianese is an accomplished lounge singer, as we see on his two CDs and in his performance in III, 13.

- Michael Imperioli (Christopher) has appeared in over 40 movies since 1980, including Steve Buscemi's *Trees Lounge, I Shot Andy Warhol, Dead Presidents, Malcolm X*, and *Lean on Me*. He was a writer/producer and appeared in Spike Lee's *Summer of Sam*, recalling the summer of paranoia caused by serial killer David Berkowitz.

I, 7:   Down Neck

Written by Robin Green and Mitchell Burgess. Directed by Loraine Senna.

Anthony Junior's delinquency at school prompts Tony to recall his own boyhood mischief and to wonder what his children know about his work. He discusses his memories with Dr. Melfi. As Tony's alienation from Livia worsens, we infer that she has always been a problematic mother.

This episode reflects upon how our personal history wields an uncertain effect on our future. As Dr. Melfi puts it, our genetic and cultural pasts may reveal our predispositions but they do not predetermine our fates. We remain responsible for our choices. Santayana's famous dictum—unless we know our history we are doomed to repeat it—here applies to both social and psychological history. In the penultimate scene, Tony watches a History Channel program about the Battle of Midway while running on his treadmill. The allusion sets the present midway between the knowable past and the unknowable future.

Tony learns from his past. As his father's cronies took their daughters to the fairground, he will arrange for several mothers to be placed in the same seniors home, as a front for their meetings. His first remark to Christopher draws on his therapy: "You're doing an excellent job. Allow yourself to take pleasure in that."

Tony's work scene contrasts to his meetings with the school authorities, after AJ is caught stealing sacramental wine from the school chapel and tested for learning disability and psychologicial problems. At work Tony is a stickler for order, using hard-hat Christopher as a "Union Safety Official" to bring a construction manager into line. But at his son's school the specialists hold sway.

During his meeting with Father Hagy and school psychologist Dr. Galati, we share Tony's skepticism about the new jargon ("Anthony has misbehaved. He should be consequenced"). Tony rejects the school psychologist's report because he considers AJ a 13-year-old boy, not a case. The specialists turn every problem "into a disease." Tony is frustrated that the modish "consequencing" does not include the time honored "whack upside the head" or the traditional tarantelle on the bottom. His own father's favorite "child development tool" was the belt. The school officials who reject spanking give AJ "a complete *battery* of testing."

We probably don't approve Uncle Junior's extreme *laissez faire* either: "Whatever happened to 'Boys will be boys'?" Ever unhelpful, Livia tells the family dinner that Tony stole a car when he was 10 and that because of his constant mischief she practically lived in the vice-principal's office.

As Tony and Carmela wonder what their children know about their father's work, they agree they should talk at least to Meadow "about the business . . . as a family." Whether it is the upper or the lower case, "family" is left ambiguous.

Tony's "history" begins with brief flashes back to Meadow's questions on their college tour and to his murder of the snitch, Peters. The flashes' briefness suggests Tony is trying to suppress them. As Livia scolded him earlier (projecting), "You only remember what you want to remember." The flashes swell into memories of entire scenes from Tony's childhood.

The episode's title refers to his hometown, where he remembers watching his father beat up Rocco Allitori, a debtor, to the sound of Eric Burdon and the Animals' "Don't Bring Me Down." Tony remembers seeing his father arrested at a fairground, along with Uncle Junior and a clown. Tony's spying on his father's Sunday trips with Janice is caught in Them's "Mystic Eyes." After his brief arrest, his father returns home while the Italian rock group, The Young Rascals, play "Lonely Too Long" on *The Ed Sullivan Show.*

The latter rock group's name suggests the American culture's affection for the outlaw, the rascal. Rocco is the first to congratulate Johnny-Boy, despite having been so badly beaten by him. Rocco even invites Johnny-Boy to join him on the Reno venture that made him a billionaire. But Livia refused: She would rather smother her children with a pillow than let them live in Nevada. Now Livia denies ever keeping her husband from doing anything he wanted. She shouts her familiar disclaimer: "I don't know what you're talking about!"

Tony's fondness for the History channel speaks to his curiosity. That abstract interest turns to the compelling concern whether his son is doomed to be like him, that is, whether his history will replay in his son. He hopes AJ is proud of him but he wants him to be different. Tony projects onto Carmela his own fears that AJ may be restricted to Tony's genetic limitations and character. Anticipating this point, Tony is shown in close-up when the school psychologist cites AJ's difficulty in both "following rules" and "weighing consequences." Tony initially believes in predestination: "You're born to this shit. You are what you are." On the other hand, genetics does not always rule, as he cites Pussy's three kids at college and—conversely—successful businessmen siring Leopold and Loeb.

Tony's sessions with Dr. Melfi open his troubled relationship with his parents and the silence in which their issues festered. He recalls his mother threatening to poke her fork into his eye if he did not stop nagging her, his jealousy of older sister Janice, and Uncle Junior hitting him with a pitch when he was distracted. *Plus ça change. . . .*

Tony responds childishly when Melfi raises his "intimate feelings" for her. He tells her about his twenty-four-year-old mistress: "How old are you?" "I find it interesting that you took so long to tell me you have a girlfriend," Melfi says in her slow, soft manner. Tony playfully parodies her. He is as belligerently guarded against Melfi's rejection as he was with his parents as a child.

When he tells Melfi what Johnny-Boy did for a living he pauses after the initial euphemism: "Retail meat and provisions—and a little numbers, loan sharking, extortion." The problem of providing for one's family appears in AJ's first response to the psychiatrist's image of a riderless horse: The rider may be off getting its food. Then AJ projects a more comfortable alternative: he is watching the first *South Park* episode, where Cartman's anal probe from aliens results in flaming flatulence. However influential the genes, AJ has his father's way with analysts.

Tony's colleagues have similar issues with their children. Silvio's daughter complains that the Bada Bing "objectifies women"—despite his paying them $1,500 a week. "Boys are different from girls," observes the large man named Pussy. To Silvio's "It's hard to raise kids in an information age," Tony adds, "To protect them." This line rings as false as Brendan's version did in I, 3. Tony's motive is to protect himself from his child's knowledge and rejection. The "information age" hardly applies to AJ learning from his schoolmates of his father's work, although a web site about the Mafia did feature Uncle Jackie Aprile. Replaying this fear of openness, Tony criticizes Chris's daylight theft of watches.

On AJ's visit to Livia (part of his punishment), he lets slip that Tony has been seeing a psychiatrist. After Livia's initial skepticism—"That's crazy. That's nothing but a racket for the Jews."—she immediately concludes that he goes to complain about what she did to him. Ironically, Livia delivers the patented self-pity of the Jewish mother.

The episode closes with Tony, sweating from his History Channel workout, pausing for a quick exchange with AJ. Like their earlier chat, over the flat tire, when AJ admitted his suspicions about his father's work, this points to their potential closeness. The episode closes on the Jefferson Airplane's musical injunction (in "White Rabbit") to "Feed your head." Tony first recalled this song when driven to his morning Prozac. When AJ says his punishment for the wine theft is not fair, Tony pats him affectionately and agrees: "You got that right." Making them both sundaes, Tony delinquently squirts whipped cream into their mouths, creating one of the better father-son memories that will feed their heads into the future.

Of course, there is an alternative reading for that last scene. Tony's quest for health is limited and self-defeating. He follows his strenuous physical workout with a huge sundae, replete with nuts, sprinkles, M&Ms, and the side shots of whipped cream straight. In his physical regimen as in his sessions with Melfi, Tony seems to take two strides back for each stutter forward. However painful his self-exploration, he undoes it with his impulsive indulgence. Self-destruction is the history he chooses.

■ David Chase may have two personal inflections in this episode. He recalls that his mother prevented the family's move to California, when his father had the opportunity to go build printing presses there. As well, Chase would sympathize with Tony's acceptance of AJ's "fidgeting." As a schoolboy in Clifton, New Jersey, the A-student Chase got an F in deportment: "I was always jiggling" (Holden, p. 22).

I, 8: Legend of Tennessee Moltisanti

Written by Frank Renzulli and David Chase. Directed by Tim Van Patten.

Rumors of indictments against New Jersey gangsters send the Family heads scurrying to destroy or to hide evidence. Dr. Melfi resists her family's pressure to refer him to another therapist. But at their session Tony erupts in an insulting rage. Meanwhile, Christopher tries to write a screenplay ("Mob stories are always hot").

This episode straddles the characters' private and public lives and focuses on the ambivalence of the Italian-Americans' image. The public life is represented by the opening scene's *Godfather*-style wedding, which dissolves on the rumor of federal indictments. The Mafiosi hustle their wives off for "spring cleaning."

When Carmela comes to take her to brunch Livia is immediately suspicious. Her instinctive dread is right: Carmela's hidden agenda is to enable Tony to stash his guns and cash in Livia's closet. So the nervous music starts up when Carmela has Livia safe in her car. Meanwhile, the newspaper and TV news make the gang families' private lives too public for comfort.

Searched by the FBI, Tony grows tenser at work and in his sessions with Dr. Melfi. Despite their growing affection, he explodes when she reminds him he will be charged for missed sessions. "I don't appreciate pouring my heart out to a fuckin' call girl," he says, who's shaking him down. "Of course, this is what it's all about, right? Motherfuckin' cocksuckin' money." Paradoxically, it is because he now has "intimate feelings" for her that he turns so abusive. As so often in this series, apparently inconsistent behavior has a psychological consistency.

Tony remains properly concerned for Chris despite claiming "I wipe your ass with my feelings." But even at his ugly worst Tony is too human for Melfi's ex-husband Richard's dismissal as "Evil." So, too, Livia, who when she tells Uncle Junior about Tony's psychoanalysis, begins with self-pity, plants a destructive innuendo, then withdraws from responsibility: "I'm sure he's told the psychiatrist it's all his mother's fault. . . . God only knows what he says. . . . But I don't want there to be any repercussions." As Richard rightly guesses, the Italian-American male client has "mother issues." As the ad said: "You don't have to be Jewish."

Though the story still centers on Tony, here more attention is paid Dr. Melfi and Christopher. In our first glimpse into Dr. Melfi's personal life, her parents and ex-husband want her to refer her dangerous client to someone else. When Richard peremptorily dismisses Tony he blames the Italian gangsters for creating the negative stereotype of Italian-Americans. Similarly, Tony accuses FBI agent Grasso of betraying his people and the FBI of prejudice in turning an Italian against him. Of course, to "grass" is to "sing" or to betray.

As *The Sopranos* has been broadly charged with stereotyping, these scenes provide an Equal Time rebuttal. As Richard argues, the 5000 Mafia members (at its peak) should not define the country's 20,000,000 other Italian-Americans. The Sopranos list major Italian inventors and innovators. Antonio Maiucci invented the telephone, but Bell gets the credit. (Incidentally, it's at a Maiucci Festival that Vincent kills Joey Zaza in *The Godfather Part III*.) Tony is proud that more Italians fought for America in World War II than any other ethnic group. But Meadow casts a pall on the dinner when she raises the history of the Mafia. These scenes rebut claims that the show perpetuates the negative stereotypy of Italian-Americans.

Rare for this series, these discussions seem arch and preachy. Lacking the usual mischief and irony of *The Sopranos*, they rather resemble the sobriety of its rival quality series, *The West Wing*. On the other hand, when Melfi's father proposes a toast—"To we, the twenty million."—he makes the Italians the subject of the phrase ("we") instead of the object ("us"). His grammatical error makes the Italian Americans the force not the victim.

But this show does not capitulate to the critics. Melfi counters Richard's paranoia. Go after Hollywood movies, she advises, not her client. "With all the poverty, starvation, ethnic cleaning and generally horrible shit in this world, you devote your energies to the protection of the dignity of Connie Stevens." In light self-satire, Melfi's son Jason refers to "ginzo gravy," as Chris calls himself a "skinny guinea." Even Richard speaks Soprano when he tells Melfi not to "bust my balls with Freud by numbers."

In their paean to the Italian-American, Tony and Carmela exchange enigmatic smiles at the climactic mention of "Francis Albert"—Sinatra. A romantic privacy plays around that public figure. Sinatra is the presiding legend in this series—more here than the titular Tennessee Williams. In I, 11 Mikey and JoJo Palmice's kid is named Frankie Albert. For Sinatra made it in America, beyond showbiz. While he hobnobbed with presidents he retained the glamour and courage of his gangster style and associations. When Chris buys the newspapers reporting his criminality, over the end credits we hear Cake's song, "Frank Sinatra."

In another ethnic balancing, Melfi, Richard, and Jason consult a Jewish therapist who takes a wacky pride in having a maternal relative who worked for Lepke. "Those were some tough Jews," he gloats. This Jew relishes the identity that the Italian resents. As it happens, the actor playing the Jewish Dr. Reis is Sam *Coppola*—confirming the *paisan*'s kinship with "the desert people." Dr. Reis suggests Melfi refer Tony to a therapist who specializes in "Mafia depression," an admittedly unfunny joke that provokes Reis's self-approving wheeze and his clients' stunned silence.

As unfunny as the Jewish shrink is the comedian working the old folks' home. Completely out of touch with his audience, he is mediocre, to boot.

His jokes broaden the show's ethnic stereotypy. In the Polish version of *Rashomon* everyone remembered the rape the same way. The Jewish Doctor Goldman abandoned tree surgery because he fainted at the sight of sap. This joke may apply to the squeamish who recoil at the show's bloodshed. Clearly any Italian-American stereotypy is only part of the show's satire. Here is Equal Opportunity offensiveness. Richard may see this as another example of Melfi's "cheesy moral relativism," but satire has its own validity.

The episode's primary psychological focus is on Christopher. It opens with his surreal nightmare that combines Czech pork sausages, the murdered Emil, and girlfriend Adriana (who in his nightmare turns into Carmela, as she would in her own). Christopher seems to fear being replaced (as Adriana's sustenance) or engulfed by sausages, that is, reduced to meat himself. In the opening shot, the cartoon pig wallpaper behind Chris recalls the real carcasses behind him when he murdered Emil. Later, when Paulie says Chris's apartment is "like a sty" the "pig" is implicit, and a reminder that Chris's life and mind are a mess as a result of that murder.

Christopher hungers for the publicity the others dread. He is indignant that Brendan is cited as a "soldier" and he is not. He ignores his "mommy's" phone call until she mentions that he has been named among the "scumbags" in the paper. Then he rushes out to buy up all the copies—out of pride rather than shame. Chris impatiently hungers for the shame of his success.

Christopher Moltisanti is also frustrated by his laptop and by his writer's block. The episode title comes from Adriana's assurance that he is her "Tennessee William"—and he is rather singular, both as a lover and as a writer. Chris has the familiar artist's problem but with no artistic purpose: "I love movies, you know that—the smell in Blockbuster." That last phrase is even more disdainful of cinema than its homonymy, "the smell of blockbuster," because it settles on cheap viewing, not success.

To judge by his (mis)spelling, Chris does not know "loyal" or how to "manage." He grows increasingly moody and irrational, complaining both to Paulie and to Pussy that he has no identity. His life does not have the "arc" (that is, the transforming experience) that a screenplay is supposed to give its lead character. The survival-bent Pussy replies: "You know who had an arc? Noah."

Christopher explodes at a bakery clerk for a perceived slight. After shooting the floor to hasten his service, he gratuitously shoots the boy's foot. "It happens," Chris says. It did. The scene and the impulse come straight out of Martin Scorsese's *GoodFellas*. There hero Henry Hill remembered that even as a young gangster he never had to wait in line at the bakery. More important, Joe Pesci's irrational character plays "cowboy," specifically Cagney's Oklahoma Kid, at a card game. To speed the boy's drinks and sandwiches he shoots at the floor, making him "dance." Then he shoots the boy in the foot—and at the next game kills him.

The bakery scene here is not just a homage to Scorsese's film—or that close relative, a rip-off. It's central to Chris's characterization. Frustrated at his attempt to make a name for himself by writing a screenplay (titled *You Bark, I Bite)*, he acts out a scene from a genre classic. Reversing the usual conundrum—the artist who writes what he cannot achieve in life—Christopher here lives what he cannot write. Tony calls that behavior—and digging up Emil's corpse—"cowboy-itis," the action of someone who wants to be caught. Chris knows he wants to make a name for himself. He doesn't realize his methods are self-destructive.

There is another twist. The actor who played Spider, the boy Pesci shot in *GoodFellas,* was young Michael Imperioli, who plays Christopher here. In a kind of meta-filmic effect, the roles seem continuous. The actor shot then, shoots now. The victim has grown into the victimizer. The casting allusion suggests that a cycle of violence operates beyond the level of the immediate plot.

- Steven van Zandt (Silvio Dante) is a guitarist in Bruce Springsteen's E Street Band, with no previous acting experience. In an in-joke, Silvio is reported to have owned rock clubs in Asbury Park. His real-life wife, Maureen, an actress and dancer, plays Silvio's wife, Gabriella.
- Tony Sirico (Paulie Walnuts Galtieri) grew up in Bensonhurst and developed a resume of 28 arrests (mainly for armed robbery) and two jail sentences (five years). Excited by an ex-cons traveling theatre group, he made his film debut in 1974 in *Crazy Joe.* Then followed *The Godfather Part II, Miller's Crossing, GoodFellas, Mickey Blue Eyes,* and his Woody Allen period: *Deconstructing Harry, Celebrity, Everyone Says I Love You, Mighty Aphrodite,* and *Bullets Over Broadway.*
- Vincent Pastore (Big Pussy Bonpensiero) was a club owner in New Rochelle, when regulars Matt and Kevin Dillon talked him into trying to act. His films include Sundance winner *True Love, Jerky Boys, GoodFellas, Gotti, Witness to the Mob, The Last Don,* and *The Hurricane.*

I, 9:   Boca

Written by Jason Cahill, Robin Green and Mitchell Burgess.
Directed by Andy Wolk.

Uncle Junior's macho status is threatened by report that he is skilled at cunnilingus. He learns that Tony is talking to a psychiatrist. The gang fathers pressure their daughters' successful high school soccer coach not to leave for a university post. But when they learn he seduced one of his Grade XI players they plan their own justice.

This extraordinarily brave episode set a new benchmark even for this benchmark series. It combines the coarsest humor with ethical challenges in two serious plots. Both involve responsibility in sexual relationships and the tension between individual liberty and societal constraints. Finally, in both stories licentious behavior conceals Puritanical fears.

In the lighter plot, Uncle Junior takes his girlfriend Bobbie to Boca Raton, where for sixteen years they have escaped for carefree pleasure. When Bobbie flatters his "real instinct" for cunnilingus, Junior reminds her that his society holds it "a sign of weakness" for a man to give oral sex. It is manlier to receive than to give. A soft, generous man is vulnerable. Indeed, in the previous episode, just before Christopher shot the bakery clerk, he indignantly asked "Do I look like a pussy to you?" In this insecure, macho society, it is derogatory to associate a man with the feminine, from pussy to palaver. "You always have to talk about everything," Junior charges Bobbie.

When Carmela learns of Junior's penchant, she can't resist jokes at dinner. Having coaxed out her secret, Tony taunts Uncle Junior at their golf game, getting back at him for recalling Tony's game-losing fielding error in Little League. Tony seethes in close-up before he starts teasing Junior on the taboo.

When Junior confronts Bobbie with the leak, he restrains his impulse to punch her but shoves her lemon meringue pie in her face. This reflex derives from the famous scene in *The Public Enemy* (1931), where gangster James Cagney shoves a grapefruit in Mae Marsh's face. When Junior calls Bobbie a "stupid fucking blabbermouth cunt," he works up to the climactic rejection of the feminine part that he has most prized. A close-up on him outside, teary-eyed and alone, suggests Junior lost more than Bobbie when—

reduced by the overhead shot—he scurries away from a 16-year relationship of open sexuality and love. In effect, he abandons his softer nature. When he mentions her again—in II, 11—he has forgotten his responsibility for their split.

As Junior feels more vulnerable he grows more anxious about Tony's psychiatric sessions. When Mikey suggests that Tony's mysterious twice-weekly meetings are with the Feds, Junior reports Tony is seeing a shrink. The two are telling the same story, but Mikey has it wrong. In the men's locker room, Junior thinks violent: "Anthony wants to play games. I taught him how to play games. I taught him to play baseball." Goaded by Livia, feeling humiliated by Tony, and sensing his nephew's weakness, Junior considers killing him.

As the stakes rise, the plot is peppered with outrageous puns. There are gags about giving head, "going down" to/in Boca, "whistling in the wheatfield," "sushi," "South of the Border, where the tuna fish play," the acquired taste for that "sweet, sweet girl," the Kalahari bushman, and Tony's ingenuous confusion of the golfer's "rough" with "muff." But then, the job Junior got Bobbie is with the Joint Cutters Union. This frisky language belies the deadly seriousness of insecure men's games.

The oral sex jokes color even the innocent language. When Bobbie remarks, "If only they knew the other side of you," Junior replies: "They'd eat me for breakfast." And Tony: "You *mange*, Uncle Joon. She'll come back." Conversely, when Tony playfully calls Allie Alphonse, his gender-blind address contrasts to her seduction by her soccer coach.

It is also hypocritical—as Carmela points out—for the men who themselves may practice cunnilingus—as Tony does once a year, presumably on Carmela's (or Columbus's) birthday—to look down on it. So, too, in the more serious plot, when the gangsters learn that Hauser has seduced a student. Silvio alternates between wallowing in the transgression and fearing for his daughter: "My daughter should know this shit? My daughter should have to think about that filth? . . . That self-righteous prick put his dick in my little girl's soccer teammate!" Silvio moves between indignation and relishing the sordidness, with appropriate hand gestures.

Of course, Silvio considers Hauser self-righteous because he rejected Brandy's free blowjob at the Bing. The coach declined, whether out of respect for his wife or because he prefers his lovers adolescent. The men's ambivalence about sex and the female is nicely caught when we cut from Tony's compliment to Meadow and her teammate—"Good job, girls"—to the naked pole-dancers at the Bada Bing.

The fathers are excessively involved in their daughters' game. Silvio offers his daughter "a hundred bucks for a goal." When the referee orders him off the field, Silvio pauses to kick dirt at him. Again, a character emulates some dubious film hero. The men's passions at the game are only exceeded by their machinations outside. In appreciation, the Bada Bing gives the Coach drinks and Brandy "on the house." Her name reduces her to a free drink for Tony or Silvio to dispense.

When Hauser is reported leaving for a university post the hoods try to persuade him to stay, first with the carrot—a free fifty-inch television—then with the stick—Christopher's implied threat to the Hauser dog. At least against the television the coach stands defiant: "Don Hauser will not be intimidated." Earlier, Hauser earlier strutted his independence by quoting the most famous line from—what else?—*The Godfather:* The University of Rhode Island "made me an offer I couldn't refuse." Of course, even the desire to keep the coach is selfish, because the fathers want him to stay till their daughters graduate.

When the men learn that the girl who had slit her wrists, Allie, had been seduced by her school soccer coach, their passions roil against him. Their immediate urge is to give Hauser an "after-school special." This could be castration, now that detentions are illegal (I, 7).

In this drama Artie is a significant figure. Without his friends' power, he feels intensely their shifting attitudes toward Hauser: their appreciation, their resolve to keep him, then their rage. In fury, Artie hacks out his frustration on the weeds in his garden. After Charmaine talks him around he tries to dissuade Tony from vigilante justice. He argues that the men's revenge would satisfy only themselves. Artie counsels leaving Hauser to the police. But Tony fears he will escape with a light sentence, then "go to Saskatchewan and teach girls soccer there." When Tony throws out Artie and Charmaine's wisdom, he denies the balance of feminine sense. He is persuaded when Dr. Melfi supports Artie's/Charmaine's argument.

The issue redefines manhood. Artie wishes he had "the balls" to punish Hauser himself, instead of leaving it to Tony. But Charmaine assures him: "Arthur, you do have balls. That's why you're not like him." For Charmaine, the vigilante hood is less of a man than the responsible citizen is. The gang tweaks Artie's manhood when Charmaine calls him home from the Bada Bing. More lightly, Artie jokes that if the soccer success gets Artie's daughter a scholarship "I'll blow the coach in midfield." Artie seems laughably presumptuous when he tells Tony Soprano what to do. But he is manliest when he wields his wife's wisdom against the macho boss.

Tony admits he is completely confused when he learns of Allie's seduction. He has assumed girls playing sports didn't do drugs or get knocked up. He stumbles from one feeble rationalization to another, before Carmela mercifully sends him downstairs so she can talk with Meadow. Tony rethinks his insistence Hauser "stick around and finish what he started with the girls."

In this episode Tony is a champion of social responsibility. He orders a young man to remove his baseball cap at the classy restaurant. Having stared the boy down, Tony then sends the couple a bottle of wine. He rewards those who obey him—and would punish those who don't. When Tony discusses the coach's transgression, Melfi returns to the same question: Why does Tony assume the responsibility to set the world right? There is a thin line between the citizen's proper responsibilities and a self-flagellating compulsion. Trying for that balance, Tony apologizes for his previous session. Calling Dr. Melfi a whore "might have been overstating the case a bit." But he still plots his vigilante justice for Hauser.

In an ironic statement of this theme, when Uncle Junior reiterates his need for Bobbie's secrecy, he dismisses her logic with "What are you going to do? I don't make the rules." Of course, as Family godfather he does make the rules. More broadly, everyone in the society of this series makes his/her own rules, or chooses which laws or conventions to accept, which to modify, which to ignore. Meadow's girlfriends, including Silvio's and Hauser's daughters, will drink in the park but will go only so far in working for a coach they can't stand. From AJ's mischief to Livia's mothering, *The Sopranos* reflects a society where people live without governing absolutes. They are responsible for themselves. They make their own rules.

Even after throwing Artie out, Tony wavers whether or not to unleash Silvio outside Hauser's house. We don't know his decision until the TV news reports that an unnamed school friend of the victim reported Hauser to the police and he has been arrested. Tony staggers home, falling-down drunk from his Prozac cocktail, and before passing out at his wife's feet mumbles "Carmela, I didn't hurt nobody." For once his profession of innocence is true.

Meadow watches this scene from upstairs, strong and clear-eyed. Perhaps she was the informer, the Soprano who took on the Hauser problem— through the legal system. After all, in the last scene she holds the high ground when Tony crashes in, hands clean for once but out of control, as if he could not do the right, the responsible, the female sensible thing without getting drunk first. Tony seems to have lost another virginity, in for the first time *not* taking brutish action; he needed to be bolstered by drink to prove this manhood too. Besides, we've seen Meadow confront Hauser before. "Go fuck yourself," she tells him, then runs her 20-lap punishment, and only then quits his team. We are not told who blew the whistle on Hauser. But in this series' gathering logic, we can respectfully suspect Meadow. After all, she has her father's sense of justice and initiative.

▪ The pie/grapefruit allusion to *The Public Enemy* evokes one of David Chase's favorite films: "Even now, he can—and does—recite most of *Public Enemy* complete with a description of camera angles. 'It blew my mind. It hooked me. I don't know why, but it did' " (Holden, p. 24). The film figures more extensively in III, 1, where we see the grapefruit scene.

I, 10: A Hit Is a Hit

Written by Joe Bosso and Frank Renzulli. Directed by Matthew Penn.

Tony and Carmela socialize with their respectable neighbors. Christopher sponsors Adriana's launch into music management by funding the demo of a rock band fronted by an ex-boyfriend. A black rap mogul pressures Hesh to pay back-royalties to the survivor of one of his music performers from the past.

The titular "hit" is both a mob and a musical term. This episode provides a variety of pecking orders—societal and musical—and the temptation to try to rise in them.

In the opening scene Paulie, Chris, and Pussy make a huge score by killing a drug runner in New York for invading their territory. In this context, they are punishing an invader, reaffirming his exclusion. As if for balance, later Tony is denied membership in the private golf club because the membership is full. Old members have to die before new ones can be admitted.

If Tony spurns the obvious strategy, it is because he does not really want to join that supercilious society, the "mayonnaisers." He is concerned what his friends would think if he were to hang out with what his father called "Wonder-bread Wops." Tony's "whites" means assimilated Italian, not Caucasian. In an episode about the racial tension between blacks and whites, the term suggests there is hegemony within races as well as between them.

Because Carmela wants to broaden the family's social sphere she and Tony mingle with non-mob (as distinct from non-criminal) American-Italians at a barbecue. The men freeze their stock market talk when Tony enquires, yet they pump him for Mafia information. At the private golf club Tony feeds their fantasies. How "real" was *The Godfather*? Did Tony have to bleed his finger for an oath? They exclude him from their circle but want the secrets of his.

At first uncomfortable, Tony proceeds to one-up them. He invents a story about John Gotti outbidding him at an auction of an ice cream truck then driving him home in it, ringing the bell all the way. His listeners know they have heard something true and poetic but they can not figure out what it means. The anecdote recalls the sinister ice-cream truck in Mahaffey's conversion scene in I, 1. The golfers are also thrilled when Tony calls Dr. Cusamano "The Cooze," because they feel admitted into mob argot. Tony later assures Dr. Cusamano that the word no longer connotes "pussy."

Even these Italian-Americans reduce other Italian-Americans to the mob stereotype. At the dinner party Dr. Cusamano relishes the scene in *Casino* (Martin Scorsese) where Joe Pesci pops a rival's head in a vise. That is, all along the social ladder people draw reference points and attitude from the gangster movies. At the other end, Paulie, when Chris uncharacteristically leaves an orgy to take Adriana to dinner, quotes another gangster classic (Mervyn LeRoy's *Little Caesar*, 1930): "Mother of Mercy, is this the end of Rico?" Of course, when Adriana becomes the FBI's target at the end of Season III, she becomes the "end" (that is, objective, target) of RICO (the Racketeer Influenced and Corrupt Organizations Act).

Tony tells Melfi that the golf game taught him what it is like to be used for someone else's amusement, "like a dancing bear." He recalls that as a kid he and friends similarly exploited Jimmy Smash, a boy with a cleft palate. When they were bored they had him sing for them, so they could laugh. The kid craved to hang out with his exploiters but he cried his way home.

But the newly sensitized Tony again makes Jimmy a joke. After explaining Jimmy is doing 20 years for robbery, Tony comically imitates the man's voice, by which he was identified in a bank robbery despite his mask. Tony persists with his joke even now he is aware the joking was wrong. His politically incorrect instincts continue unrestrained. Typically, Tony's incorrigibility is the basis of both his evil and his charm. As Carmela admits, about his episode-ending mischief with the sandbox, "You look kind of cute when you're being a bad boy."

Perhaps that dynamic is also at work in the episode's first scene, the New York mugging. The murder scene is entirely at odds with the comedy in the rest of the episode. While the episode satirizes the Italian-American film stereotype, the opening plays a cliché scene straight. Tony repeats the ridicule he is embarrassed to have made, feeding the golfers a fiction that fulfills their expectations, the episode itself starting off with a gangster film cliché—in each case the art plays to a prejudice.

As Carmela grows insecure about what she would do if "something happened" to Tony, she acts on a stock tip she gleaned from her society outing. Her first purchase does well. A headline reports that because of the success of its impotence drug, American Biotics Tumescent splits three for one. Presumably, the women learned the promise of this drug from their husbands, whether from their bull market or their bed.

But Carmela will never enjoy their comfort level. The respectable wives know they are secure: "We don't just play [the stock market and, one assumes, anything else]; we win." And they're legitimate. In fact, Tony earlier plans to invest his windfall score in something "legit"—like "some insider trading shit." This, Cusamano's cronies—and their wives—clearly practice.

Because Adriana doesn't want to be a housewife like Carmela, she talks about running her own restaurant or managing musicians. As the ambitious/frustrated Christopher envies the glamour of Massive Genius, the black rap mogul, he decides to launch her. But Chris remains Chris. To encourage the lead singer he smashes a guitar on his head. When he drops the mediocre band and suggests Massive Genius was interested in her, not them, Adriana charges that Chris is still trying to "keep me down." As for his macho silence: "You're either screaming your head off or fucking dead." Having discovered her own ambition, she now resists her recessive role in the relationship.

Chris flashes his bigotry when he's impatient for service at the burger shop. To a black customer Chris replies: "I'm looking for a burger, not converted rice." This Uncle Ben aspersion recurs around Tony's aversion to Noah in III, 2. Despite his racism, Massive Genius accepts Chris as a useful tool.

In fact, Chris's racism only confirms Massive Genius's assumption about the Italian and Jewish gangsters. In a collision of pecking orders, Massive Genius expresses his respect for Chris's "people" by praising *The Godfather*, which he saw "200 times." Moreover, he pretends to a special sensitivity by defending *The Godfather Part III* as "misunderstood." Regrettably, he does not elaborate. Perhaps he relishes the honky overlord's suffering—diabetes, debility, heartbreak, and death. Or he may simply be trying to ingratiate himself, as Chris called out to "Martin Scorsese" about another unvalued film, "*Kundun*—I liked it!" (I, 2).

Massive Genius flexes his new power by trying to shake Hesh down for $400,000 in royalties he says Hesh owes the family of Little Jimmy Willis, one of Hesh's old music partners. The singer died penniless, having—as Silvio quips—blown on horse (heroin) the money Hesh invested in his horse farm.

Massive lumps Hesh in with the history of whites, especially the Jews in the entertainment industries, who exploited the black. Hesh claims "My people were the white man's nigger when yours were still painting your faces and chasing zebras." That animal can pass in both the white and the black worlds, so it is an appropriate emblem for Hesh to confront Massive. When Hesh calls Massive "Tatteleh" (Yiddish: "little father," but not quite "Daddy-O"), he provides his own ethnic version of "Bro."

In contrast to all the episode's wannabes Hesh is a self-sufficient, solid integrity. He seriously considers Massive's moral and legal argument before deciding not to pay. Threatened with a lawsuit—with Massive's *Jewish* lawyers—he counters with pertinent savvy. Hesh notes that one of Massive's hit songs plagiarized one of his songs' rhythm track. More than a legal ploy, this proves that Hesh knows rhythm and blues music. That is, he has a plausible claim for composer royalties on the songs Massive contends Willis wrote alone. Of course, in I, 6, Tony teased Hesh by joking that he took the credit for songs the black kids wrote. But Tony could have been teasing his friend. Here, when sound engineer Squid criticizes Adriana's singer for poor structure in his songs, he shows how Hesh might have contributed to Little Jimmy's composing.

Later Hesh dismisses Chris's group's demo—and Chris's charge that Hesh's musical judgment is obsolete. Unaffected by Chris's ambition, Hesh judges from his own solid core. If the song he calls a hit—Dori Hartley's "Nobody Loves Me but You," from his album, *Blue Djinn*—happens not to have been a hit, that only confirms the independence and solidity of Hesh's judgment: He's talking quality, not sales. Whether Adriana's group is called Defiled or Visiting Day, Hesh knows they are not good. In contrast, Massive Genius likes "any music that turns shit green" (that is, makes money).

The zebra also emblematizes the assimilated Italian-Americans. When viewed in their natural habitat—the Cusamanos' dinner party—they reveal their own pecking order. One guest wonders how Mafia neighbors affect their god, "property values." Dr. Cusamano shares the Monte Cristos (Cuban cigars, illegal) Tony gave him, but condescends even in his defense. With its bribery and bugging, "Sometimes I think the only thing separating American business from the mobs is fuckin' whackin' someone." The "closed" membership at the Cooze's golf club recalls Tony telling Chris that the "made" membership is full. As the doctor's diction has been inflected by exposure to Tony, the distinctions between legitimate and illegitimate business have blurred. Melfi bravely opposes one woman's denigration of the Sopranos' taste: "I like Murano glass."

But Tony has the last laugh. He enigmatically asks his neighbor to keep a package for him for a few weeks, which The Cooze and his wife assume is important and likely illegal but are too nervous to open. It is just sand. Here Tony's evil is safely "so much fun." When the episode closes on the Cusamanos scared of their box, we are brought full circle to the opening scene, where Tony's gang grabbed someone else's stash. The closing tone is much lighter than the opening. A playful hoax is not a bullet between the courier's eyes.

And yet . . . and yet, we and the Cusamanos hear a couple of pained screams from next door. They recall the screams that Dr. Melfi heard when she left the dining room to see Tony's house from the Cusamanos' bathroom. Tony denied hearing them, when she asked, but she heard definite screams. Now we see their source: Tony, as he strains under the weights in his basement exercise room. Logical enough in their literal import, the screams additionally express the strain and the pain of someone trying to improve his condition, in a melting pot America that maintains prohibitive social barriers not just between but within its ethnic hierarchies.

In the episode's most delicate exchange, Dr. Melfi tells Tony that she was at the Cusamanos for dinner and she saw his house. She does not tell him that she went out of her way for the excuse to go to the bathroom, flushing for a cover, and that she climbed the bidet for her glimpse. Nor her delicacy in taking a piece of toilet paper to lower the seat, a gesture that reminds us how far apart Melfi's and Tony's natures are. As Tony leaves he pauses in the doorway, then says "You saw my house." With another shuffle he is gone.

His line hangs in the air. That she saw his house suggests to him that she wanted to look at it. She has sought an insight, an intimacy, outside their sessions. Perhaps Tony even entertains the thought that Jennifer Melfi may have been impressed by it. Moved to regard him more respectfully, she may perhaps now be more open to him. We detected her squirm when The Cooze said his patient gave him the Monte Cristos because he was "very happy" with his referral (that is, Melfi). Though none of this is spoken, in the glimpse, the report, its consideration, the shrink's relationship with her client has reached a new intimacy, despite the patient's aggression and the therapist's recoil.

I, 11:   Nobody Knows Anything

Written by Frank Renzulli. Directed by Henry Bronchtein.

Pussy collapses in a brothel from his back problems. A police raid on Jimmy Altieri's social club uncovers a cache of weapons in the pool table. Pussy and Jimmy are arrested, but Pussy is released immediately. Vin, Tony's police source, reports that Pussy has been wired to incriminate him. Meanwhile Livia, angry that Tony has sold her house, tells Uncle Junior that Tony meets with three other *capos* at the seniors residence, where they have put their mothers. When Vin is arrested in a brothel raid and suspended, he kills himself. As Tony concludes that Jimmy is the traitor, Uncle Junior decides to have Tony killed.

This episode unleashes a variety of betrayals against one surprising and maverick loyalty. As the first season nears its conclusion the emphasis is on the disorder still to be settled.

Much of it deals with Tony's pain at the idea that Pussy might be the traitor. "Like him, I fuckin' love him" he tells his detective Vin Macazian. But Pussy is the Feds' favorite target for "flipping" because he "loves his family above all else." Trying to prevent his treachery, Tony assures Pussy that he would never be out of options (that is, bound to the Feds); he has friends who would die for him. But when Tony jokes that the convalescing Pussy is a "beached whale" he anticipates his marine death.

To ascertain whether Pussy is indeed wired, Paulie takes him to a steam bath. Pussy pleads his doctor's insistence that a *schvitz* (Yiddish for sweat) would be bad for his high blood pressure. Tony insists on being "110-percent sure" before ordering what he has to. He requires Paulie to see the wire on him before acting. This is Othello's "ocular proof." If he demands less evidence before shifting his suspicion onto Jimmy, it's because Tony does love Pussy and fears wrongly condemning him. When Pussy disappears, Tony physically attacks Paulie for perhaps having acted prematurely.

Tony's loyalty to Pussy—and Paulie's loyalty to Tony, in taking on Pussy's punishment for him—contrasts to Livia's betrayal of her son. Livia maintains her martyred innocence in the face of Carmela's bluntness: "I want you to cut the drama. It's killing Tony." Livia fires Uncle Junior against her son, when she seems to let slip Tony's conspiracy with the other *capos*. As usual, her dangerous innuendo begins as a complaint: "I suppose he would have found it harder to have his meetings at my house than in the nursing home. . . . Maybe it was you they were talking about, who knows? . . . Now I just don't like being put in the middle of things." When Junior decides to have Tony killed, "Blood or no," Livia feigns concern: "Oh, God, what did I say now?" Junior is so paranoid that more than one meeting of the *capos* becomes a disease: He says "pleurisy" for "plural."

The other regulars have minor roles in this episode. Melfi allows that Pussy's bad back could result from his secret and guilt. At breakfast Meadow remarks upon America's backwardness in still criminalizing prostitution and in persecuting the president (presumably Bill Clinton, unnamed) for his vagrant sex life. Tony confirms his loyalty to old values (as to old friends): "Out there it's the 1990s. But in this house it's 1954."

The episode's most surprising case of loyalty is Tony's bought detective, Vin Macazian. When Vin objects to Tony's insults, we assume Tony disdains of Vin for being disloyal—albeit to the police. Disloyalty is bad in itself. But we later (in III, 3) learn that in Tony's most traumatic childhood experience, his father used his brutality to teach Tony not to gamble. So Tony hates Vin for gambling. In II, 8, Tony tells Melfi that his victim Davey is "a fuckin' degenerate gambler." In I, 1, he called Mahaffey "a degenerate fuckin' gambler." To his face here Tony calls Vin "a degenerate fuckin' gambler with a badge." Even Livia dismisses the elderly Millie at Green Grove as "a degenerate gambler." Johnny-Boy made the phrase a moral unit. Of course, whatever risks he may take Tony does not gamble.

Moreover, as that trauma associated gambling and raw meat with violence and sexuality in Tony's mind, there is also an irony in Vin's earlier quip (in I, 4) to Melfi: "You have prime rib at home. Don't be going out for hamburgers." Assuming Melfi is one of Tony's conquests, Vin cites Tony's weakness, his phobia for meat, as if it were his strength. Again, the irony in the language shimmers across episodes.

To some extent, Vin embodies the weaknesses that Tony has suppressed in himself. Tony is surprised at this bond. Having assumed that Vin's service is out of strictly mercenary motive, he is touched when the madam Debbie tells him that Vin always liked and trusted Tony. She recalls his assurance: "As long as he had you in his corner there is nothing really to worry about. . . . At least with Tony Soprano you know where you stand." In the episode's last scene Tony stands contemplative under the bridge from which his unappreciated friend dove.

In an earlier conversation Tony found something of his own experience in the turned cop's. As a boy, Vin recalls, he used to hide under his bed all night to escape his parents' violence. Especially now Tony knows the need for such refuge. He could also identify with Debbie's summary of Vin: "He was not happy with himself. How he turned out." The reason why may be inferred from Vin's pinning his badge back on before diving to his death. When Vin sarcastically applauds Tony's "amazing ability to sum up a man's whole life in a sentence," his complexity and ambivalence parallels Tony's.

For years Vin went to Debbie for friendship and mutual support. Tony comes to regard that relationship as a variation on his with Dr. Melfi. As Debbie remarks, "Who wouldn't want to sleep with their shrink? . . . You would be amazed how much easier it is to open up when you're naked and in the arms of someone who cares for you." Although we do not see much of the Vin-Debbie relationship, it seems warm, understanding and healthy—especially when compared to the vituperative marriage between Mikey Palmice and JoJo. The latter bristles harsh even after Mikey hears Junior has ordered Tony's murder, which would lead to Mikey's promotion.

In this episode about trust and betrayals there is a metaphoric resonance in Paulie's report from the doctor: "When it comes to backs nobody knows anything, really."

I, 12: Isabella

Written by Robin Green and Mitchell Burgess. Directed by Allen Coulter.

Worried about Pussy's disappearance, Tony is overcome by depression, despite his diet of Prozac and Lithium. For Uncle Junior, Mikey puts out a contract on Tony. Chris unwittingly thwarts the first attempt by parking in the assassins' way while spying on Tony. On the second, Tony wrestles the assassins in turn through his car windows, has one shoot the other, then grabs the second's gun. Laughing exuberantly at having escaped, Tony smashes his car and is briefly hospitalized for stitches on his ear. He spurns the FBI's offer of the Witness Protection Program. His encounter with a beautiful, nurturing Italian exchange student is revealed to be a fantasy. AJ goes to his first prom, escorted by Silvio and Paulie in a limousine.

From the opening shot, the corpse of the woman Uncle Junior nostalgically remembers giving him his first handjob behind the chicken market, this episode is about death in life. The outdoor shots show the trees turned yellow, the autumn of desiccation and chill. When Jimmy Altieri tells Junior "How many of these [funerals] do we have to go to?" we know he has just his own left. Suspected of informing the Feds, Jimmy will be killed in the next episode. Uncle Junior points to the spiritual void of his time when he wonders why Saints cards don't sell like baseball cards: "Thousands of bucks for Honus Wagner and jackshit for Jesus." In addition to the righteousness and alliteration, the phrase shows how Junior, not unlike the Metaphysical poets, unites the profane and the religious in one passion.

When Tony is not cowering slit-eyed under his blankets, he stumbles through his days in a depressed stupor. In his first session he and Dr. Melfi are unusually framed in the same shot, as if he needs her to prop him up. Denying any pain, he says: "I don't feel nothin'. Nothin'. Dead. Empty." He stumbles out of bed to his drugs, against the Tindersticks's song, "Tiny Tears," a spare, melancholy lyric about someone lying in bed week after week, "too busy looking into your head, To see the tiny tears in her eye."

Tony's one vitality in this episode turns out to be a fantasy. He sees a beautiful young Italian woman hanging white laundry next door. He walks over and sniffs the slip he picks off the grass. Isabella is an exchange student studying dental surgery, house-sitting while the Cusamanos are golfing in Bermuda. When he meets her downtown and takes her to lunch she guesses his people are from Avelino. Tony envisions her in a rural house, nursing their baby. We might infer he's projecting a fantasy of them together, but he later tells Melfi the fantasy was set around 1907 and she was whispering to baby Antonio not to cry, not to worry, everything will be alright, she loves him. The sexual, idealized Isabella is the mother Tony never had.

When Cusamano returns Tony realizes that he imagined the entire experience. But for Melfi it points to Tony's need for a loving, caring woman in his life, at a time when Livia keeps reporting news stories about mothers murdering their children and when she has prodded Uncle Junior to kill him. Tony denies his mother's possible involvement in what he insists was a carjacking. The FBI and the TV news say it was a failed assassination attempt; Silvio and Chris assume it was at Uncle Junior's order.

There are careful clues to suggest Isabella is a fantasy figure. For one thing, she's too beautiful to be true. Her whiteness and full-bosom ethereality recall Claudia Cardinale wafting through Federico Fellini's *8½* (1963). Tony meets Isabella outside a pharmacy that has an antique window display and a sign, CHEMIST SINCE 1907. Their conversation bristles with the fugitive metaphors of a dream. She knows where he's coming from (including Avelino). If she's studying dental surgery it's because Tony has a cavity to fill (and has an episode ago had a flat tire while driving AJ to a dentist for his braces). When Tony—and a close-up—focuses on her perfect mouth, her beauty may embody the pre-sexual orality of the child. Her interest in gum tumors and soft tissue points to Tony's need for a woman of healthy softness, who would replace his malignant undermining (the tumors/rumors of his mother wanting him whacked). His own anxieties reflect in her wondering why a "hero" would be trapped in a sandwich and why his foundation should be shaken by a "hurt-quake."

When Carmela sees the woman she is concerned that he took her for lunch ("If I had an ounce of self-respect I would cut your dick off"). But that verification of Isabella is immediately undercut. The shot of Tony in bed rotates 90 degrees, so that the prone Tony seems erect, and the maid tells him Carmela has gone to New York to buy a suit for AJ's prom. As we know Carmela has already done this, the line declares this exchange— and therefore the previous one with Carmela—fantasy. Even as Tony fantasizes a nourishing woman he generates a balancing punishment. Both his fantasy love and his fantasy of his wife are a way to avoid thinking of his mother.

Of course, Livia is at full venom. She drives Tony from the dinner table with her insults. Why should he be depressed, she snorts: "Nobody threw him into the glue factory and sold his house out from under him." A scene outside a cinema could be either real or part of Tony's fantasy. As she and Junior line up for tickets, Livia details how dead Tony already acts and how non-existent he is as a father. "Don't talk about Tony any more," Junior snaps, "It's done." This scene is so consistent with the plotters' realistic scenes that it could be happening. On the other hand, as everything in the scene is gray and it is blown with the same strong wind that blows around the radiant Isabella, it could be Tony's fantasy, in which his subconscious finally admits the conspiracy against him. This confusion between reality and dread confirms the death-like state of Tony's life at this point.

The characters react variously to the failed assassination. When he hears of the first failure Junior vomits out of his car. After the second he panics over Tony's likely revenge. Carmela wants to take up FBI agent Harris's offer of witness relocation: "This is our chance to get out." But Tony would not break his oath of *omertà*—nor retire to sell souvenirs roadside or to ranch rattlesnakes in Utah.

As she watches the TV-news report with Uncle Junior, Livia is shocked: "How could this happen. . . . My son got shot—and he got away! . . . He's my only son." She shifts from the obligatory shock that Tony was shot, to the genuine disappointment that he got away, to maternal rhetoric. Her first words to Tony are unconsoling: "Your ear—it's disfigured." When she doesn't recognize Meadow, Junior angrily confronts her about her convenient loss of memory. She gives her usual bold reply: "I don't know what you're talking about." A chastened Junior senses that his dangerous action was based on an unreliable, vengeful old woman.

Tony's session in Melfi's car seems almost romantic. When Carmela drives him to the dark country road, she avoids looking at Melfi as if she were his *goomah*. "Did you ever tell anyone about you and me?" he asks Melfi, as if they were furtive lovers. Though she answers that truthfully, she tells a lover's white lie: that the cigarettes in her car are her son's. We know (I, 8) Jason moved to a smoke-free dorm. Her eyes fill with tears as she explains how his fantasy of a nourishing Isabella addressed his situation with Livia. When they part, he caresses her cheek with his knuckles.

And how does Tony feel after his brush with death (from the other end of the scythe)? "To tell you the truth I feel pretty good." Getting shot "gives you a nice kick start," he tells Dr. Melfi. (In this violent context he says "kick start," vs. the "jump start" he used in the sexual context in I, 6). When in his depression he wanted to die, now "every fuckin' particle of my being was fighting to live."

We glimpsed his revived spirit earlier, when Father Phil dropped in to express his concern and suggested a circle of prayer: "Why don't you grab a sandwich and we'll talk later. You are sleeping over, aren't you?" The incorrigible Tony S. is back alive and kicking—especially at the freeloading family priest. Fitting that the episode closes on Cream's "I Feel Free." The last line we hear could speak for Tony's post-assault cockiness: "I can walk down the street and there's no one there." Of course, it also reflects his solitude, the solitude that comes with the mark of Cain.

▪ As usual, the script sparkles with incidental information. Carmela opens the windows on Tony: "In Alaska they wear these little light hats in the winter so they don't get depressed." And as Silvio points out, "Winston Churchill, he drank a quart of brandy before breakfast. And Napoleon, he was a moody fuck, too." No theme is too bleak to go unlightened by this series' dark comedy.

I, 13: I Dream of Jeannie Cusamano

Written by David Chase. Directed by John Patterson.

As Livia shows increasing signs of Alzheimer's she is transferred to the nursing unit. She tells Artie that Tony burned down his Vesuvio. When Artie confronts Tony with a shotgun he is talked out of his anger. Tony violently attacks Dr. Melfi for suggesting that Livia might have been involved in his assassination attempt. But he is persuaded when the FBI plays their tapes of her Green Grove conversations with Junior. Tony, Chris, and Silvio kill Junior's two aides, but before they can get to Junior he is arrested in an FBI sweep. Junior refuses the FBI offer to implicate Tony instead. When Tony comes to the hospital to smother his mother he is thwarted by the fact she has suffered a stroke. In the last scene Tony, Carmela, and the children, trapped in a heavy storm, are given refuge in Artie's restaurant.

In the first season's finale there is a general clearing of the air and the conclusion of several issues. Tony secures his position by having traitor Jimmy Altieri and Junior's two henchmen, Chucky Signore and Mikey Palmice, killed. Though Junior is saved by his arrest, his power shifts to Tony. Tony finally realizes his own position when the FBI plays tapes of his mother and Junior plotting against him.

Livia continues her subtle destruction. When Artie visits her she pretends confusion—remembering that husband Johnny-Boy, not Tony, played Little League with Artie—before letting slip her lethal revelation: "You're such a good boy, Artie. . . . After what my son did to you, how can I look you in the face? . . . You don't blame him for starting the fire? I guess we have to be grateful that nobody was incinerated to death." Between the compliment and the relief comes the shiv.

Tony's denial to Artie is false but it is literally and emotionally true: "I didn't burn down your restaurant. I swear on my mother." In fact, he only commissioned the arson; nor would he object if Livia suffered divine retribution. To Artie's correct statement of Tony's motive for the arson Tony makes the only possible defense: "Here's a question for you. Am I that fuckin' stupid?" Thus persuaded, Artie smashes his rifle on his own station wagon—not the action of a smart wiseguy—and speeds off, even more overwrought than on his arrival.

Even after Tony knows about his mother's and uncle's plot, he hosts them at the traditional Sunday dinner. In this world the relatively virtuous can be as duplicitous as the vile. "I don't have to admit anything," Livia responds to an innocent remark by Carmela. Over dinner Livia pretends not to remember Artie Bucco.

In a bedroom chat Tony blames himself: "What kind of person can I be, if my own mother wants me dead." Carmela wisely shifts the blame to Livia. When she adds that she's a peculiar duck, the innocent colloquialism recalls Tony's dream (I, 1) of a bird flying off with his penis, which to Melfi represents Livia emasculating her son. Tony blames his razzing of Junior and the fear of what he may have told Melfi for the war: "Cunnilingus and psychiatry brought us to this." For Tony, that is a doubled fear of the feminine. Tony declares that he will take of care of Junior and Mikey "and I'll get some satisfaction. But inside I'll know"—the inexpressible: that his own mother tried to have him killed.

In the episode's most dramatic scene, Tony leans over his mother as she is being wheeled up the hospital hallway and tells her: "I know what you did. Your only son. . . . I heard the tapes!" When the orderlies say she can't understand, Tony fights off them and their illusions about her: "Look at her face. She's smiling." Under her oxygen mask, the indomitable Livia seems indeed to be.

Artie's explosion against Tony clears their air as well. When Artie later thanks Father Phil for his counsel, we infer that the priest has been urging Artie to tell Charmaine and the police that Tony was responsible for burning down the Vesuvio. His "You must be strong" apparently means "strong enough to turn Tony in—or to let Charmaine do it for you." All the while Father Phil has been assuring Carmela of his concern for Tony and enjoying his steaks and DVD player, he has been counseling Artie against him. The priest is disappointed when Artie finds peace in not squealing. Doubting Tony "would only add to the quotient of sorrow in the world," Artie rationalizes, like a good sermon.

After Carmela learns that Rosalie Aprile gave Father Phil her Jackie's watch and finds them snuggled over the lunch she brought him, Carmela rebukes Father Phil's pretended interest in Tony and affirms her independence from her priest:

He doesn't give a flying fuck. . . . I think that you like the . . . whiff of sexuality that never goes anyplace. . . . I think you need to look at yourself. . . . I think you have this m.o. where you manipulate spiritually thirsty women. And I think a lot of it is tied up with food somehow as well as the sexual tension game.

In her wisdom and articulate coolness, Carmela shows a remarkable strength here. Her self-awareness ("spiritually thirsty women") and courage to abandon a false support contrast to the helpless Livia's demonic strength. Carmela's strength is all the more impressive given that she has been shaken by the sweeping arrests and by seeing Mikey's wife crying on television about her husband's disappearance. The reaction shot shows Carmela identifying.

Unable to respond, Father Phil retrieves his DVD and leaves. He represents the supposedly superior alternative to Tony but is exposed as equally self-serving, self-indulgent, and predatory. As exasperated Carmela points out, "I get exactly the same 'who me?' shit from Tony." From the priest's sanctimoniousness Tony is attractively free.

This scene begins with Carmela coming home with groceries and finding the priest in her kitchen, having checked the fridge. He brought a DVD that Carmela does not want to see (in her one curious lapse of judgment Carmela is not a Renee Zellweger fan). The only *One True Thing* about Father Phil is the title of the film he says he brought for Carmela's interest.

Far stormier is Tony's confrontation with Melfi. Tony hears her apposite definition of a "borderline personality disorder." But when she suggests Livia may be behind the assassination attempt he leaps on her, swearing and threatening. Tony has to overcome her fear before Melfi admits him again—having slipped precautionary scissors up her sleeve. In their brief discussion Tony says his only dreams have involved him having sex with Jeannie Cusamano, doggie-style, and he refers to her "big ass," which as Melfi observes does not apply to the slender Jeannie. As he fantasizes to avoid confronting the real women in his life, he turns to others' cheeks. When Tony warns that Melfi's life may be in danger she slips into the mob argot: "I can't lam it. . . . Jesus fucking Christ!" But—still not of Tony's world—she calls Pussy "Booty" by mistake.

When Tony tells his three aides about his therapy and invites their response, they react sympathetically. "I'm sure you did it with complete discretion," Silvio offers, confident he also speaks for the still absent Pussy. Paulie surprises: "I was seeing a therapist myself about a year ago. I had some issues. Enough said. I lacked some coping skills." Chris doesn't know what to think—"Was it like marriage counseling?"—so he just runs out.

The first season closes on a note of familial warmth and grace. When Artie lets Tony bring his family in from the storm he overrides his suspicions about the arson and Charmaine's rejection of the mob. As Tony toasts his family, he beams at his children: "You two'll have your own families someday soon. And if you're lucky you'll remember the little moments. Like this. [pause] That were good." The pause suggests that perhaps most of the family's "little moments" may not have been so good.

The prospect of these children having their own families harkens back to the episode's start. Livia's unexpected visit interrupted Meadow petting under a boy on the sofa and AJ masturbating in his room. The road toward having children indeed begins with such fumbling adolescent sexuality.

More seriously, this conclusion returns to the season's opening episode. The nostalgia about "little moments . . . that were good" recalls Tony's remarks to Carmela in I, 1, when she attended his CAT scan: "We had some good times. Some good years." In the first episode Tony cried when his lost ducks portended his loss of his family. His toast here shows that the 13 episodes of tribulation and self-discovery have reconciled him to that natural cycle of growth and life. Though the last episode is propelled by the energy of Buddy Holly's "Rave On" and Bruce Springsteen's "State Trooper," two classical pieces—Gabriel Faure's *Pavane* (a rock version of which was played in "*Pax Soprana*," [I, 6]) and Samuel Barber's *Adagio for Strings*—close the season on notes of peace and warmth.

- In an apparent continuity error, the FBI tape ostensibly made at the retirement home includes some of the cinema line-up conversation, Livia on Tony seeming already dead and Junior's "Don't talk about Tony. It's done." Similarly, in the previous episode Livia complains that Tony has sold her house. In the next season, it has not been sold and it accommodates Janice's romance with Richie. These are minor trespasses in a series of such remarkable coherence. For example:

When the FBI agent tells Junior he really wants to get Johnny Sack and his superiors, Junior replies: "I want to fuck Angie Dickinson. See who gets lucky first." Junior dreams he marries Angie—still in the context of turning informer—in his anesthetic dream in III, 7. One presumes Junior loves the Angie of *Rio Bravo* (Howard Hawks, 1959), not that of the later *Police Woman* television series.

When Tony pulls a gun out of a fish's mouth to kill Chucky Signore, he sets off a string a "sleeping with the fishes" incidents, alluding to *The Godfather*. It culminates in the murder of Pussy—and Tony's torment thereafter.

- With regard to Tony's "Cunnilingus and psychiatry brought us to this," Chase considers this line too literary, self-conscious, and arch—"but I couldn't resist it" (Season One DVD, disc four).

Season Two

II, 1:   Guy Walks into a Psychiatrist's Office

Written by Jason Cahill. Directed by Allen Coulter.

Pussy returns to a suspicious Tony. Tony's older hippie sister Janice comes from Seattle to care for Livia, who has recovered from her "stroke" but is still hospitalized. Christopher cheats to get his stockbroker's license so he can operate a crooked brokerage firm. Tony has the jailed Uncle Junior's gunsel aide Philly Parisi killed. Tony suffers panic attacks but cannot find a therapist.

The second season opens in the un-Soprano setting of a classroom, with an authoritative black man in a suit presiding over a room of individual desks and computers. An Oriental man about to take the stockbroker's exam identifies himself as Christopher Moltisanti. Chris requires this certification for a new scam that derives from Tony's plan to invest the windfall (I, 10) score in something "legit." The surprise and meaning of this scene depend on our knowing what Christopher looks like and is. This in-joke is a playful way to welcome back a familiar audience.

A montage reintroduces the major characters, accompanied by Frank Sinatra's "A Very Good Year." In addition to the song's usual nostalgia, here it implicitly celebrates the series' successful beginning. The montage begins with a pan from an IV to a hospital patient—Livia, apparently recovering. Then we see Tony playing the emblematic solitaire, the gang passing in a bag full of money, Junior in jail, Carmela cooking, the FBI labeling Tony's picture as the new "Street Boss," Dr. Melfi meeting clients in a motel, Silvio flashing new shoes and suit, AJ starting to take an interest in his looks, Livia at therapy, Paulie (ditto) screwing a stripper on the Bing pool table, Chris snorting coke in front of an Edward G. Robinson gangster film on TV, Meadow taking a driving lesson from the affectionate Tony, Carmela still cooking, Tony under his mistress Irina, then tiptoeing home, throwing his perfumed shirt in the washer, then joining Carmela in bed. She awakens long enough to turn away from him.

While it is business as usual, some old habits (Carmela, Paulie, Chris, Tony) are interwoven with new beginnings (Livia, AJ, Silvio, Meadow, Melfi). There is often a fugitive connection between the Sinatra phrase and the visual it attends—e.g., a comment on woman's vanity for Silvio and AJ preening, the mellow sense of life as vintage wine, from the brim to the dregs, over Tony and Carmela in bed together—usually ironic.

The plot resumes with a threat and its apparent resolution. When Tony goes out for the morning paper he recoils from a suspicious car in the driveway. Out steps the long-missing Pussy, whose suspicions of Tony are reciprocated. Pussy says he went for back treatments to Puerto Rico, where he became involved with a 26-year-old acupuncturist. Now he's back because he needs the money to support his family, two kids in college and one marrying. He hadn't contacted anyone because his friends had turned "their hearts of stone" against him. They read his weakness as treason. He knew he was in trouble when out of the blue Tony came at 3 P.M. to assure him he had friends. He knows Tony's embrace is to frisk him for a wire. His bad back may denote a suspect spine. Even as his cronies welcome him back and convey (most of) his territory earnings, Tony has Paulie check out Pussy's story. At the Bing, when Silvio performs his *Godfather* Pacino for Pussy, he concludes with the prophetic: "Our true enemy has yet to reveal himself."

In addition to the treacherous Pussy, Tony is afflicted with his older sister, Janice, a Seattle hippie who now calls herself Parvati (after a Hindu goddess). Janice's scam is total disability insurance for her chronic carpal syndrome. After promising to take Livia back to Seattle, to look after her, Janice tries to prevent Tony's sale of Livia's house and to grab what she can from Livia. Janice is equal parts New Age Flake—looking to the Chelsea set to fund her new video—and schemer, as she reveals in her poolside chat with sister Barbara. Notwithstanding her lack of work ethic and her general dysfunctionality, Janice plans a self-help video titled "Lady Kerouac; or, Packing for the Highway to a Woman's Self-Esteem."

With no Melfi to help him, Tony disintegrates. At first he seems in control. Though he is off therapy he is self-medicating and confident. After whacking Philly, Tony feels secure enough to tell Melfi that she can safely resume her normal business. She is shocked and angry that he knows her motel phone number and seems to be watching her. Being as safe as Tony does not mean she is safe from him.

Apart from Pussy's danger, Tony's main problem at work is Christopher, who neglects his duties as their brokerage's SCC Compliance Officer. The operation hustles sales of a bad company to fixed-income pensioners. Even Tony's lawyer, Neil Mink, has sold some of his Disney to buy the inflated "Wobistics" (the name seems to institutionalize Elmer Fudd's "robbery"). Chris's two loose-cannon aides, Matt Bevilaqua and Sean Gismonte, assault one broker for giving a client honest advice. When Chris corrects them, he demands a cut of their car thefts. He slaps Adriana for mentioning his drug use in their presence. When we cut from Chris's assault of Adriana to Tony's approach to Melfi, Chris seems to personify Tony's negative potential. That is, he represents Tony's Achilles Heel not just in the gang but in his own psyche. Both men need "to exercise impulse control," as Tony counsels Chris.

From this stress Tony's composure crumbles. Happily driving along to Deep Purple's "Smoke on the Water," when his CD sticks he loses his temper and blacks out. Happily, the airbag saves him from injury and the crash cures the CD. At his barbecue, Tony is enraged by Janice's machinations. Carmela orders him to join his friends for some fun. Even with them, he is belligerent and almost passes out. When he goes to a male therapist, despite claiming to be "Mr. Spears" he is recognized. The therapist refuses to take him on as a patient. He has seen *Analyze This* (1999), Harold Ramis's comedy of a shrink (Billy Crystal) and his gang-boss patient (Robert De Niro). (Once again, film demonstrates its dangerous public effects.)

Realizing Dr. Melfi is his last hope, Tony imposes himself on her at a roadside diner. They sound like ex-lovers. "That was a different time for us," Melfi responds to his nostalgia. Though Tony is apologetic ("I don't deserve your help"), Melfi remains angry. When his danger forced her practice into a motel, one client killed herself. She orders him out of her life: "How many other people have to die for your personal growth?"

In the closing scene Tony drifts around Carmela at home in the afternoon. She nukes him a bowl of cold pasta, fixes his collar while he eats, then sits with him to check the mail. Their silence expresses marital comfort. This scene provides a mellow conclusion to the season opener, which has refreshed our memories of the characters and introduced Tony's problems old (Livia), new (Janice), and resurrected (Pussy). Their kitchen comfort is a rebuke to what Livia told Carmela on her wedding day: "This is a big mistake. Tony will get bored with you." The closing song, Skeleton Key's "Nod Off," ironically comments on patterns of marriage and their violation: "Someday, she'll marry someone just like Daddy." Carmela's husband would not be commanded off—as her father is—to buy canned peaches for a pound cake.

▪ Aida Turturro (Janice) played James Gandolfini's wife in the 1992 revival of *A Streetcar Named Desire*. Her films include *Bringing Out the Dead, Mickey Blue Eyes, Sleepers, Manhattan Murder Mystery, What about Bob?*, and *Play It to the Bone*. She also played Fran on *As the World Turns*. She is the cousin of actors John and Nicholas Turturro.

II, 2:   Do Not Resuscitate

Written by Robin Green, Mitchell Burgess, and Frank Renzulli. Directed by Martin Bruestle.

Tony has tense visits with Uncle Junior, first in prison then, when he is on house arrest, at the doctor's office. When Tony takes over Junior's territory he leaves him reduced earnings and the title of boss (to keep the FBI's focus on him). When FBI agent Skip Lipari drives Pussy home from therapy we learn that Pussy has been informing the Feds for two years, but remains reluctant to rat on Tony. Rev. Herman James Jr. leads a picket of the Massarone Bros. Construction site, demanding jobs for black joint-fitters. Tony pays him a private kickback after providing goons to break up the next demonstration.

The range and intensity of betrayals in the Soprano circle still surprise us. The joint-fitters plot is a parable of betrayal. Reverend James co-opts his 83-year-old war veteran father in his campaign to win construction jobs for African Americans. But under the reverend's "business arrangement," Tony charges the construction company for breaking up the next demonstration—five non-existent positions on the payroll. Tony and the reverend share the money for these "no shows." No African Americans are hired. The reverend betrays both his community and his father (who dies ignorant of the deal). The revelation poignantly reflects on what the father told Tony: "Never underestimate a man's determination to be free." For his son, the freedom of choice is to "fill his pockets," what he accuses the white bosses of doing.

The father represents a genuine piety of which his son—like Father Phil—is a self-serving pretender. Herman James Sr. is so real he even has his original teeth. He dies right after we—and Tony—meet him. Cynically, the kickback payment follows the reverend's philosophizing: "When the last one goes we become the old ones at family functions." Herman Sr.'s passing is the end of the church's "Old School."

There is no equivalent to the virtue of Herman Sr. in Tony's ambivalent relationship with Uncle Junior. They agree to whack Green Grove owner Freddy Capuano, whose indiscreet gossip includes Tony's attempt to smother his mother. Junior tries to salvage his own honor by exhorting Tony to make peace with Livia. "Nobody played me," he avows, "She didn't know she was setting you up to get whacked." But Tony insists: "She's dead to me." Livia shadows Junior's invective use of "motherless." (For example the prison guards are "motherless fucks who listen to everything.")

Despite their tensions, however, when Junior falls in the shower Tony rushes over to help him. He carries him out like a bride, to the end-credit song "Goodnight, My Love," by Ella Fitzgerald and Benny Goodman. Ella's "Remember that you're mine, sweetheart" provides an ironic twist to this irregular relationship. Despite their animosity, the uncle and nephew remain devoted.

There is a false suggestion of betrayal when Uncle Junior appeals for medical release from prison. When he compares the electronic bracelet to Nazi Germany, his Jewish lawyer senses that Junior has offended the Jewish judge. In a soft, oily voice the lawyer suggests "I don't think we should let our shared sorrows or biases enter into this, Judge." That is, he tries to exploit their ethnic connection. But the honorable Judge Jacob Greenspan rejects this manipulation and imposes the bracelet to prevent Junior's flight.

The domestic machinations continue. At dinner Janice evades Tony's ban by talking about how wicked Livia is. To ingratiate herself she calls Meadow's driving examiner a "Fascist martinet"; as soon as Meadow gets her license she is maneuvered herself. From Meadow Janice learns that Livia likes "that Mario Lasagna guy" (translation: Mario Lanza). Janice flatters Livia with opera records and fond memories of watching the tenors on *The Ed Sullivan Show* together every Sunday eve, though she admits to Meadow "I hated that shit." But Livia knows her daughter: "You're here because you want to take my house." When Janice proposes to live with her, Livia switches to prefer Green Grove.

Despite Livia's malevolence she is archetypal: "Some day I hope you have children of your own and they treat you like this." Livia generously offers Janice "some of my tapioca"—from which she has recoiled. With more mischief than care Tony agrees to take the house off the market and let them live there: "You deserve each other. It'll be like *Whatever Happened to Baby Janice.*"

As with Tony's therapy, AJ unwittingly betrays him by telling Livia that Janice and Tony discussed her DNR—the DO NOT RESUSCITATE instruction that the nurse requested, in case of emergency. Livia uses this knowledge. Why should she move home with Janice, "So you can not resuscitate me?" Livia teases Janice with suggestions that she has stashed a large sum of money. Livia phones Carmela, insisting she doesn't know what she did to upset Tony and warning her that Janice is "a snake in the grass." Faithful to her husband, Carmela hangs up on her. In its snarl of manipulations and betrayals *The Sopranos* adds the grab of a good soap opera to the wit of classic drama.

II, 3: Toodle-Fucking-oo

Written by Frank Renzulli. Directed by Lee Tamahori.

A friendly policeman calls Tony to Livia's house, where Meadow's party has been taken over by druggies. Carmela rebukes Janice for interfering in their daughter's discipline. After Richie Aprile is released from prison, he bullies and beats pizza seller Beansie, for refusing to pay him tribute. Richie courts Parvati (Janice) at a yoga class. Dr. Melfi is embarrassed when she, in a group of imbibing women, encounters Tony with his gang.

The episode's title comes from Melfi's embarrassment at the restaurant. As she tells her psychiatrist, Elliot, when she met Tony she departed with the coquettish "Toodle-oo." When her "Jennifer" dominated her "Doctor Melfi," she "regressed into the girl thing to escape the responsibility of abandoning him as a client." She regressed because "young girls are not accountable for their behavior" (a view both Meadow and Janice implicitly share here). Hence, too, Melfi's nightmare—which we see as an event—where Tony's panic attack causes his fatal car crash, accompanied by the "You're out of the woods" song from *The Wizard of Oz*. Oz represents

Tony's strange world and his death, her recovered safety. Clearly, he affects her still.

The loss of control, both of others and of self, is the theme of the episode's other two plot lines. Both plots are covered by Janice's "That's what this is all about—ego and control." In the first, Meadow's party runs out of control when it is crashed by delinquents with designer drugs. That design causes chaos. The combination of health and danger in the teens' grab for independence is caught in the stretcher case who overdosed on Special K and Ecstasy.

Discussing her punishment, her parents know they no longer control their teenager. While Carmela insists Meadow must face consequences, Tony is more pragmatic: "I yelled. What the fuck else am I gonna do?" The parents should not overplay their hands "Cause if she finds out we're powerless we're fucked." Meadow knows this. She discusses her strategy with Hunter, who controls her parents through threats of bulimia: "Start purging. They won't say anything." Meadow's proposal—that she be punished by the brief withdrawal of her credit card—leads to ritual negotiation. The teens are in control. Meadow leaves her parents the same illusion of authority that the gangsters leave the cops. For Meadow, her parents' punishment is hypocritical: "How do you think my father makes a living?"

Other characters assert independence by changing their names. Livia tells Richie that Janice became Parvati just to shame her mother. In return, Janice's son Harpo has—not surprisingly—changed his name to Hal and moved to Montreal with his father, Eugenio, who is with the *Cirque du Soleil* (a less metaphoric circus than the Sopranos).

In another form of domestic control, Richie Aprile tries to reclaim his territory after 10 years in jail. Richie shaking down the pizza dealer parallels Meadow's shakedown of her parents—wangling extra cash to make up for the lost card. In their first meeting, Richie smashes Beansie's face with a coffee pot, then bashes him with a chair and fists. Later he shoots at him, then runs over him with his car, permanently crippling him. Richie's behavior is worse than Meadow's revolt, of course, but both show a lack of self-control and both reject Tony's authority. As Tony loses control over Meadow, Richie promises to serve Tony but he casts his lot with Uncle Junior. To Junior's rhetorical "What are you gonna do?" Richie responds "Whatever you tell me. . . . I'm yours, Junior."

Janice/Parvati unites Tony's domestic and business tensions when she interferes in Meadow's discipline and resumes her teenage affair with Richie. In both plots Janice undermines Tony but proves inconsistent, even hypocritical. Having supported Meadow's independence and opposed her punishment, she turns against her when—"beyond outrage"—she sees the damage done "her" house. In their yoga she and Richie both claim to have advanced their consciousness since they first dated. But there is little yoga in Janice's scheming or in Richie's sadism.

Richie's double entendre here suggests a non-spiritual bent: "Did you ever think you'd see Richie Aprile doing Downward Facing Dog?" That yoga position suggests the traditional "doggie style" that Tony dreams of doing with Jeannie Cusamano (I, 13) and that we will later see (II, 10) Richie and Janice engaged in (pistol to head optional).

When Richie tells Janice he did "a lot of stretching" in jail, more is involved than his work on his physical flexibility. Having served his "stretch," he is now bent upon over-reaching. In fact, his courtship of Janice is precisely ambiguous. It mingles Richie's family and his Family ambitions. That scheme is implicit in this exchange:

TONY: Go fuck yourself.
RICHIE: How's your sister?
TONY: Hey. There's no need for that kind of talk.

Richie opposes Tony by courting Janice through Livia, bringing flowers to the hospital. This romance would advance his status in the Soprano crew. Actor David Proval suggests Richie's feral cunning, from his hard but warm voice to his steely nose-to-nose confrontation of Tony. Richie uses Janice's affection—like Uncle Junior's suspicion—against Tony. After their yoga meeting, we cut from Richie thoughtfully watching Janice walk away, to Tony scratching his back as he waits for Richie in the mall. Romancing Janice is Richie's phantom stab at Tony's back.

Perhaps a minor theme lies in the running reference to fellatio, as it is associated with macho power and selfishness. In the first restaurant scene Tony lets his leering cronies assume Melfi is a conquest. "Pipefitter Lips," Pussy poetically names her. Richie's release is celebrated by homages at the Bada Bing Club and a blowjob in the backroom. Though the latter was Silvio's treat, Richie insists on paying: "Whose joint did you just cop, mine or his?" Richie insists on control. Men will be boys. As he tells Tony, "What's mine is not yours to give me."

Against the macho posturing, violence and strategizing loom two strong characters. Carmela shows her integrity first in criticizing and then in reconciling with Janice. It would not be Christian to let Janice leave their home, she tells Tony, after asking Janice's forgiveness. Carmela's family sense overrides such heated differences. In the parallel world, Beansie, so crippled he needs Tony to blow his nose, reiterates his "Old School" fidelity: He won't tell the police. In contrast, Richie's "Old School" warning to Christopher is not to beat Adriana (Richie's niece) unless he marries her first.

The episode ends as it began, with Tony surprised to find Meadow at his mother's house. This time she is scrubbing the floor, gagging at its stench. The episode closes on Tony's thoughtful close-up, as he considers his daughter's new responsibility. The Mafia-American Princess shows a surprising self-control as she persists in her nauseating task. This duty no-one urged on her. In her emerging maturity perhaps Tony sees he may not need to try to control her much longer.

- Director Lee Tamahori is a New Zealander who made a remarkable international reputation with his first feature film, *Once Were Warriors* (1994), which won a PEN Award. Two years later he made his American directing debut with *Mulholland Falls*. He went on to direct *The Edge, Along Came a Spider, In Search of the Assassin*, and *10th Victim*.

- Melfi's shrink, Dr. Elliot Kupferberg, is played by the well-known film writer and director Peter Bogdanovich. He directed *Targets; The Last Picture Show; What's up, Doc?; Paper Moon; Daisy Miller; Nickelodeon; Saint Jack; Texasville*; and *Noises Off*. As an actor, he appeared in several Roger Corman B-classics (*The Wild Angels, The Trip*) before moving up to Agnes Varda's *Lions Love*. His documentaries about filmmakers are especially well regarded. His experience as a film critic and historian is apparent in his interviews with David Chase on the Season One DVD (discs one and four).

- David Proval (Richie Aprile) studied acting with Uta Hagen and William Hickey. In *Mean Streets* he played the genial bar owner, Tony. He also appeared in *The Shawshank Redemption, Innocent Blood, Four Rooms, The Star Chamber*, and *The Siege*. He won the Toronto Film Festival Best Actor award for the title role in *Nunzio*. After he was killed later in this series (read on) he played a rabbi opposed to capital punishment on *The West Wing*.

II, 4: *Commendatóri*

Written by David Chase. Directed by Tim van Patten.

Paulie smashes a stolen DVD because it won't play. Two hoods car-jack a family's Mercedes ML430, which Tony's gang will sell to part-ners in Italy. Tony takes Christopher and Paulie to Naples to meet boss Zi Vittorio. Meeting with the Number Two man, Tony offers to supply the Mercedes ML cars at $90,000. Don Vittorio is wheeled in by his beautiful daughter, Annalisa, whose husband is the acting boss but serving a life sentence. Tony agrees to sell Annalisa the cars at $75,000 provided she lets him have her best man, Furio. Meanwhile, Angie tells Carmela and Rosalie Aprile that she wants to divorce Pussy. When Pussy's meeting with his FBI contact is interrupted by a friend, Elvis impersonator Jimmy Bones, Pussy kills him.

This major episode critiques its male heroes' ethic and satirizes the self-importance of their style, both their Italian and their macho. The title, *Commendatóri* ("commanders" or "knights commander"), is the honorific with which the Naples hotelier greets our heroes. Paulie enjoys the title, but when he addresses some locals with it they ignore him. The episode questions male honor both in Tony's trans-Atlantic business world and in Angie's and Carmela's discussion of marriage.

In a comic version of this theme, the wus rages at the men who stole his new Mercedes: "Fuckin' niggers! . . . Well, who else?" But this is in the safety of his family, after the thieves are safely out of earshot. Far from resisting, he cowered with his family. Of course, the Sopranos are the "Who else" behind the theft.

In the opening scene the gangsters' silly strength turns to destructive frustration. When they can't get their stolen DVD to run their advance bootleg of the—what else?—*Godfather* outtakes, they break the machine. The episode opens on a close-up of the FBI warning that starts the DVD. That makes the FBI comically futile: A bootleg copy of buried material is about to be played on a stolen machine.

"You know the scene I love most?" Paulie asks. Of course, what and how men love is one of the episode's major questions. " 'It was you, Fredo.' " In that scene in *The Godfather Part II*, Michael Corleone grips his brother's (John Cazale) head and identifies him as the traitor. To keep the mood light, Paulie does not finish the quote: "You broke my heart!" Now Pussy—Tony's traitor—asks about his visit to Junior. After resisting the men's "favorite scene" nonsense—"What, you gonna call Coppola with ideas how to fix it?"—Tony relents. His favorite scene is the Don's trip to Sicily, with the crickets in the silence at Don Cicci's villa. (For the implications of Tony's choice, see the appendix.) But in the event, Tony's Italian experience does not live up to the *Godfather* model. The Don's modernistic villa does not live up to Don Cicci's.

In Italy, Tony's discipline contrasts to his colleagues' weakness. Though Christopher is determined to view the topless beaches and the crater of Vesuvius, he misses both—and neglects Tony's assignments—by sharing a hard drug stupor with the hood Tanno. Chris rushes to buy Adriana's Italian presents from the Duty Free at home.

Paulie wants to discover his roots in order to match his doctor (!) brother's experience. Italy is his "mother country. Here they make it real." But he proves a misfit in that reality. At the first dinner Paulie rejects the Italian food and asks for macaroni and tomato sauce, to the disdain of the Italians: "And you thought the Germans were classless pieces of shit." Paulie wants to rush back to the hotel to avoid the restaurant toilet. He bores the prostitute with his delight that she is from his grandfather's home town. Another local, assuming the American must be from NATO, blames him for cutting the ski lift cable. But at the airport Paulie reports "I felt right at home" and urges Pussy to visit his roots there as soon as possible.

Tony's business trip is a success. His final deal doubles Uncle Junior's profit. And he secures Furio Giunta, who speaks English and is from the Old School. That is, he honors the code of silence, respects the family, and shows his strength of character when he beats up a young boy who frightened the entourage with firecrackers. While the mother cries for mercy, the boy begs to join the gang, and the *carabiniéri* drive discreetly away, Furio pounds the kid while others hold him. "This is Naples University." From Tony's pensive response to the sight we may infer revulsion, but it is covetous respect.

None of our Italian-American heroes understand the spoken Italian, so they are helpless without our privilege of subtitles. Furio translates Nino's "Why is he busting my balls? Tell him to get to the point" to "Happy to be at your disposal." This shows (1) Furio may be a brute but he is diplomatic, and (2) the Italian thugs speak the same language as the American even if it is different. Tony's first negotiation with Annalisa ends with her "Fuck you" and his "Up your ass." The American rap record Annalisa's son plays is paralleled by the Italian rap played over the end-credits (Jovanotti's "Piove").

It may even be an uncharacteristic success for Tony *not* to screw Annalisa. He shows an unexpected honor. When she leads him into the Cumae, a pagan sybil's cave, the layered hallways present them as archetypes. Behind Tony is a fountainlike column, behind Annalisa an open cave. The contrast suggests the Romantic balance of the archetypal Male and Female. Against that background they reach their agreement and she offers herself. Tony declines because of conflict of interest: "I don't shit where I eat."

In this surprising abstention, that business principle may be less important than some other factors, such as the self-awareness to which Dr. Melfi has led him or his guilt at not having brought Carmela along. Or he is comfortable only with submissive women, like Paulie with his Neapolitan whore. Annalisa is a hard case: "My husband. Fuck you. He is never coming back, so you have to fucking deal with me." Tony can do his business deal with her but he cannot deal with such a strong woman, albeit available. In motivation the show prefers the enigmas of life over literary simplification.

Annalisa's power is ambiguous. With wiry strength she commands the all-male operation, while sustaining her warmth and softness as a mother and in caring for her incoherent father. The song in her domestic scene is Wyclef Jean's "Blood Is Thicker than Water." As Annalisa relates the myth of the sybil and burns her toenails (to keep them from any enemy), she is a primitive parallel to Melfi's psychoanalysis—yet she is an effective modern manager. The close-up on Annalisa's mouth, devouring a prawn, recalls the close-up of the dream with Isabella's luxuriant mouth in I, 12. But like the villa, this reality falls short of Tony's fantasy expectations. In contrast to Isabella's feminine delicacy, Annalisa's robust chew suggests a masculinity that could lead a gang.

Tony's dream of fucking Annalisa—from behind, Roman wolf-style, the woman in a hiked toga and the man in the classic breastplate—parallels Pussy's nightmare about a "too quiet" Jimmy. Whether it is the Jimmy Bones he fears will squeal on seeing him with the FBI agent or the Jimmy Altieri who was killed (so is now bones) in Pussy's place (an unwitting impersonation), the nightmare reveals Pussy's guilt and fear for talking to the Feds. He protects Tony by reporting that Raymond Curto took over Junior's stolen car exports.

When our heroes drive home, Paulie, who found the trip miserable and frustrating, beams while Tony, who enjoyed such success, broods. Tony's pensiveness may center on Annalisa, recalling Uncle Junior's continuing regret that he "never went." "It ain't over yet," Tony consoled him. But the "serious man" Junior remembers is now a wheelchair invalid who is only interested in reciting American place-names. His "Wheel-share Pool-apart" refers to his own immobility more than LA's Wilshire Boulevard. The senile Italian's blurry fascination with American clichés parallels the deracinated Italian-Americans' remoteness from the real Italian.

Carmela's disappointment at being left home feeds the marriage doubts prompted by Angie Bonpensiero's decision to leave Pussy. In fact, an Italian love song bridges Angie's "I'm getting a divorce" with the romantic shot of the men's plane flying the night sky to Naples. At lunch with Carmela and the widow Rosalie Aprile, Angie's happy pretense crumbles. She thought she missed Pussy and was worried but his return made her want to vomit. She shocks her friends by saying she wants a divorce.

Although we know Pussy is profoundly preoccupied, Angie thinks his insensitivity proves their marriage a waste. When she mentions her biopsy, her husband goes back to putting WD40 on his pocketknife. Even after hearing the good news, she is so nervous she drops a dozen eggs. But he responds: "Good, I'll be back later." When he wordlessly brings her roses she whips him with them, then runs upstairs. Pussy is not entirely without sensitivity. Angie says he cried when he heard their daughter could not bear children. But—manfully—he buries it.

Angie wonders how he could dare "To just come and go like that." "Have you reached out to him?" Carmela naively asks, sounding more like a marriage manual than a woman who lives a similar void. Carmela defends the sacrament of marriage and reminds Angie of her responsibilities to their three (grown) children. When Angie reports her lawyers will file for divorce on Tuesday, Carmela assumes she is taking another day to rethink it. No, Monday is a Jewish holiday so Angie's lawyers are unavailable.

Carmela's opposition to divorce rationalizes her own marriage with reflex arguments. Her thoughtful close-ups after these exchanges suggest she doubts her position. Perhaps for her as for Angie, it is—as Sarah Brightman and Andrea Bocelli sing her favorite song—"Time to Say Good-bye."

In her feminist wisdom Janice defines Italian men as "swaggering mama's boys, fuckin' hypocrites . . . emotional cripples . . . [who] expect their wives to live like the fuckin' nuns at Mount Carmel College." Annalisa confirms this view when she tells Tony why she's accepted as a leader: "Italian men in love to their mothers so obeying woman is natural." Janice seems to have persuaded Carmela until she avows that prison made Richie sensitive to the plight of women. At that Carmela can only laugh, but she stops for a serious thought anyway.

Among themselves the gangsters' women can be as tough as their men. This Tony learns from Annalisa, as well as from Carmela, who in the next episode slams the door on Uncle Junior when he comes to the reception for Furio. Here in the restaurant, the melancholy widow, Rosalie, yells at the woman at the next table. The Family ladies can give as good as they get. That's perhaps why they rule out divorce.

When Tony comes home, Carmela is upstairs, putting away the laundry. Tony, bearing his usual gifts, is diminished by the high-angle shot—what director Van Patten calls his "high-wide-and-stupid shot" (Season II DVD, disc one)—while Carmela fills her screen. As she remembers Angie she wonders if Tony's return is more nauseating than nice. Or would she rather stash her family's laundry than air it? In any case, the wives have lost their respect for their *Commendatóri*.

- According to director Tim Van Patten's excellent commentary on the Season II DVD edition (disc one), the show's general rule is to shoot the gangster scenes with a wider angle lens, bringing them closer to the viewer, and the family scenes with a longer lens, giving them a softer register, more detached. He reports that it is not uncommon in Italy for strong women to take over their man's gang, though they tend not to last long as leaders.
- Because of scheduling problems, the Naples restaurant and hotel interior scenes were filmed in New York and New Jersey, with the Italian actors flown in for their parts.

II, 5: Big Girls Don't Cry

Written by Terence Winter. Directed by Tim Van Patten.

Though Furio's advent disturbs Tony's crew, he handles a brothel owner's unpaid debts more persuasively than Chris did. Chris takes an "Acting for Writers" workshop with some evasion, some success, and a violent outburst. Tony is infuriated to learn Janice is trying to get a bank loan on their mother's house. Dr. Melfi takes Tony back as a client.

As the title suggests, this episode deals with how different characters handle their emotional pressures. "Each his own, Tony. Each his own," as Richie explains his interest in Janice, after Tony remarks: "There are men in the can better looking than my sister."

As the show shifts away from Carmela, the primary "Big girl" here is Dr. Melfi, who discusses with her therapist her guilt for having abandoned Tony. Under her client's absent influence, Melfi is eating more, gaining weight, and against her will thrilled by his danger. She even stomps out of her first session à *la* Tony: "Fuck you. You think this is funny. You smug cocksucker. Fuck you." Dr. Jennifer Melfi's Soprano accent raises her therapist's eyebrows.

When Melfi tells her shrink that seeing Tony "will be very therapeutic for me," she reverses her responsibility. When Kupferberg asks if Tony lies behind her over-eating, she retreats to a Livia line: "I don't know what you mean." Melfi admits "feelings on a personal level" for Tony but denies they are sexual: "He can be such a little boy sometimes." But this context is harsher than his box of sand (I, 13). The scene cuts to Tony in his car, enjoying his cigar to the sounds of Furio torturing the brothel owners. When Melfi puts down her glass of wine to call him, her invitation seems romantic. Though Tony declined, he appears at the appointed hour, like a lover who has feigned disinterest.

Chris finds a release for his emotions in the acting workshop Adriana gave him for his birthday. When the teacher describes the actor as the instrument for conveying ideas, she also covers Chris's Family role, in which he has just been out-performed by Furio. Feeling socially inferior to the other students, especially Mitch, a BA (English) now selling Porsches, Chris introduces himself (not entirely wrong) as working with stocks. He evades the assignment with which he can not identify: the Gentleman Caller in *The Glass Menagerie*. When Chris can not understand why this "player" would try to screw Laura the gimp, he reduces the character to his own experience. The play recalls the singular reduction of Adriana's "my Tennessee William."

Chris performs passionately as Jim in *Rebel without a Cause*, weeping as he begs his father's help. His emotional release confirms the irony of the episode title, because men as well as "Big girls" are expected not to cry. In a more abstract exercise at the next class, Chris explodes at the actor who played the father, punching and kicking him. As Adriana suggests, because his father died so young Chris has unresolved issues, which emerged in the class and drove him out of both workshops in which he revealed himself. When he rises at night to throw out his screenplay he again runs away from self-exposure. His false class-name, "Chris McAvity" suggests he senses he has a cavity to fill but hides it (even in his pronunciation: Mac-a-vee-tee).

Furio's arrival creates some possible problems for Tony. He coaxes Artie into providing a job front for Furio's immigration, as master cheesemaker. Only later, meeting outside The Lou Costello Memorial, does Tony inform Paulie. The site suggests the comical sidekick that Paulie fears he is becoming. Lou's statue stands parallel behind Paulie in one shot, and looms over him, hat befouled, in another. But that is rather Pussy's fate, as Tony promotes Paulie and Silvio and leaves Pussy to report to them.

Embittered by this slight, Pussy asks "Foolio" if he stomped the grapes for their wine. When he is pointedly excluded from a discussion, Pussy leaves ("I've gotta make a call anyway"). Then we see him and FBI agent Skip Lipari both complaining about being bypassed for promotion. The respectable world again parallels the mob's. When Lipari says Tony doesn't "give a flying fuck" for Pussy, his phrase recalls Carmela's description of Tony's feelings for Father Phil and the church (I, 13). In this parallel Tony is trapped between opposing expectations, his gang code on the one side and conventional morality on the other.

No such dilemmas for young Furio. He amuses little children at his welcoming party, warmly engages with all, and is delighted to be in the land of AFC old movies. Now at his spiritual home, he trims the title of his favorite TV show to "PD Blue." Yet the same affable Furio wreaks efficient havoc at the brothel.

As Tony imported Furio to distance himself from his dangerous business, he is all the more concerned when he loses his temper. At word of Janice's mortgage, Tony smashes the phone, to AJ's shock and Carmela's anger. "Why don't you grow the fuck up?" she properly advises. Angry that Irina is feeding Cheezies to the boatside ducks (!), he attacks the Russian next boat for suggesting Irina date his brother.

We don't share Melfi's surprise to see Tony back for his appointment. For we've seen him impose on Hesh with long outpourings about his short fuse. Tony is oddly reassured when Hesh tells him Johnny-Boy, Tony's father, used to get stress attacks once or twice a year and once cracked his head open on a cigarette machine.

From their sessions, Tony tells Melfi, he wants to stop the panic attacks and blackouts so he can "direct my power and my fuckin' anger against the people in my life who deserve it." The "power" may come from a manual but the rest is pure Tony. Addressing his mix of self-defense and self-destruction, Melfi asks how he felt about Furio's devastation in the brothel. "I wished it was me in there." "Giving the beating or taking it?" Tony tries to smile away her somber question, but he considers it. Perhaps the episode's last shot—Christopher throwing his self-expression (his screenplay floppies and hard copy both) into the dumpster outside and striding back into the dark house—speaks for Tony too, as he swaggers back to the supposed strength of silence. Big guys do not cry—or even talk.

• The feral Furio is played by Naples-born Federico Castelluccio, who came to the United States in 1968. In 1982 he earned a BFA in painting and media arts at the School of Visual Arts in New York. Since 1986 he has had remarkable success acting on stage, film, and television, while maintaining his career as a painter.

• The Lou Costello Memorial honors the junior partner of the Abbott and Costello vaudeville and B-film comedy team. He was born Louis Francis Cristillo in Paterson—where Castelluccio grew up. Costello is yet another great Italian-American who is not connected with the Mafia.

II, 6: The Happy Wanderer

Written by Frank Renzulli. Directed by John Patterson.

At their high school College Night, Tony and Artie meet school buddy Dave Scatino and his son Eric. Tony rejects Dave's request to let him into the Executive high-stakes poker game that Tony took over from Junior. At Richie's game Dave runs up a $7,000 debt, which Richie demands be paid before he plays again. Richie explodes when he finds Dave playing in Tony's Executive Game, where he incurs another $45,000 debt. When Artie can not lend Dave $20,000 for "breathing space" he gives Tony Eric's jeep. Meadow's joy at getting the SUV turns into anger when she learns its source. She and Eric have been rehearsing "Sun and Moon" (from *Ms. Saigon*) for the school's Cabaret Night to score extra-curricular activity points for college admission. Eric turns on Meadow and walks out on Cabaret Night, damaging his college chances. This leaves Meadow with the advantage of performing a solo, "My Heart will Go On," the theme from *Titanic*.

The loser's pall hangs over this black comedy. Perhaps because the characters' ambitions are so twisted satisfaction is impossible. Here even the winners are losers. Meadow's triumphant solo comes from the film about the sunk Titanic so it is a success based on a disaster, as her getting the jeep was based on Eric's dad gambling losses. Meadow's cabaret success pales beside the loss of her friend, because of their respective fathers' doings, and her realization that—as Tony yells—"Everything this family has comes from the work I do."

Innocent Meadow is herself compromised by having to scramble for nonacademic points to bolster her college application. As the Brown College representative advises, admission is highly competitive: "Get all your academic and extra-curricular ducks in a row."—that fugitive promise of Tony's lost ducks again—"Leave nothing to chance." In one way the students' plotting for college admission is antithetical to the gamblers' world of chance and risk. Yet university acceptance does not depend on academic standing but a system of maneuvering, not entirely unlike the mob poker game. Thus one friend parlays her black mother into early admission to Wesleyan. Whether she wants to or not, Meadow "wins" by getting both the jeep and the solo. Eric loses the first innocently and abandons the second. Both fine kids are damaged by their fathers' wrong-headed ambitions.

The loser's gloom is introduced lightly in the second scene. When Tony jokes about what heroes Dave and Artie were at school, he implies that they are since fallen. Great and boisterous quarterbacks Y. A. Tittle and Joe Namath shrink to the merely affable Phil Donohue and Alan Alda. A close-up holds on Artie's sad recognition. Perhaps it was Tony's gibe that spurred Davey on to the risky, high-stakes game in which he "got no business being."

Though Dave has a successful sporting goods store, he's doomed by his compulsion to gamble. His weak face and nervous eyes stamp him a loser, as both card games prove. While Tony naps at the Executive Game, Dave raises his initial debt from five to forty-five thousand dollars. Tony's five-percent weekly interest charge puts Dave's business and his family at risk. With Mickey and Sylvia's "Love Is Strange" playing in the background, Dave tries to borrow money from one friend, Artie, to stave off another, Tony. His faith in his friends' love is naive, desperate, and irrelevant. For Tony as for Richie, the financial screws on Davey are purely business, "Nothin' personal."

Dave fares even worse as a father than as a gambler. When he takes back Eric's jeep, he pretends to punish him for "going off-road" (Eric drove the cheerleaders onto their practice field). "Accountability is everything,"

Dave shouts to his wife and son. This hypocrisy loses any sympathy we might have given him.

At least Tony scores points for his relative integrity. He warned Dave not to play in the Executive Game, warned him not to expect favors on his "short-term" loan, and then does what he has to do to save face in his world. For that reason, too, he "taxes" Richie for "disrespecting" Tony's game. Tony is also the more—albeit harshly—honest with his child. He admits that Eric's father "something like" sold him the truck. Not to mention his: "So take that high moral ground and go sleep in the fuckin' bus station if you want." Though everything is going well for Tony, he suffers from his anger at his mother, his defensive anger at his therapist, and his veering between self-respect and guilt.

Adding to the Sopranos' history of loss and sorrow, Uncle Junior tells Tony that there was another brother, Hercule (reduced to Eckley), born between Junior and Johnny-Boy, who was as strong as a bull, handsome like George Raft, but "slow." As was the custom, the brothers kept him in a home until he died. Tony tweaks Uncle Junior when he recalls Livia "talking about my father's feeble-minded brother. But I always thought that was you."

The episode focuses on Tony's anger. He tells Dr. Melfi that he is so upset he could smash her face into hamburger—but won't. She has turned him into one of those yappy "fuckin' pussies," not the strong, silent Gary Cooper type he always admired. Tony's confusion points to the heart of the episode: "I got the world by the balls and I can't stop feeling I'm a fuckin' loser." Though Tony rejects Melfi's claim that his parents kept him from joy, whenever Livia surfaces—at the cabaret, at a funeral—her very presence enrages him anew.

As Tony describes his free-form anger, when he sees someone happy, "always fuckin' whistlin' like the fuckin' Happy Wanderer," he wants to tear out the whistler's throat. "Why should I be angry at guys like this? I should say *asalut'*. . . . Good for you. . . . Go with God." Later Melfi suggests Tony should be heartened by the death of sister Barb's father-in-law, who the day after retiring is fatally blown off his roof while installing a satellite dish. Without Tony having to do anything, the man "joined the ranks of the unlucky." And isn't Ercole "enough of a sad tragedy that you can join the rest of the douche bags" who are always whining at their therapy? Seeing such others fail, she suggests, should enable Tony to see Melfi without guilt. Since resuming their sessions Melfi is more aggressive toward Tony.

The episode closes on a tauntingly happy note. Gudrun's opera solo at the school cabaret—a soaring German song about a heavy heart—gives way for the end credits to "The Happy Wanderer."

Because of Tony's values, built into his every success is inevitable frustration. He and Silvio luxuriate in now owning the Executive Game, which his father and uncle started 30 years ago and from which Uncle Junior used to chase them away. Even as he nets $80,000 from this game, though, Tony "loses" because of his entanglement with Dave, the mixed blessing of the jeep, and the deepening of his differences with Richie.

After the funeral service's "not the first to rise from the dead," the camera pans from a sleeping Livia to her malevolent resurrection in Janice. She goads Richie against Tony, saying the $50,000 Tony gave him on his prison release is what her father gave someone in that situation thirty years ago (equivalent to half a million now). Richie brings Meadow a bigger bouquet than Tony's. Tony's every satisfaction brings more loss.

In contrast, at Richie's game Artie cashes out when he is ahead. He is free from the macho vanity that keeps Dave losing: "I got to go now or Charmaine will have my balls on the menu." This episode satirizes the macho element in the high-stakes card game. Though Christopher tells his two aides this is no "nickel and dime" game, he slips matches under the scales to reduce the cost of seafood for fifteen—then accuses the clerk of cheating. His two gunsels pettily complain at being treated pettily. Silvio ludicrously explodes at one aide for trying to sweep up the cheese under his chair.

Among the players are real-life celebrity Frank Sinatra Jr.—whom Paulie calls "Chairboy of the Board"—and fictional Dr. Fried, whose specialty is penal implants. Only Tony and Dr. Fried smoke Tony's Macanudos. Sometimes a cigar may be just a cigar, but not in this context. Especially not a Macanudo, with its heft and outlaw strut. Foreshadowing the resurrection of Meadow's Cabaret solo, Paulie reports that a crate of Viagra is being lowered to "raise" the Titanic. In an apposite pun, Silvio opines that Dave "ain't got dick." Similarly, when the idealistic Hasid, Hillel Teittleman, complains at partner Furio's taking so many rooms free for his whores, he loses the high ground when a prostitute admits his custom.

In the moral universe of *The Sopranos,* there is no uncontaminated virtue. Meadow clearly does not have the voice or training that Gudrun has, but she still gets her solo in the cabaret—because she is a Soprano. However much she tries to distance herself from her father's work, Meadow suffers its advantage. All that keeps Tony from being the Happy Wanderer himself is his inability to know joy, his refusal to sing.

■ In the card game, Sunshine is played by Paul Mazursky, who acted in *Blackboard Jungle* and directed such films as *Bob and Carol and Ted and Alice*, *Blume in Love*, *Harry and Tonto*, *An Unmarried Woman*, *Down and out in Beverly Hills* and *Scenes from a Mall*.

II, 7: D-Girl

Written by Todd Kessler. Directed by Allen Coulter.

On a joyride in Carmela's Mercedes, AJ breaks the sideview mirror. When scolded, AJ defends himself with the Existentialism he has learned in school from Camus' *The Stranger*. Tony asks Pussy to advise AJ. Agent Lipari pressures Pussy to wear a wire to AJ's confirmation party at Tony's house. Meanwhile, Chris meets his lawyer cousin Gregory's fiancée, Amy, a woman in film development (the titular D-Girl), who introduces him to director Jon Favreau. She reads Chris's discarded screenplay, *You Bark, I Bite* (of which Adriana faithfully preserved a copy). After Chris has sex with Amy he turns more callous toward Adriana and Tony. At the confirmation party Tony gives Chris ten minutes to decide either to dedicate himself completely to his service or to leave Tony completely. After thinking about it outside, Chris returns to the fold.

In the series' most openly philosophical episode, Chris as much as AJ comes of age. AJ "stumbled into Existentialism" (in Dr. Melfi's sympathetic phrase; Tony blames the "Fuckin' Internet"). The concept exposes Chris's shallowness: "I love movies. But I want to be a player." He won't bother with "all that other shit" such as working, acting, qualifying, that is, actually becoming something instead of just affecting the role. He wants to be a player rather than learning to play a real role.

As AJ questions the meaning of life in an Absurd order, the other characters are defined by whether they respond with dedication or with betrayal. They are all as insecure as AJ. For defending her brother's proper "education," Meadow is sent to her room. Pussy is torn between serving the FBI to stay out of jail or to serve Tony.

Adriana is clearly dedicated to Chris, despite his unreliability and his evasion of marriage. Mind you, Tony's advice to Chris doesn't help her case: "When you marry you'll appreciate the importance of fresh produce." But Adriana is herself star-struck and upset when Chris toured Amy and Favreau through his old neighborhood without her.

Livia, as usual, instinctively thwarts Tony. She nourishes AJ's adolescent *angst*: "Who says everything has a purpose? The world's a jungle. You want my advice, Anthony, don't expect happiness. You won't get it. People let you down. I won't mention any names. But, in the end, you die in your own arms. . . . It's all a big nothing. What makes you think you're so special?"

In the series' most self-referential episode, Amy brings Chris to Jon's set, where the two lesbian heroines—played by Janeane Garofalo and Sandra Bernhard—shoot each other. Chris becomes a hero by proposing Sandra's last epithet be "*puchiacha*" (cunt) instead of "bitch." "Cunt. I like that," concludes Favreau.

Despite its Brooklyn authenticity, however, from another perspective Chris's suggestion is wrong. "Cunt" would not be the ultimate pejorative for a lesbian that it is for these men. Chris's bright suggestion may be true to its social background but it remains a man's view, a male invective. (True, Svetlana uses the term in III, 3, but that's her Profanity as a Second Language. Gloria uses that term for Irina in III, 12, but that episode is about characters proving their "balls.") The term seems inappropriate for the lesbian character to call her lover, even in dying anger.

Chris fascinates Jon with his gun and with his stories, including the Sinatra background to the Johnny Fontane plot in *The Godfather*. But a playful skirmish terrifies Jon. As Amy is fascinated when Chris dominates the Morgan Stanley rowdies at the bar, Jon is taken with Chris's gun and his aura of danger. But Amy pursues her attraction. Critiquing Chris's script, she starts listing the seven-part hierarchy of human needs that motivates characters. By the third, "the need to understand," she is on him.

Later Chris discovers Jon's new script has stolen Chris's story about Joey Cippolina, who poured acid on a she-male for seducing him. "*Crying Game*," says Amy, who lives through the filter of film. Later, to Chris's rueful expression of affection she replies "This is getting kind of William Inge here, isn't it?" Though he betrayed Adriana and Gregory with Amy, Chris feels betrayed and endangered by their use of his anecdote.

Chris's introduction to the filmmaking world parallels AJ's confirmation. As Chris learns its systemic lures, exploitation, betrayals, and abandonment, he loses the innocence that tempted him to drop Tony and Adriana for Hollywood. Chris becomes a man when he drops his improbable Hollywood fantasy and rededicates himself to Tony. Even if that means exchanging one Hollywood role for another, the writer for the hood, the dedication is better than the vain and treacherous pursuit of a phantom.

AJ's existentialism is equally shallow. His passengers' mortal risk in his joyride prompts: "Death just shows the ultimate Absurdity of life." Not without grounds does Tony question AJ's claim to manhood. Two years after bedwetting at camp he is reporting "Nitch's" claim that "God is dead."

Pussy's youngest son Matt shows more authority. After correcting AJ's "Nietzsche"—that is, AJ has not yet found his proper niche in philosophy—Matt rejects Nietzsche for his lunacy and Sartre as "a fucking fraud [who] copped it all from Husserl and Heidegger." Matt recommends Kierkegaard: "Every duty is essentially duty to God." Not bad for a gunsel's kid who has just proved his prowess in the batting cage and who dismisses current Rap as "marketing."

Pussy says his kid won't hit sacrifice flies. But Pussy is about to sacrifice Tony—and thereby himself—to avoid serving "thirty to life for selling H." At the beginning of Pussy's end, the cemetery lies just behind Pussy's house when agent Lipari coerces him against Tony. Pussy is so torn that he assaults Angie when she almost catches him wiring himself for AJ's confirmation party. Matt has to pull his raging father, bleeding from the mike, off her.

In his first session with Dr. Melfi, Tony is less disturbed with AJ's delinquency than with his brooding. Melfi spells out the implications of Existentialism. In a world without absolute values—"In your family even motherhood is up for debate."—people are solely responsible for themselves. The only absolute is death. Though he agrees "the kid's on to something," with AJ Tony hardens his position: "Even if God is dead you're still gonna kiss His ass" (that is, be confirmed).

When AJ is caught smoking pot Carmela confirms the family's religious approach: "What kind of animal smokes marijuana at his own confirmation?" Is it too much to ask to "be a good Catholic for fifteen fuckin' minutes?" But AJ defends his grass: "Even Grandma says the world has no purpose."

When Tony asks Pussy—as AJ's godfather (no film reference intended)—to counsel AJ, he leaves his *Waste News*. But Pussy's "You gotta learn to appreciate the value of things" refers to the dented Mercedes. There is some self-justification in Pussy's advice: "Sometimes you got to do things you don't want to." Pussy approaches AJ after the marijuana incident: "I'm your sponsor. We need to talk. You need to listen." The line is ironic, because the "We need to talk" really means "I need to talk to you" and the

"You need to listen" hides the fact that the FBI agents are listening on Pussy's wire, hoping Tony will incriminate himself. Instead, all the agents hear is Pussy telling AJ what a generous man Tony is. "He'd take a bullet for you. . . . He's a stand-up guy."

Absent from the family picture ("Where's the godfather?"), Pussy is up in the bathroom sobbing because he is betraying his best friend. This godfather has crumbled into Fredo. In the last sequence, the high passion of opera, Emma Shaplin singing "*Vedi, Maria,*" unites Chris's decision to serve Tony and Pussy's to betray him. Chris and Tony both face the Existential choice the hero of Chris's screenplay faced: to shit or go blind.

The Kierkegaard line—"Every duty is essentially duty to God"—shadows every small duty and its converse betrayal in this episode. For example, Pussy weeps because fidelity to Tony would be closer to serving God than serving the FBI would be. The irony of AJ's brush with Nietzsche is that his father has the makings of the Nietzschean hero. At his best—that is, worst—Tony Soprano rises above convention, above the law, above the reflexes of traditional morality, and stamps out his own code and values. What pulls him short is his regression into societal convention, his "Old School" nostalgia and the colleagues who betray him. Tony is especially Nietzschean in the instinctiveness of his ethic, uncontaminated by philosophy or instruction.

• Jon Favreau wrote and produced *Swingers* (1966) and directed a TV movie, *Smog* (1999) and a feature *Made* (2001). He is also well known as a film and TV actor.

II, 8:   Full Leather Jacket

Written by Robin Green and Mitchell Burgess. Directed by Allen Coulter.

Meadow hopes to go to Berkeley, but Tony and Carmela want her closer to home. Chris proposes to Adriana. He and his two aides, Sean and Matt, crack some safes. The new hoods embarrass themselves by addressing Tony in the toilet, then visit Richie who says "If there's ever anything you can do for me let me know." Richie begrudgingly agrees to have his nephews, the Spatafores, build a ramp at the crippled Beanie's house. To improve their relations, Richie gives Tony a prized old leather jacket and is devastated to find he gave it to his maid's husband. Hoping to impress Richie, Sean and Matt shoot Chris. Chris kills Sean and when Matt seeks help, a furious Richie chases him away.

This show's major theme is "leaving the nest" and the parents' or mentors' challenge of knowing when to guide and when to withdraw. As Richie quotes the Tao: "You got to shut one door before another one can open." This high-blown sentiment is undercut by Bobby closing a car trunk in the background, while Junior says: "Was that so hard to do?"

As usual the family drama is played out both in Tony's home and in his business. And where they merge: Richie gives Tony the jacket he admired as a boy because "I got to let go of the past." The gesture shows an unexpected sentimentality in the vile Richie. He is understandably hurt when Tony—because he wants to let go of the same past—gives it away. In giving Tony the jacket—and then mentioning it at every opportunity—Richie seeks to recover his position as Tony's senior and benefactor. It's a way to win their war—as the title parodies Stanley Kubrick's war film *Full Metal Jacket* (1987). Tony's slight increases Richie's discomfort with him as boss. To mollify Tony Richie agrees to build his victim Beansie a ramp but proceeds half-heartedly. For his part, Tony wants Richie "where I can see him." "That's what we mean when we say 'family,'" Carmela replies, with a kiss.

A second metaphor inflects the first: the "profile toner" advertised on TV. Often the mentor's "generosity" here is insincere, a matter of improving one's public appearance. Concerned about his "profile," Richie threatens Beansie for presumably asking Tony for the ramp instead of asking him. In a comic version, Richie jokes with Matt and Sean about Chris's "camel nose," which is emphasized at the end when the camera pans down his unconscious body's profile. Carmela strives to improve the "profile" of Meadow's college application because marks are not enough anymore.

When Meadow challenges Carmela's right to have her room cleaned, Carmela suddenly agrees. On the verge of leaving home for college, Meadow is old enough to look after herself. "What right do I have to interfere?" Carmela also corrects her attempt to hide Meadow's letter from Berkeley, requiring additional materials for her application.

Before that recognition, however, Carmela first asked her neighbor Jeannie, then approached Jeannie's lawyer sister Joan, for a reference to help get Meadow into Georgetown, Joan's alma mater. "You don't understand. I want you to write the letter," Carmela tells the lawyer firmly, having softened her approach with a ricotta pie. The Soprano pie with peaches becomes an offer Joan can't refuse. Perhaps the threat of a broken leg may lurk in Carmela's remark that her mother's foot specialist is in the neighborhood. When she returns the pie plate Jeannie conveys her sister's face-saving insistence that she was persuaded to write by Meadow's remarkable transcripts and her teachers' comments. Apparently, honest lawyers—not to say apparently honest lawyers—need to tone their profile as much as Mafiosi do. Joan's acquiescence undermines her earlier advice to her sister: "You want to be a doormat for the rest of your life? Just deal with it."

Carmela first helps her daughter, then lets her mature. In contrast, when Chris proposes Adriana's mother—who risibly preserves her bottled sexpot image—interferes and threatens her daughter: "When you get hurt next time, this door is closed to you." If Carmela will continue to "interfere" in her daughter's life, she will keep a lower profile.

In his session with Dr. Melfi, Tony wonders why he gave Meadow her friend Eric's jeep when he knew "she would freak out." Melfi suggests that unconsciously he must have wanted to stop shielding Meadow from his work—especially since the gambler Dave was such a respectable citizen. Tony was helping Meadow adjust to the reality she will inevitably meet when she "leaves the nest" ("Not those fuckin' ducks again!"). Tony wonders how he can be accused of doing something noble when "I give my girl a car to rub her nose in shit." Helpless before yet another psychiatric paradox, Tony pledges silence—but at least he does not stomp out.

Tony's surrogate child, Chris, is grateful that Tony straightened him out with his ultimatum of the previous episode. After some great sex with Adriana (which always helps one appreciate education), Chris summarizes his mentor's lesson: Stay focused, no distractions or drugs, keep your eye on the prize.

Chris is less fortunate in the hoods whom he chooses to mentor. Sean and Matt are transparently immature and indiscreetly eager to meet and to impress Tony. Matt won't marry because he can hire women for all his domestic relief. Not that Chris is much more mature. In post-coital candor he blames his fights with Adriana on his failure to "communicate my needs," as if she might not have any.

Indeed, there is an ironic cut from Tony advising AJ to "crack the books" and the safecrackers. Sean's habit of leaving a bowel movement at the safe-crack scene confirms his infantilism. When Matt is whacked in II, 9, he wets his pants and cries for his "Mummy." Both men feel insulted that Tony sent Furio for his money and that Furio exacted an additional grand. Hoping to win Richie's favor by whacking Chris, they prove their independence premature.

Ironically, when Sean is killed because he can't get out of his seatbelt, he seems to justify Livia's irresponsible warning AJ against seatbelts (II, 7). But life is a tragedy of the Absurd. So Chris is nearly killed just when he assumes a new maturity. Or as Pussy in the next episode mechanically tells Tony, he believes in God even though He moves in mysterious ways his wonders to perform.

"How could this happen?" Tony asks rhetorically at the end of the episode. How could it not happen in a world of unbridled ambition and misdirected mentoring? With no music over the end credits, the beep and thwock of Chris's life-support system attest to the starkest level of existence.

■ Beansie was earlier described as a Mummy in his hospital bed, after Richie ran him over (and over). Here, as Richie approaches them, Uncle Junior describes a black market film scam to Tony: "He had *The Mummy* before it was in the theatres." Even without the sharp focus of a pun the language often provides such fugitive echoes and coherence. So, too, in the next episode Carmela is moved to concerns for religious vision, after hearing that a hood's *goomah* has borne a child "by C-section." *The Sopranos*'s scripts offer extraordinarily intense language.

X, 9:   From Where to Eternity

Written by Michael Imperioli. Directed by Henry J. Bronchtein.

After coming out of a clinically dead state, Christopher tells Tony and Silvio that he crossed over to Hell, where he saw his father. The dead Mikey gave him a message for Tony and Silvio: "Three o'clock." Tony dismisses this but Silvio is spooked into nightmares. Meanwhile, Carmela wants Tony to have a vasectomy. Overwrought, Tony snaps at Dr. Melfi and at AJ. Tony and Pussy whack Matt Bevilaqua for trying to kill Chris.

In a script written by Michael Imperioli (who plays Christopher, aspiring screenwriter), Chris's shooting moves the characters to reevaluate their lives. For several, it's a wake-up call to their mortality. But over the episode presides Otis Redding's "My Lover's Prayer," a love song in religious language. It plays over Adriana's vigil at Chris's bedside, through Carmela's quarrel with Tony and over their reconciliation at the end.

In business as usual Tony and his men don't tell the detectives anything about the suspect, Matt Bevilaqua. Christopher's mother proves more of a virago than we expected of the woman angry that the paper named her son among the "scumbags" (I, 8). Here, amid the muted grays of the hospital and the somberly dressed family, she rages against the shooter: "I want that motherfucker to suffer." "Don't worry," Silvio assures her, "we'll do the best we can." Like the "bad eminence" of Milton's Satan, here "the best" means "the worst."

When Chris regains consciousness he is certain he has visited Hell—an Irish pub where every day is St. Patrick's Day. There his father loses every hand he plays and he is painfully whacked again every midnight. Tony is skeptical about Mikey's message. After all, would all "the heavy-hitters" Paulie has whacked choose Mikey as their leader? As Tony summarizes his religious beliefs: If in India you go to Hell for eating steaks and in New Jersey you don't, then "None of this shit means a goddam thing."

Unassured, Paulie stays awake to see 3 A.M. tick by safely. He dreams he's being dragged to hell. He argues that Christopher visited purgatory not Hell (no horns on the bouncer, not very hot). So Paulie negotiates himself a deal: His life's crimes will only require 6,000 years there, which he could do on his head, like a couple of days here—just "a little detour on the way to Paradise."

His séance is a comic collision of the mundane and the supernatural. The psychic, his suburban furnishings, the other clients, all are spectacularly ordinary, as if they came from Wal-Mart. Tea and cookies will follow the messages from Beyond. Despite this bathetic normalcy, the psychic contacts Sonny Pegano, Paulie's first hit, and reports Mikey Palmice's tease about Paulie's poison ivy. At this Paulie runs amok, throws a chair and yells "fuckin' queers" before stomping out. With that reaction the séance parallels Tony's discomfiting sessions with Melfi. But where Paulie drags "a bunch of fuckin' ghouls around," Tony's baggage lives.

In a delicious irony, Paulie cuts off his parish priest. After 23 years of donations Paulie "shoulda had immunity for all this shit." The racketeer is angry that his church has not provided the protection he bought. Father

Felix, a bald man who sits at his desk coolly smoking, looks like a "Waste Management Boss," especially with the big trucks passing outside his window. He dismisses the medium as a charlatan, but makes no case for his religion, just: "You should have come to me first and none of this would have happened."

That defense is exactly what Don Vito Corleone (Brando) tells his first supplicant, the undertaker, at the beginning of *The Godfather*. When the priest echoes the Godfather, his moral vacuity justifies Paulie's charge. The church is equivalent to the mob's protection racket. The allusion validates Paulie's goofball assumption: "You left me unprotected. I'm cutting you off for good." After a scolding glare at Jesus, Paulie leaves the church, slamming the door on God for having broken their deal. The down-shot leaves Jesus balefully viewing his diminished territory.

Notwithstanding Paulie's comic function, this episode also provides our sole glimpse into his warmer nature. In two scenes he relates to his obviously loving mistress and her children. Paulie's comfort with them is as dramatic—and more touching—than his large (and real) tattoo. As in the Tony and Melfi plots, Paulie's gangster experience intrudes upon his more important private life.

Against that Catholic background, the Jewish Hesh provides more pragmatic consolation. He assures Adriana that Chris is in the best trauma unit in the Tri-state area, then questions the doctor from a position of medical knowledge.

In contrast, Carmela prays to Jesus to save Chris and to "Deliver him from blindness and grant him vision . . . [to] see Your love and gain the strength to carry on in service to Your mercy." Her faith seems confirmed when Chris recovers and Tony tells her Chris saw Heaven. But Chris tells her it was Hell he visited and to Hell he was told he was going. Though she doesn't confront Tony with his lie, it confirms Carmela's insecurity: "If you can't be honest with me at least have the balls to be honest with yourself."

Carmela also wants Tony to have the balls to get a vasectomy. She is affected by the gossip that Ralph Rotaldo's Brazilian *goomah* had his child. Carmela fears her children's humiliation if a mistress bore Tony's child. Tony denies he is having an affair: "I told you I cut it off." Normally, he would say: "I broke it off." But "cutting" it off hangs in this episode's air, from Paulie "cutting off" Father Felix to Carmela's demand of a vasectomy. Even in his care Tony is insensitive: "I had her tested for AIDS!" Outraged, Carmela stomps out to sleep alone. Otis Redding marks Tony's solitude: "What you gonna do tonight / When you need some lovin' arms to hold you tight?"

Despite their anger, when Chris's emergency brings them back to the hospital, Tony and Carmela enter holding hands. Their differences are suspended in the crisis—but they resume. Tony takes his nerves out on AJ for dropping a dish of pasta after dinner: "I'm supposed to get a vasectomy when this is my male heir?" To make amends Tony brings a pizza and pop into AJ's room to apologize. He assures AJ that he sees himself in his son. "I gotta learn to control my emotions around the people I love. . . . I couldn't ask for a better son, AJ. I mean that."

When Carmela overhears Tony's apology, she rejects the "snip snip." Touched at Tony's fatherly warmth, she considers having another child. Of course, she came to get Tony for Pussy's call—the summons to deal with Matt.

At episode end, Carmela plugs Tony's habitual pledge of fidelity with "Just prove it." In perhaps their most intimate scene in the series, Carmela is tender toward Tony, massaging him, holding him, as if to alleviate his burden she subconsciously knows he feels from having just avenged Chris. In the last shot, the camera pans away from the couple's lovemaking—with its corporeal climax in their clenched hands—past a row of approving ornamental angels, still to "My Lover's Prayer."

For all his stress, Pussy enjoys his community here. In the hospital Pussy consoles and hugs Adriana. He rejects Richie's "negative energies" and wants "positive vibes only" around Christopher. But in an opening pan across the waiting room, over Carmela's prayer, while the others sit together in their private thoughts, Pussy is isolated alone in the background. Perhaps to ease the FBI pressure, he tells Lipari that Tony seems to suspect he has turned. But Skip assures him: "You're the one who's seeing through different eyes."

When someone does report Matt's whereabouts—"for points,"which is what Matt tried to score with Richie by shooting Chris—it's to Pussy. Is he being blessed for his treachery? Or do singers of a feather attract each other? Tony insists on shooting Matt himself—with his faithful Pussy—rather than delegating the duty.

From whacking Matt, Tony and Pussy go to dine at the restaurant Pussy first brought him to on the night Tony "popped [his] cherry." Whether that initiation was sexual or his first murder, in Tony's vulnerability toward his betrayer he is once again like a virgin. The stained glass window behind Pussy recalls Paulie's abandoned church, to which the men's steak dinner is a heartier alternative. Pussy affirms his faith in God, whose mysterious ways have helped him, but that glass recasts him as Judas.

The character who fares least well through this drama—with the obvious exception of gunsel Matt—is Dr. Melfi. After Paulie bolsters himself with his ludicrous calculation of Purgatory, we find the more intelligent Melfi crumbling. She is unusually aggressive with Tony and shakey in her own position.

Tony's self-justification is as transparent a rationalization as Paulie's tally for Purgatory. Tony contends that he and Christopher won't go to Hell. Hell is for molesters and sadists, Hitlers and Pol Pots: "We're soldiers. Soldiers don't go to Hell. It's war. Soldiers kill other soldiers. Everybody involved knows the stakes." His logic seems undercut by his impulsive, animal scratch. His argument parallels Carmela's prayer—"We have chosen this life in full awareness of the consequences of our sins"—but where she acknowledges her sin Tony strains to justify himself.

Angered by Melfi's skepticism, Tony argues history (incidentally also answering the critics of the show's treatment of Italian-Americans). The American government opened the floodgates for Italian immigrants "because they needed us, to build their cities." But not all wanted to lose their identity. Some wanted to preserve their culture of family, honor, and loyalty—Tony's "Old School." Not all wanted to remain "worker bees," feeding the moguls, "Some of us wanted a piece of the action." At Melfi's skepticism, Tony turns on her: When he's worried about the "nephew" he loves, "This is the time you pick to take a stand?"

We next see Melfi crying to her therapist, Elliot, guilty for having been insensitive to her patient. "Do I hate him?" she wonders. She has been drinking alone, to face Tony's "moral Never Never Land." Having taken a moral position, now she's scared and regrets having told Tony her son's college. Melfi's strong character has been shattered.

While everyone reacts to Chris's crisis differently, Chris finds his own characteristic response. While his friends and family come and go, his cronies avenge him, his mother rages, Carmela prays, Chris quietly ratchets up his morphine drip.

II, 10: Bust Out

Written by Frank Renzulli and Robin Green & Mitchell Burgess.
Directed by John Patterson.

A witness makes Tony a suspect for Matt's murder, which tightens the FBI hold on Pussy. Tony uses Dave's sporting goods store as a front to order goods that will not be paid for. Carmela sympathizes with Dave's wife Christina about her husband's gambling. Carmela and Christina's brother, Vic Musto, are instantly attracted to each other. He retreats after Dave tells him that Tony has bankrupted him. Faced with jail, Tony draws closer to his children. When Richie tries to turn Uncle Junior against Tony again, he is warned about Janice.

This episode is about the relationship—sometimes direct, sometimes ironic—between the immediate experience and the larger contexts beyond our awareness. According to the end-credits song, Journey's "Wheel in the Sky," "The wheel in the sky keeps on turnin' / I don't know where I'll be tomorrow." This song also accompanies Carmela's attraction to Vic. However sentient and focused a character may be, there is always some influence beyond his awareness. The arc is redefined by its whole, the unseen, larger circle. As superstition evolves into religion, those invisible forces are what Annalisa's sybils, the medium Colin's séance, Father Phil's Christianity, and Dr. Melfi's psychoanalysis are supposed to access for us.

At the plot center, Tony's confidence about Matt's whack is shaken when he learns that a witness espied Tony and a "heavyset" accomplice leaving the murder scene. Suddenly Tony faces the threat of jail—or of fleeing to "Elvis country" (where there are no Italians or Jews). As he tells Dr. Melfi, "I could be goin' away for a very long time—for something I didn't do." That he rewords from a broader context: "I didn't do nothin' wrong." As the witness is not identified, Paulie cannot dissuade him. As Melfi detects in Tony's swagger—"the government can do what it wants" to him, once AJ has left home—Tony for the first time appears scared.

Here the turning wheel is felt first in the witness, then correctively when the newspaper identifies Matt as a Soprano associate. The witness is an intellectual: he plays avant-garde music and reads *Anarchy, State and Utopia*. He is caught between the hope for a crime-free Utopia and the more immediate dangers of criminal anarchy. He tries to be a responsible citizen (that is, "a flag-salutin' motherfucker") but when he learns of the Soprano involvement he understandably panics. With his wife's support ("I knew it. I knew it. But no, you had to be The Big Man!") the witness rejects the FBI ("lying cocksuckers"), withdraws his identification and leaves Tony safe again.

Even in Tony's relationship with his children the visible moment is redefined by the larger context. He misses AJ's swim meet because he's stashing, with lawyer Neil Mink, $400,000 to be paid out to Carmela in the event of his absence. Where Carmela sees only the apparent neglect, Tony's larger movement serves his familial care.

The parent's relationship with the child is affected by both the larger patterns of the parent's other concerns and the natural cycle of the child's maturing toward independence. As Melfi describes this "bittersweet" stage, "You're glad that they're growing up but you're sad to lose them." When Tony suggests they share a movie and pizza, AJ is committed to meet his friends at the mall. When Meadow finds Tony maudlin from brandy she sends him to bed (as he earlier did the game-playing AJ). "Sometimes we're all hypocrites," she says, negating her earlier criticism of his profession.

In the last scene, Tony having "dodged the big bullet" takes AJ sailing. In their exuberance they are unaware of the larger arc they are cutting, as they unwittingly capsize a small boat in their wake. Oblivious of the danger in their power, the father lets his son steer *The Stugots* in all its—dangerous, suspect—masculine glory.

The theme also applies to the Janice-Richie scenes. When they make love—on Livia's sofa in the living room, as if they were still adolescents—Richie holds a pistol to her head and she spurs him on with hot monosyllabics. He can handle the "Boss" and "You're the best" but he withdraws from her "It should be you." "I can't think of shit like that when we're having sex," he complains, limply: "You're not in the moment." Richie's lust for power is checked by his compulsion "to be loyal . . . I'm Old School."

When Richie sympathetically needles him about Tony's abuse, Uncle Junior warns him about Janice's dishonesty. Now the arc of fealty is redefined by the larger arc of betrayal, which is redefined by another arc of fealty. So, too, the traitor Pussy's "Thank God" when Tony learns the witness is not an insider. On the other hand, Pussy feeds the FBI information (the list of duped investors in Wobistics). Yet Pussy does not betray Tony's murder of Matt.

In contrast, in Carmela's impulsive dalliance with Vic Musto—the "artist in wallpaper"—both characters are swept away by their feelings. It is ironic that Vic introduces himself to a Soprano as "bonded, state-certified but I'm still dangerous." He soon learns about that family's danger. Carmela, we know, is virtuous and faithful. Vic, we learn, was the perfect husband through his wife's fatal breast cancer. We see his generous character when he confronts Dave and resolves to pay for Eric's college. (In Tony's Executive poker game Dave lost his son's education fund.) But when checking out the confining powder room, Carmela and Vic seem driven to their kiss. They both pull back, apologizing simultaneously, shocked at their own impulses.

They are cooler but still forced to have contact with each other when they agree on the phone that Vic will work alone the next day and Carmela will prepare a gourmet lunch. When his co-worker Ramone arrives instead, Carmela's (and our) hopes are dashed. Vic has shown his extraordinary virtue—and his sensible fear of Sopranos—again: resisting the force of the wheel driving him to Carmela. In addition to their powerful attraction, Carmela is influenced by her marriage difficulties, Tony's insensitivity toward AJ, and of course, the literature she is reading *(Memoirs of a Geisha)*. Vic's control of his temptation contrasts to his brother-in-law Dave's self-destruction.

When Tony learns he is safe he is watching a History Channel program about Patton, another figure who both turned and was turned by the wheels of history. As the show intones, Patton too "knows the controversies that have swirled around him have tainted his reputation." Tony would also identify with the TV remark that Patton's "hatred of his enemy is matched only by his concern for his men." When Tony goes into the powder room for a deep sigh of relief, he is unaware of the second threat he has dodged: Carmela's romantic temptation within that same tight space, with its vertical-bar wallpaper and the camouflaged door out. In moving to a private space to express his relief Tony celebrates one close call on the site of another.

As with the capsized boat, Tony is often the larger wheel that influences other's lives. In this case his destruction of Dave frightens Vic off Carmela. Just the Soprano name renders the murder witness amnesiac. Tony drives Dave into bankruptcy by ordering large quantities of designer bottled water, coolers, designer running shoes, and airline tickets on his store account. We see Tony's invisible reach when Artie offers Christine and Carmela the water Tony gave him "such a deal on" (at the expense of Christine, who nominally owns Dave's store). More positively, Tony thanks the crippled Beansie for agreeing to accept his $50,000 cash gift. For her part, Carmela meets with other mothers to plan their kids Graduation Night parties, hoping to impose a circle of their control on the celebrants' exuberant arcs.

We also find this dynamic in the editing strategy of ironic bridges between scenes. For example, right after the police tell the witness that it's people like him who enable the police to stop criminals, we see the merry-go-round where Tony meets Richie. It images the police's inability to break out of the circle of arrest and release, charge and acquittal, identification and withdrawal. Similarly, Tony will pass Richie's complaint—that Barone Sanitation is over-charging him—on to the company, of which Tony is half owner. In this example of the arc governed by the circle, Tony gives Richie a runaround. The merry-go-round metaphor relates back to the police and ahead to Richie.

Similarly, we see Dave playing Russian roulette on his pool table at home so we know he has a gun. When Tony finds Dave sleeping in a tent in the store, they have a candid chat. Tony admits he let Dave into the disastrous game because "I knew you had this business. It's my nature," as in the fable of the scorpion and the frog. Dave breaks down when Tony says the end is Dave's bankruptcy. When the scene ends with a gunshot, we assume that Dave has killed himself. But the shot is the starter's pistol in the next scene, AJ's swim meet.

The scene bridge is something that relates back to the previous scene and is redefined in the next one. The element means one thing in the context of the first scene, but something else in the next. Thus a woman concerned about "Little Eric" (presumably Dave's and Christine's son) turns out to be a character in a television-soap opera to which Uncle Junior has become devoted. The sausage-spewing machine that could represent Richie's and Junior's churn of malice is what Livia is watching on her TV. When it turns to make chocolate pasta Livia gives Meadow $20 to celebrate her college admissions at Berkeley and NYU, her wait-listing at Columbia and Georgetown—and her unaccountable rejection at Bowdoin and Penn. The student proposes and the college disposes—more mysterious grindings of an unseen wheel.

In this theme *The Sopranos* replays on the level of dramatic irony one of its recurring issues: At what point are we responsible for our selves and our actions? When Tony tells Melfi about Annalisa's "You're your own worst enemy," Melfi replies: "The question is 'How do you stop?' " Tony stops—the therapy—and goes sailing with his son instead. As he gleefully revs up his 120 seahorse-power *Stugots* he upsets the smaller boat. The tangled web of responsibility and determinism ensnares us in every action, large or small. Our soul—like God and the devil—is in the details.

II, 11: House Arrest

Written by Terence Winter. Directed by Tim Van Patten.

Restricted to his house, Uncle Junior reunites with an old friend, Catherine Romano, whose late husband was a cop. At lawyer Neil

Mink's suggestion, Tony starts biding his time at his garbage company office, instead of at the Bada Bing. He's disturbed that Richie—with Junior's approval—continues to sell cocaine along his collection route. From his stress Tony collapses, has breathing difficulties, and develops a severe rash. Meanwhile, Dr. Melfi braces herself with a long vodka before Tony's session and is ordered out of a restaurant for quarreling with a smoking woman.

Confinement and nostalgia form the cohering theme of this episode. It is introduced in the song when Carmela leaves Tony alone to go for her eyebrow treatment. As Tony contemplates changing his life habits, that aging symbol of 1960s liberation, Bob Dylan, sings "You're gonna have to serve somebody."

Literally, Uncle Junior is confined under house arrest. Abhorring restriction, he rejects the bedpan because "I'm not a cat. I don't shit in a box." When Michael McLuhan of the marshal's ("Marshall's") office restores his electronic bracelet, Junior learns that the tedium is the massage. In even closer confinement: he spends six hours with his hand stuck in the kitchen drain—and needs to be relaxed and lubricated by Richie to be freed. Junior's physical condition, apnea, literalizes his feeling smothered.

When Junior fails to attract the young nurse, Tracy, he is forced to acknowledge that he can no longer score with the women that he would have as a younger man. So he settles into a relationship with Catherine Romano. He assures her that her dead husband Lou, "a real straight shooter," was not on the take. In the funhouse mirror of this world, "straight shooter" means a sympathetically bent holster. The futility of living on the past is expressed in the closing song, Johnny Thunders' "Can't Put Your Arm around a Memory." In contrast, Catherine relishes Junior's company because of their common past: "I enjoy you, Corrado. I always did."

Richie feels confined by his small garbage route and high costs, especially when Janice wants an $850,000 home. He chafes under Tony's restrictions—for example, forbidding his drivers' dangerous sale of cocaine—and takes risky initiatives. In the opening scene—to The Pretenders's "Space Invaders"—Richie has a garbage truck dump its load in front of a deli whose owner complained at having to pay double for missed pickups. Parodying a guarantee, the company gives the complainer double his garbage back. Continuing to turn Junior against Tony, Richie deploys Livia's evasive innuendo: "I don't want to say anything disparaging."

Of course, another form of constraint is a nagging memory, the past that won't stay buried. That's what Livia marshalls when she tells Junior that her Johnny-Boy once said that the nice, sweet Catherine let him feel her up behind The Sons of Italy Hall. Even the innocent are confined by their storied pasts. Earlier, Junior briefly recalls his lost Roberta, the 16-year affair he ended when she betrayed his cunnilinguistic genius (I, 9). He is heartened that she has bought a house: Bobby saw her buy a fountain of a urinating boy.

As Tony complains to Dr. Melfi, he is so bored even a polished thriller like *Se7en* is uninteresting: "It's all a series of distractions till you die." Interestingly, when Tony mentioned watching a Brad Pitt and Gwyneth Paltrow movie, Melfi assumed it was *Sliding Doors*—though Pitt isn't in it— an optimistic movie about discovering one's alternative life. But Tony sticks to his gangsters. Even his passion for history now fails him. He does not rush down to see the gang's shipment of World War II memorabilia, including the jeep Patton drove in Sicily, Eisenhauer's dinner service, and Goering's guns. In ominous comedy, the false Pussy parodies the TV-and-Hollywood Nazi: "I know nothing. Nothing. . . . Vee have vays of dealing vit you, Mr. Soprano."

When Tony's lawyer advises him to insulate himself from the gang's shenanigans, this turns into a self-imposed, painful form of house arrest. For long days at his garbage company office Tony doodles, scrapes his rash till it bleeds, and sets up an office basketball pool. When his doctor suggests he talk to his therapist about "stress management" Tony takes a more direct approach. In his office he screws (doggie-style) the stacked secretary ("a Born-again Christian," he was warned), while a dog barks madly in the background. Stress spreads.

Another form of constraint sounds in the characters' language. Though the profanity seems outlaw, even blasphemous, it slips into the formal order of a pattern. Junior's "Mother of fuckin' Mercy" is echoed by Tony's "Son of a fuckin' bitch." The black Michael McLuhan from the marshal's office seems unaware of the larger pattern that his name and occupation set on him, even when the nurse calls him Marshall McLuhan. Like the song by the other 1960s icon, Dylan, this man's name serves a larger pattern. Similarly, the country club's reception sign, "Couples Invitational," assumes a second meaning from our downview on a passing cleavage.

Dr. Melfi herself is restricted by her relationship with Tony. She feels she cannot refer him to another doctor, yet she suffers from their association. When she humiliates her son in the restaurant, Melfi claims her concern was for his well-being. So, too, she insists Tony is not ready to be referred elsewhere. When her son says he is studying Lacan's deconstructivism, Melfi jokes that his grandfather was a contractor. But the subject's irony relates rather to her disintegration. She finally accepts Kupferberg's prescription for an anti-obsession drug. When Tony finds her "mellow," we credit her vodka bracer.

In a variation on the theme of constraint, perhaps Melfi has her own compulsive behavior in mind as well as Tony's when she cites the psychological disorder, alexithymia: "The individual craves almost ceaseless action which enables them to avoid acknowledging the abhorrent things they do." Without this activity, they have to face their feeling empty and the self-loathing that has haunted them since childhood, so "they crash." In one shot Tony and Melfi both seem to be patients, turned away from each other, their heads held in the hand in opposite directions. Of course, Melfi resumed seeing Tony for her therapy as well as his.

Melfi's disintegration proves Tony destructive. Under his unintentional influence even someone of Melfi's sensitivity, knowledge, wisdom, and both psychological and moral self-awareness proves helpless. She breaks down from trying to bridge the abyss between Tony's charm and his evil. When Melfi embarrasses her son at the restaurant, she expresses her pent-up rage at not being able to control her life—a frustration perilously close to what she was treating in Tony. Stress spreads.

In different ways, the characters are moving out of themselves. Uncle Junior falls asleep in front of the televsion with Catherine holding his feet. To subdue his snoring she puts his oxygen mask on him. At last he has friendly, relaxing company—and she packs a seductive *manicott'*. Carmela broadens her horizons by hosting a book-club discussion of Frank Mc-Court's novels, *Angela's Ashes* and *'Tis*, which focus the Italian-American women on the Irish characters' dysfunctional families and drinking problems. Melfi promises Dr. Kupferberg that she will to go to an AA meeting.

Tony escapes his office rut—and rutting—by returning to the Satriale backroom for gags with the gang. A car crash takes them outside. There the lads shuffle around, Tony lights up his Cuban, and Paulie suns himself under a reflector. FBI Agent Harris drops by to introduce his new partner, Joe Marquez. The rising camera takes a detached, clinical view on the street life below. This is not the microscope used to burn live ants (as Tony joked was his pastime), but a bemused and sympathetic gaze down on people making the most of their empty day. In the absence of high drama, the pulse persists.

These last mundane details—like the comforts of Catherine and Junior—exemplify the "series of distractions" by which we divert ourselves until we die. This consolation helps to bridge old animosities. If no lion lies with any lamb here, at least Tony and Agent Harris comment amiably on the Nets's basketball game, the erstwhile quarrelers Hesh and Chris play cards, and Pussy shares a girlie magazine with his once resented Furio. The peace survives the collision caused by Carmine's speeding.

II, 12:   The Knight in White Satin Armor

Written by Robin Green and Mitchell Burgess. Directed by Allen Coulter.

Pussy starts to fancy himself an FBI employee. Though Tony and Carmela throw an engagement party for them, Richie plots to kill Tony but Janice kills him in a domestic tiff. Tony breaks up with Irina but is drawn back when she attempts suicide.

The season's penultimate episode returns to the tension between loyalty and betrayal. Of course, the most dramatic case is Janice's engagement to marry Richie, heralded as the union of the Sopranos and the Apriles. Scene after scene opens in harmony and dissolves into bitterness, because the sentiments are false.

The opening seems to be a dream: An unfamiliar couple dance elegantly through the empty mansion. When Tony and Janice carry in a loveseat, and the couple are identified as Richie's son Rick and his competition ballroom dance partner, it seems the dream has become reality. In their loving speeches at the engagement party Janice and Richie avow as much.

But that dream scene carries the seeds of its destruction. If Tony enters ("ass first," director Allen Coulter instructed) helping Janice carry in the love seat, he exits telling her to "shove it up [her] ass." So, too, the young man dancing turns out to be Richie's son, Richard Jr. As Tony expects and Janice denies, his dance career profoundly disappoints Richie. Jackie Aprile Jr.'s introduction is also ominous, as his cigar suggests he aspires to become another Tony.

The fatal kitchen incident is defined by the TV-boxing match, which plays behind Janice as she nags Richie. Initially, he is irked having to make decisions about the wedding, then by the mounting house costs, then by Janice's snarling hatred of Tony ("Tony just can't handle that our house is nicer than his fuckin' house."). In return, she objects to Richie's attitude. She drugged Livia so they could have sex but says that is unlikely now.

The irritants collect. Richie flares up when she calls his son "Ricky" instead of Rick and wishes he had a son like Jackie, not a dancer. When Janice would accept Rick being gay Richie punches her mouth. Removing the *New Jersey Bride* magazine from his chair, Richie sits down to eat, and says coldly: "You gonna cry now?" Janice gets the gun they use for sex and kills him.

Ironically, this happens right after Tony has authorized Silvio—who glowers like the mask of Tragedy or the hunched bitterness of Richard Nixon—to kill Richie. The murder verifies Uncle Junior's last advice to Tony (as to Richie earlier): "You have to wonder where Janice is in all this. My little niece." With her new hair, wardrobe, and domestic assertiveness, the hippie niece is transforming into mob wife—until she arrests the engagement.

Though both Richie's violence and Janice's murder are shocking, they are consistent. In Richie's first appearance (II, 3), he warns Chris about slapping Adriana: "You want to raise your hand, you give her your last name." That is how Richie is from the Old School. Janice's violent outburst confirms the shallow faddishness of her various New Age idealisms.

In her post-murder need Janice turns to the brother she has been sabotaging. In the opening scene Tony explains he is hosting the engagement party, despite his hatred of Richie, out of obligation to his sister. Janice is even more aggressive against Tony than Livia is. To provoke Richie, Janice reports that Tony does not want him near his kids. But when she needs help she calls Tony and he saves her. Tony enters the kitchen warily, his gun drawn, as if he might be entering a trap.

Despite their differences, Tony sympathizes with his sister. Livia is delighted to hear Richie did not come home: "He probably jilted her. That's the story of her life." Tony defends Janice: "What chance did she have, with you for a mother?" Livia passes through an encyclopedia of emotional pretense here, inviting Tony's kiss and dismissing him as "cruel." When he falls on his face outside, Livia laughs—as in Tony's only warm memory from childhood (I, 2), when the family laughed at Johnny-Boy's fall. At the bus station Tony tells Janice that his shrink has diagnosed Livia as a narcissistic personality who cannot allow joy. This episode shows Janice as an equally destructive narcissist.

In contrast to Janice's and Livia's betrayal of Tony stands the quiet, unquestioning loyalty of Silvio, Chris, and Furio. And ostensibly Uncle Junior. At first, Junior's frustration and financial needs ($400,000 just to challenge the wiretap evidence) make Junior sympathetic to Richie's desire to whack Tony. But when he "couldn't sell it" to Albert Barese, Junior concludes Richie is "a fuckin' loser." He is better off with Tony.

When Junior warns Tony about Richie's plot he claims his cocaine selling (earlier his "lifeline") was a strategic ploy. "I've been playing him." Junior hides his self-interest in avuncular warmth: "If I didn't come to you your fuckin' wife would be a widow and your children wouldn't have a father. Go fuck yourself." But however self-serving, Junior still loves his nephew. Even when he's angry enough to want him killed, he still loves him. In the Family family, blood is thicker than . . . bloodshed. Uncle Junior's simple hominess is expressed in his kitchen, with its pictures of kittens, the domestic instruments, and cake-plates. When he hears of Richie's failure the green half-wall behind him seems an image of his nausea.

Dr. Melfi, who seems to be recovering her composure and stability, remains Tony's faithful counsel. She indignantly denies ever being judgmental about his—or any other client's—sex life. She even tries to temper Tony's guilt about Irina:

TONY: I was bangin' her for two years.
MELFI: Was that a hardship on her?
TONY: That's cute.

Now that Melfi seems to have regained control of her negative feelings toward Tony and their relationship, Tony again enjoys their exchanges.

In Pussy's tension between loyalty and betrayal, he moves from his closeness with Tony to wear a wire to the engagement party and to turn in Chris for hoisting a truckload of Pokémon cards (more "nickel and dime" stuff for the unwise guy whose brokerage certificate was a "license to steal" via the stock market). Tailing Chris, Pussy puts a 7–11 clerk into a coma, smashes his son's car, and needs Skip's intervention to avoid the charge of leaving an accident. More than the capsized boat victims, the clerk is a serious reminder of the innocents our heroes hurt.

To resolve his conflict, Pussy generates a new loyalty. He defines himself as an FBI employee. He suggests that after this assignment he could resettle under the Witness Protection Program in Scottsdale, Arizona, and give lectures to the FBI. He acts like an operative, giving Skip a present and using official language and code on his reports: THIS IS THE FAT MAN. WHO? SAL?

Pussy rationalizes his switch of loyalty: Tony treated him like "an errand boy" when he sent him to find the teacher's car. He conveniently overlooks

Tony's more recent trust in their whacking Matt Bevilaqua together, though—to show how comfortable he now feels "in" the FBI—he admits his involvement to Skip.

Like Pussy, Carmela loses faith in Tony when she smells Calvin Klein One on Tony's shirt after he claimed to have left Irina. Of course, Carmela understands her situation. When Janice tries on her wedding gown (thanking Jesus for her cleavage), Carmela advises her: "In a year, tops, you're going to have to accept a *goomah.*" As the scene is shot almost entirely in a mirror the image of radiant bridal bliss seems an illusion. Mirrors always suggest pause for reflection.

Nor does Irina's suicide attempt arouse Carmela's sympathy. When Janice phones Tony for help, Carmela moves from suspicion—"You better get it. Maybe she slit the other wrist"—to skepticism. She phones Livia's to check if Tony is there.

The characters' lives make for inverted values. So Richie tells Junior, "This country is going through boom times. There's more fuckin' garbage than there ever was." Amid the formal elegance of the bridal shop, Janice reveals Richie's need to hold a gun to her head during sex: "It's ritualistic. Fetishistic. That's all." Anyway, "usually he takes the clip out." After her suicide attempt, the Russian Irina refuses to talk to the hospital psychiatrist because he's Rumanian. She is depressed because she's too old to model for salad spinners. Though her salad days are over, she is still green in judgment.

When Carmela thanks Vic for "thinking" and "being strong" for both of them in curtailing their relationship, she suggests a possible future: "Maybe someday I will be free." When the scene opens, the sound of the paint-mixing machine sounds like machine gun fire, especially as it follows Albert Barese's refusal to join "a move against Tony Soprano." The sound-cut connects Vic's and Barese's submission to Tony. In Tony's life, murder is as common as redecorating. But Carmela resists the idea that Vic withdrew simply out of fear of Tony. Director Coulter kept Vic and Carmela in profile to express their unease with each other (Season II DVD, disc 4), with the paint-chip rack between them "like a ski-slope toward her." Again, this TV show has the visual artistry of a feature film.

At the end, Carmela asserts a new independence. She announces that after Meadow's graduation she and Rosalie Aprile will take a three-week holiday in Rome to shop and perhaps to meet with the Pope. Tony will chauffeur AJ and find Meadow a tennis clinic "because if I have to do it, Tony, I just might commit suicide." The wife assumes the rights and strategies of the *goomah*. The scene begins with a pan up from Carmela's Italian travel brochures. At the end Carmela walks out, leaving Tony shrunk between the living room column and the wall, as usual behind a rock and a hard place.

In his own way, Tony maintains fealty if not fidelity to his lovers. When he breaks up with Irina it is partly to force her to make her own life, to get a career, to find someone who will marry her and give her children. This explanation is not just a rationalization. Irina is unhappy in their sporadic relationship. Her friend Svetlana's Bill carried her off when her prosthetic leg fell off in the—where else?—Gap store. So it's understandable that Irina will ask: "Where is my knight in white satin armor?" The malapropism admits Irina's desire for a wedding gown, like Janice's, that would be her armor against the world.

In part, Tony leaves her so she will find her knight. His response to her suicide attempt shows that he is concerned for her, in his fashion: "Fuckin' ambulance. They pumped her stomach. Cost me three grand." Having suggested modeling prospects and a therapist, Tony finally breaks with her by sending Silvio with $75,000 cash and his usual sage advice: "Time is a great enemy" for a woman, but "Something always comes along. . . . It's called *Passages*. It's a book."

Primarily, Tony breaks off with Irina because he loves Carmela. Dr. Melfi is surprised that he ends the affair now, given his obvious feelings for Irina. But now his concern for Carmela outweighs his vagrant lust. He protectively refuses to tell his wife what happened to Richie: "Carmela, after eighteen years of marriage, don't make me make you an accessory after the fact." Despite the discretion of his words, his first hand gesture suggests a gun. But with Carmela his words and deeds are rarely at one.

When she hears that Richie is "gone" and Janice decamped to Seattle, Carmela concludes: "That was not a marriage made in heaven." The camera provides a couple of different views of Tony and Carmela sitting together on the sofa, like Carmela and Father Phil in I, 5, and Chris and Jon in II, 7, apart but together. Particularly given Carmela's recollection of her wedding—

CARMELA: Remember how radiant I looked walking down the aisle?
JANICE: You must be depressed.
CARMELA: No, not depressed. I leave that for others.

—her marriage was not made in heaven either. It was made on earth, where real people live, with real problems and few illusions, and it has adjusted to the challenges and compromises necessary to sustain it. The white satin wedding gown is not a suit of armor, not a protection against outside threats, but a ritual no stronger than the people's loves within it. In that spirit of familial acceptance Tony can see Janice off with "All in all, I'd say it was a pretty good visit."

As all the relationships are tested and redefined in this episode, it seems to grow out of the previous one's Dylan song, "You're gonna have to serve somebody." But when the dust has cleared Tony can relax with a more satisfied song over the end credits, The Eurythmics's "I Saved the World Today": "Everybody's happy now / The bad thing's gone away / Everybody's happy now / The good thing's here to stay." The Richie and Irina threats are gone and the Tony and Carmela marriage remains, in whatever new terms she may negotiate.

II, 13: Funhouse

Written by David Chase and Todd Kessler. Directed by John Patterson.

Livia is rejected by her daughter, Barbara, and by the Green Grove Retirement Home for having abused the staff. When she insults Carmela, Tony washes his hands of her by giving her two first-class airline tickets to go live with her sister in Tucson. Tony and Pussy meet at an Indian restaurant to collect on their new prepaid phone card scam. Suffering severe food poisoning, Tony experiences six nightmares, mostly set on the Asbury Park boardwalk in winter. In their climax, a tilefish with Pussy's voice admits having betrayed him to the FBI. Tony finds Pussy's wire under his cigars. Tony, Silvio, and Paulie take Pussy out on a boat and kill him. On the eve of Meadow's graduation the FBI arrest Tony for possession of stolen airplane tickets. Out on bail, he attends the graduation ceremony and party.

David Chase concludes the second season with an episode focused on purging and cleansing. Not all the examples are scatological. The literal purge, of course, is Tony's epic reaction to food poisoning. Tony spends a night of cramps, upchuck, and the richest orchestration of flatulence since *Blazing Saddles* (Mel Brooks, 1974). The less sensitive Pussy had "a slight touch of diarrhea but that all passed." Of course, apart from the safecracker's wind-breaking in II, 8, the only previous note of flatulence in this series was also struck by Pussy on his release in I, 11. The purge theme gives new meaning to the framing Rolling Stones song, "Through and Through" and Tony's episode-end regret, "I blew an easy one. I blew everything. . . . I got predicates up the ass."

In a psychological form of purge, Tony's nightmares pour out his waking anxieties. The dreams grow out of Tony's playful surrealism when he claims his coat has grown hair and is attacking him (It's the sable for Carmela). His suicide flame in the first nightmare points to the *gee* which Artie blames for the food poisoning. In India that clarified butter is used to prepare the body for the funeral pyre. His first nightmare transforms the supplier of Carmela's new fur, Patsy Parisi, into his brother Philly, whom Tony had whacked in II, 1. Pussy is notably absent from Tony's suicide.

In another dream Tony watches himself shoot Paulie—then admit to Melfi that this was an excessive punishment for Paulie's sending out a family newsletter every Christmas and whistling television commercials, especially since he is such a good earner. (He doesn't mention Paulie's worst trait: repeating—in self-congratulation—his own jokes.) This dream prepares Tony for the execution of a close aide.

In the second dream Dr. Melfi speaks through Annalisa, agreeing that he is still his own worst enemy. In the next dream his new clean-up guy Furio hands Tony a roll of toilet paper as Adriana and Chris drive Tony to find Pussy. Tony's subconscious is zeroing in on Pussy.

In a dream session with Dr. Melfi, Tony enters wearing his sweatshirt and a fairly impressive erection (actually a strapped-on dildo, according to Director John Patterson, in his commentary on Season II DVD, disc four). This Melfi refers to as his "friend," then his "friend Pussy." This recalls the confusion in I, 1, between Pussy Malanga (whom Junior planned to kill in Artie's restaurant) and Big Pussy Buonpensiero. As Tony told Hesh, "You think he's going to fuck with Big Pussy? My Pussy?" Now Tony is uncertain whether Melfi is talking about Pussy or pussy: "I got pussy on the brain. Always did. I want to fuck you. Always did."

The ambiguity confirms Pussy as the unacknowledged source of Tony's anxiety, his uncertainty about his safety and identity. Tony has Pussy on the brain but suppresses his intuition that his best friend has turned. As Pussy has been singing to the FBI, he is Tony's weak spot, the lowest-case soprano. This dream ends with Tony taking Melfi on her desk, as his weakness for pussy edges out his vulnerability to Pussy one last time.

In Tony's last dream his anxiety would not be deflected. From a market stall a tilefish confesses in Pussy's voice: "You know I've been working with the government, Tony. . . . Sooner or later you've got to face facts. . . . You passed me over for promotion." In telling Tony what he already knows, the fish surfaces Tony's suppressed intuition. Through the magic of digital imaging, the fish is morphed with Pussy's mouth.

As Tony has to get past the pussy to Pussy in his nightmares, he has to go beneath the Cuban cigars in Pussy's bedroom to find the wires, mike, and mini-recorder that confirm his treachery. As if to indulge a Freudian analyst, Pussy hid his betrayal under his cigars. Pussy's identification with fish was set up in the opening restaurant scene, when a waiter passed Tony's and Pussy's table with a platter of fish.

The confrontation on the boat is poignant, as it unwinds over the surreally inapt, "Baubles, Bangles and Beads," by the god Sinatra. As the song is about small mementos that evoke a shared, loving past, perhaps it does suit the scene where the three men kill the traitor who was "like a brother" to them. As well, the "singer" Pussy is confronted on the line "Her heart will sing, sing-a-linga."

After a reflex denial Pussy minimizes what he gave the FBI: "Picayune shit. . . . They know about the calling cards, Scatino, the phone card scam." From his defense of helplessness—"I was going away for pushing H. . . . Thirty to life. I had no choice"—he turns to brag about deceiving the FBI: "I'm mind-fucking those donkeys like you wouldn't believe." After a few tequilas Pussy recalls his 26-year-old acupuncturist in Puerto Rico: "Her ass was the second coming." The men laugh along until Tony punctures the illusion: "Did she even really exist?"

Exposed, Pussy still asks, "Not in the face, ok? Give me that? Keep my eyes?" In *GoodFellas*, Tommy (Joe Pesci) is shot in the face so his mother cannot have an open coffin. As Pussy is at sea he should be beyond that concern. But then his admission that his "inner ear balance is off" speaks to a failure in balance as well as conscience.

Tony's physical purge points to several other poisons. From the Green Grove point of view—shared by Barbara's husband, Tom—Livia has been properly expunged. Tony thinks he has managed that, too, until his scam tickets backfire, she is stopped by airport security and he is arrested.

Meadow seems to purge herself of any last shame about her father, especially after her friends see him taken out in handcuffs. As she assures Carmela: "This is who Dad is. My friends don't judge me. And fuck them if they do. I'll cut them off." Coming after Tony's submission to the arresting FBI boss—"You think this bothers me, you fuckhead?"—Meadow's line shows her father's strength.

The sable coat is enough to wash away Carmela's recent anger at him. The WATCH US MAKE IT sign on the Saltwater Taffy shop bridges their making love and the first of his boardwalk nightmares. The juxtaposition suggests the flow between his real and dream lives.

Even Dr. Melfi comes clean. She tells Tony that she didn't push him to confront his mother's "psychic injuries" to him because she was afraid of him. Now she declares his flaming rage—as expressed in his dream of self-immolation—is his distraction from the profound sadness he refuses to confront. Tony pretends to confident cheer, with his feet on her table, arrogantly. He exits jauntily singing down the hall: "Maybe, baby, I'll have you." As he projects into life the sex he dreamed, he continues to ignore his sorrow.

Pussy has purged himself of his qualms about betraying his best friend. As he tells Agent Lipari, "President Franklin is my best friend and he's in there"—the envelope in which Pussy regretfully turns over his take on the phone-card scam he has just exposed.

Dave's animosities are also purged when he meets Tony over the—of course, given Dave's luck—empty coffee machine. Without blaming any-one, the haggard Dave reports that son Eric was accepted into Georgetown but is going to State College for financial reasons. Dave invites Tony to hang out with him on the ranch outside Las Vegas, where he has taken a job. That is not the most promising location for a compulsive gambler with "cowboy-itis." It is no surprise when, in the next season, Meadow reports that Dave is in a mental ward.

The last episode of the second season closes the elements introduced in the first. Tony's dream replays Silvio's Pacino performance for Pussy: "Our true enemy has yet to reveal himself." The stock hustle started there is closed down here. Tony nominates Chris for "the button." As Chris, like Meadow, graduates, he shows far more control and maturity than in the first episode. Melfi is back in normal business and has reconciled herself to dealing with Tony. As before II, 1, Angie wonders where Pussy is and is angry he isn't there—so she could leave him. Other characters—Chris's two sets of useless aides, Richie, Janice, Irina—are one way or another out of the way. As Tony exults at the start of the episode, "All my enemies are smoked." But he still feels angry with himself for the airline ticket mess. Otherwise, Tony has survived his depression.

Paralleling the season opener's montage, the last episode intercuts Meadow's graduation and the family's celebrations with a survey of the Soprano business interests: a Barone garbage truck, a porn theater, the phone cards, a junkie Hillel has to clean away at the Teittleman/Soprano motel, the gutted brokerage office, money raining down on the Executive card game. These support Meadow's celebration. As Tony smokes his long (and did I mention illegal?) Cuban, all seems well in his world. But Melfi knows the profound sorrow Tony is hiding.

The closing shot of the pier and the swelling, frothing tide, the waters at which Tony stared when he left Pussy to the deep, remind us that there are hidden depths under Tony's security that may not prove so peaceful. Not if there is a Season Three. Fear of what the tides might wash up adds a sinister note to the love song that ends the season: "Waiting for a call from you." When the phone rings in the Soprano home, everyone holds a breath.

- Yes, Virginia, there was an actual Big Pussy and a Little Pussy in New Jersey crime, back in the 1940s. David Chase adopted the names.

Season Three

III, 1:   Mr. Ruggerio's Neighborhood

Written by David Chase. Directed by Allen Coulter.

Their phone taps having failed, FBI Agent Ike Harris and his team plan to wiretap Tony's basement. To plant a mike in a lamp, they tail each resident. Meanwhile, Tony is concerned about the melancholy of Patsy Parisi, who was brought over from Uncle Junior's crew after Tony had Parisi's twin brother Spoons whacked. AJ tries out for the football team, Meadow deals with college and her troubled roommate, and Carmela gets a new tennis coach.

David Chase launched the third season with a humorous program that focused on Tony's FBI hounds as much as on the Soprano family. The title reference to Tony's plumber, Mr. Ruggerio, parodies *Mr. Rogers' Neighborhood.* The FBI's covert operations evoke the notorious "Plumbers" of Richard Nixon's White House. The FBI focus makes this a shaggy dog story—like Paulie's lunch monologue about befouled shoelaces. It belies the opening scene suggestion that the topic will be—as Tony's morning paper headline puts it—MOB COMPETITION FOR GARBAGE CONTRACTS HEATS UP—VIOLENCE FEARED.

The agents' tailing of the household reintroduces the characters more fluidly than the montage in II, 1. Again, the familiar audience is flattered with in-jokes—this time at the FBI's expense. The earnest agents have everything wrong. Pussy did not end up in some compost heap but in the ocean. Livia is one mother who would testify against her son—even *sans* immunity. The more certain they are, the more wrong: "Richie Aprile! No doubt about it—the cartel had him whacked." They still have Tony's picture labeled "Underboss," when he has effectively become the boss.

When the Sopranos rush home to their basement flood, the agent is certain it "must be a crisis with one of the children." The FBI man is right about the family's devotion—hence Carmela's "Save the pictures!" But they don't know a leak when they get one. They say they have no idea what went wrong—but they knew Tony had a problem water heater.

Even when the agents are onto something they prove wrong. Watching the video tour of Tony's basement, an agent spots a rust point in the 120-gallon hot water tank. Skip Liparski, a plumber's son, confidently predicts the tank will blow in six months. Wrong again: the tank blows the following Tuesday, aborting the bug. In their dealings with the Sopranos the FBI can't deal with even that leak

The FBI is also comic in how it follows the law. The agents are hobbled by the legal limits on how long they may listen to their bug. They hear Tony assign a "messy job" but it is only their maid's husband planning a sump pump. When they return they hear Tony and Carmela discuss his roughage, dental floss, and the problems therewith.

The series plays the FBI as if they were a gang like Tony's, only not as effective or smart. The FBI and the mobster have more in common than their Black and Decker. The agents case the joint. They pick locks to get in. The agent watching Carmela can't stop ogling Adriana, as she joins Carmela's tennis lessons and attracts the apparently lesbian coach. He even sounds like a wiseguy: "How green was my fuckin' valley." The spotted spy reports "They fuckin' made me." The FBI's need to move before "our warrant goes stale" parallels Tony's tank blowing post-warranty. The FBI "agency" is similarly parodied when Tony says he hired his mother's Russian caregiver from "an agency." She is his ex-mistress Irina's one-legged cousin, Svetlana.

The agents have their own argot. The agent has no idea "what went down." They report on the family as "Bings," with Meadow "Princess Bing," AJ "Baby Bing" and Tony "Der Bingle," in homage to Bing Crosby—like whom perhaps they hope he will "sing." The home is "the sausage factory." Having laughed at Pussy for playing his word game (II, 12), we can't take the real FBI agents seriously either.

In contrast, the gangsters show a surprising knowledge of Shakespeare. For example, in II, 12, Uncle Junior resolves "to screw [his] courage to the post" (after Lady Macbeth's "Screw your courage to the sticking place"). In I, 4, Junior is "waiting here like fucking Patience on a monument for discipline to be handed down" (*Twelfth Night*). Even Johnny-Boy was reaching for his Coleridge when he called young Livia "a fuckin' albacore around my neck" (I, 7). Here one of Tony's mugs describes Patsy in a paraphrase of Hamlet's "That a man may smile, and smile, and be a villain."

Of course, I am not accusing the Mafiosi of reading Shakespeare. In their alert intelligence they accrue language—and literature—the way they snap up business opportunities, as Tony does the Teittlemans' motel and Mahaffey's medical practice. That is how Tony uses what he learns from Dr. Melfi. He is not always accurate, as in I, 2, when he mistakes Melfi's Cape d'Antibes as "Captain Teebs." But usually the gangsters are more alert, opportunistic, and clear than the FBI. The crooks can seem classier than the cops.

Nor is the FBI entirely trustworthy. When the judge warrants two entries to plan and to place the hidden microphone, he insists they "limit both entrances to the basement only." But one agent rifles the family's mail and sneaks a peek into the kitchen fridge. Perhaps to extend the target beyond Italian-Americans, one agent is off to Denver for state espionage at a *mosque*. The agents seem fastidious about process when they debate whether to move the table back to its original placement, after the flood. On the other hand, one agent runs Stasiu's name past Anti-Terrorism "just for laughs." Well before September 11, this was an unjustified intrusion. After, that satire is nullified.

In fact, Stasiu is—understandably—embittered about America. He answers all his wife's Citizenship Exam questions with "Martin Luther King" and insults the composer of "The Star-spangled Banner." She scolds him for losing a test point by translating the sign STOP MEN AT WORK as "Stop all men who are working." But that is Stasiu's experience of America. In Poland, he was a mechanical engineer who supervised twenty employees and had a full time grant for autonomous research. In America he drives a cab. But that's no reason for the FBI to investigate him. While they track him, his wife steals the Soprano silverware and glass.

In a more somber scene, Patsy Parisi stumbles drunk into Tony's yard and aims his pistol at him to avenge his twin's murder. But his resolve weakens and he lowers the gun, weeping. He satisfies himself by pissing into Tony's pool. When Parisi aims to kill Tony the FBI agents watch him—and don't know what to do. Preventing the murder would blow their cover. They don't even say what they said when they spotted the flawed water tank: "It's a shame we can't warn him." Tony is protected by the would-be killer's weakened will, not by these Keystone Kops, ensnarled in their strategy, whose only "executive decision" is to move back the basement table.

Later, Parisi assures Tony that he is happy to be working with him, feels well rewarded, and has "put the grief behind me." The camera holds on his stolid non-commitment when Tony suggests Parisi bring his young son over to "hang out with AJ" and "go in the pool." The irony is both verbal—there are two ways to "go" in the pool—and dramatic—Patsy won't want his son to go in the pool that he "went" in. The "Hamburger Patties" sign behind Tony is framed as "Hamburger Pat" when he probes Patsy's mood, as if to suggest what Pat's wrong answer might make him. The episode's most somber scene—Patsy's intention to kill Tony—turns into comedy and Patsy stays the patsy.

The central characters' natures are also advanced in this episode. Tony's handling of Parisi is generous, certainly more humane than Paulie's "option," whacking him like his brother. The "excellent jersey" draws AJ out of his apathy to try out for the school football team. When his training scene is introduced by the FBI agent's cry of "Touchdown!" (re: the completed bugging), the FBI agent is again played unaware of his context. Meadow handles her college and New York freedom better than her at first frisky, then depressed roommate, Caitlin. And Carmela finds herself again shunned romantically, when the new tennis coach lusts for Adriana.

The Sopranos gain sympathy by how they are victimized here. Jeannie Cusamano nearly betrays them to the undercover agents, their maid steals, and—reduced to that level—the FBI subverts their privacy. Each time Tony wafts down the driveway for his morning paper, in his open robe, t-shirt and boxer shorts, he seems open and vulnerable, a sympathetic figure. When the FBI pretends to be a mosquito-control unit, they treat the Sopranos as their target pests. They are more honest when they claim to protect their power line.

The program advances two plunging lives. In the last dorm scene Hunter tells Meadow that Eric Scatino hates Montclair State and has been doing a lot of LSD. As Meadow knew him as "straight," he becomes another victim of Tony's amiable profession. Similarly, the Caitlin who partied so freely in her first scene here falls into obsessive depression. This recasts her earlier confidence that "New York is an experience that unalterably changes a person."

Notwithstanding these shadows, the episode remains comic. Its lightness informs the choice of music. Tony sings along with Steely Dan: "I'm a fool to do your dirty work," when he drives to work, unaware of the FBI's dirty tricks against him. At the end, as the camera zooms in on the miked lamp, Elvis Costello (in "High Fidelity") asks "Can you hear it?" At several points the FBI's seriousness is undercut by the theme from the old *Peter Gunn* series. That was another hero whose solitary search for justice showed up the law-enforcement institutions. Satirizing the FBI's skullduggery, the Gunn theme is mixed with Sting's "Every Breath You Take," with the spy's threat: "I'll be watching you."

• Paulie's tirade against the danger of germs on one's shoes has its own poetry. In contrast to men's washrooms, some women's are so clean "you could eat maple walnut ice cream from the toilets." But the riff fits: He's paranoid about bugs, including the FBI breed. Tony frequently has the Bada Bing toilet "swept" for bugs. Furio's delicate dusting of Tony's car plays into this concern about cleanliness and against his rather rougher nature. This cleanliness fetish harks back to II, 9, where Paulie wipes his hands with some cleaner, to Pussy's disdain, in the hospital waiting room.

III, 2: *Proshai, Livushka*

Written by David Chase. Directed by Tim Van Patten.

Tony tells Meadow's college friend Noah Tannenbaum, an African-Jewish-American, to stay away from her. Livia dies. Janice's return revives familiar tensions. Carmela and her father add a welcome candor to the falseness of Livia's funeral.

Again the episode begins with the garbage gang war. This opening scene fulfills the violence promised in the previous episode's opening, then veers off into the tragic-comic mode, with Livia's death.

The title comes from her brusque Russian caregiver's toast: "Good-bye, little Livia." As Svetlana admits, Livia was a difficult patient and "She defeated me." But to honor Livia's wishes Svetlana insists on keeping her very valuable collection of opera and American show-tune records that Janice tries to pry away. Janice's search for Livia's supposed stash of cash in the basement wall cuts to another hood's being wired for Livia's wake. The greed and malice unleashed by Livia's death make this a black comedy. In its funereal context, Les Paul's "I'm Forever Blowing Bubbles" over the end credits lightly reflects on the evanescence of life and its petty acquisitions.

Livia's funeral occasions massive hypocrisy. Everyone struggles to be respectful toward the not very dear departed. "At least she didn't suffer" is the most common obsequy. Tony's chorus is "What are you gonna do?"—which is what the crooked Reverend James said at his—far superior—father's passing (II, 2) and what Tony said about Spoons Parisi's death (III, 1). From the background, Fanny—still in the wheelchair from when Livia ran her over—offers that Livia was her "best friend" because she always called to tell her who had just died.

When Janice forces the confessional circle, the coerced Hesh musters something like a compliment: "She didn't mince words. Between brain and mouth there was no interlocutor." Hesh always rises to the occasion. Ironically, he provides a more appropriate reflection on Livia in the Jewish joke he told at the funeral home earlier. In his story, the only positive anyone has for the deceased is "His brother was worse." In contrast, the stoned Christopher irrelevantly questions the claim that "there's no two people on earth exactly the same." His conclusion—that there could be "another Mrs. Soprano just like her"—consoles nobody.

When Artie is about to recount Livia's report of Tony's arson, Carmela cuts him off: "This is such a crock of shit!" Obligated not to teach her children hypocrisy, she remembers Livia as dysfunctional: "She gave no one joy." Carmela's father rises (against her mother's silencing) to support her: "We suffered for years under the yoke of that woman. She estranged us from our own daughter." Carmela notes that Livia's children did not disobey her until after her death, when they staged the funeral Livia had forbade. She didn't want a funeral because she was afraid no one would come. Livia neglected her grandchildren's memory books because she thought no one loved her enough to read them. In her frank criticism Carmela shows a sympathetic understanding of the poor soul.

Janice's true feelings also emerge, despite the artifice of her expression and the "California bullshit," as Tony banned it, of her confessional circle. Though she planned not to come—until Tony paid her fare—Janice arrives at the Sopranos' in full weep. She uses her homage in the "circle" to promote her own "visual interpretive skills" and declares her critical mother "the reason I make videos today" (presumably, instead of pursuing the drawing and painting on which Livia was "tough" but "right"). To introduce Tony, Janice reports that Livia preserved all Tony's schoolwork but none of hers and Barbara's. Janice's homage is as self-serving as Charmaine's announcement that the desserts now ready are by the New Vesuvio's newer pastry chef.

Tony feels guilt for feeling relieved his mother is dead. Though he can tell Melfi his mother was a "selfish, miserable cunt," he cannot accept that she planned his murder. But she was the source of all his problems: "So, we're probably done here, right? She's dead." Of course, Tony tries to end his therapy in most of his sessions with Melfi.

Tony finds refuge in the classic Jimmy Cagney film, *The Public Enemy*, several times. Where Junior relived its grapefruit-in-the-face scene (I, 9), Tony emphasizes the dying gangster's last scenes with his maudlin mother. The video applies to Tony's family life in two opposite ways. First, its hero's loving, supportive mother is a pole away from Livia. When gangster Tom (Cagney) is wounded his mother says "I'm almost glad it happened," because now he will return to her. As Livia wanted her son's murder, she was disturbed that he survived. If Tony identifies with Tom, it is by their contrasting mothers; their fathers were harsh disciplinarians, Tom's a cop and Tony's a hood. Tony does not cry at his mother's death until he's overwhelmed by the last scene in the movie. Tom's corpse falls through the doorway while his mother is cheerfully readying his room for him upstairs. Before another sip of scotch stops him, Tony cries—less for Livia's death than for the mother's love he never had.

Second, that video recalls Meadow's alienation when Tony banned her friend, Noah Tannenbaum, because he was half-black (and the other half Jewish). For Noah, in this film "Cagney is modernity"—and Tony personifies archaic racism. But Noah seems naïve in his zeal for the college film course titled "Images of Hyper-Capitalist Self-Advancement in the Era of the Studio System." For that theme applies equally to the post-studio system, to *The Sopranos* as a mass media entertainment like the old genre films, and to both Noah's father's and Tony's jobs. Like so much academia (and books analyzing American TV series), the pompous academic overstates the obvious. If *Public Enemy* is "modernity," *The Sopranos* is postmodern in its shifting viewpoints, non-linear narrative, cultural allusiveness, and reflecting back on itself.

Hence this episode's rare bit of technical gimmickry. When Carmela finds Tony unconscious on the kitchen floor, she asks: "What happened?" The scene—including Tony's exchange with Meadow and Noah—is run backward to its starting point, then replayed. This device emphasizes the filmic nature both of *The Sopranos* and of the Sopranos' experience. It is especially appropriate for a scene that deals with (i) Noah's filmconsciousness and (ii) Tony's regressive nature, seen especially in his racism. It also suggests that in life, too, we can move backward, though only in the sense of regressing. You can't rewind life to edit it. The rewind reminds us we're watching a movie.

This technical self-consciousness parallels the moral self-consciousness of the title with which the video introduces the Cagney film: "Tom Powers in *Public Enemy* and Rico in *Little Caesar* are not two men, nor are they merely characters—they are a problem that sooner or later we, the public, must solve." Clearly, Tony Soprano is a problem that we have to solve, a moral question that troubles our affection for him, though not in the pseudo-sociological terms of those two films. *The Sopranos* clearly shares the intention of *The Public Enemy*: "to honestly depict an environment that exists today in a certain strata [sic] of American life, rather than glorify the hoodlum or the criminal."

In another form of self-reference, Furio describes a plan to hijack the popular *Survivor* television series by scoring protection money from the competitors. With his own spin on "surviving," Furio would bring that show's artificial reality closer to his reality—that is, to the reality already inflected by the gangster film. As the fictional and real worlds meld in the media, we glimpse (the dead) Pussy in the hallway mirror when Tony opens the door. As it is not Tony's perspective, our memory is imaged within the fictional world.

When Tony returns from the garden to find Carmela, Meadow, and AJ arrayed in wait, our assumption—and probably his—is that they are set to attack him for insulting Noah. Instead, they sympathetically report his mother's death. His first response is "You're kiddin'. I mean, Jesus Christ!" Then he repeats "She's dead"—as if to make sure. The homilies follow: "She was in no pain, Tony" (Svetlana); "We all know—how much you loved her" (Silvio); "I can imagine how you feel" (Paulie). Tony's first expression of genuine emotion after Livia's death is his "Goddam fuckin' bitch!" (which refers not to his dear departed mother but to Janice, who plans to miss the funeral).

In an interlude, Meadow helps AJ write an essay on Robert Frost's poem "Stopping by the Woods on a Snowy Evening." Its discussion of death and the rigors of life reflects on the Livia plot. When Meadow relates the "miles to go before I sleep" to Death as "The Big Sleep," Robert Frost meets film noir (*The Big Sleep*, Howard Hawks, 1946). The poem also reflects on Tony's rejection of Noah. Meadow explains that the cold, white snow is an image of death. "I thought black was death," AJ replies. "White, too," Meadow says. As she now sees the half-black Noah as a life force, she associates Tony's racism with death, emptiness, and the chill in their relationship. In a related joke, Tony assures Janice that the Richie murder investigation is "colder than your tits." As the motherhood of Livia and Janice (whose son is now a street-person in Montreal) is cold and killing, Tony's rejection of Noah places him in their camp.

Tony exults in racist terms for Noah that avoid the N-word. In III, 2, he calls him "Moe," as the generic Jew. There is glee and vitality in his anti-black barrage: "charcoal briquette," *ditsou, moolinyan*, "Those old Tarzan movies?" "Maybe if I say it in Swahili." In III, 3, Noah is "Sambo." In III, 9, he is "Jamal Ginsberg, the Hasidic Homeboy" and in III, 10, "the Oreo cookie." In III, 5, the black cop Wilmore is "this fuckin' smoke" and "affirmative action cocksucker." Colorful, clever, Tony's offensive language is as unscrupulous, dangerous, and charming as his more criminal behavior.

As they watch her graciously accepting condolences, Tony remarks to Carmela that Meadow is becoming "a robot, like the rest of us. . . . All her innocence is gone." Her cold look at her father confirms his fears that she is no longer his little girl.

III, 3: Fortunate Son

Written by Todd Kessler. Directed by Henry Bronchtein.

After Christopher is finally "made"—that is, admitted into the gang's inner circle—he has trouble meeting his new responsibilities. Janice moves into her mother's house and steals Svetlana's prosthetic leg, to leverage her demand for Livia's record collection. Dr. Melfi probes the causes of Tony's panic attacks. Meadow confirms their alienation and AJ succeeds at frosh football.

As the title suggests, this episode centers on the ambivalence of being a son—the mix of benefit and burden. In the central episode, Tony remembers that when he was 11 years old, he saw his father chop a finger off the butcher Satriale for not paying his gambling debt. As Dr. Melfi points out, Tony's current panic attacks are triggered by his associations with meat. His latest attack was not, as we assumed, prompted by the Uncle Ben rice logo and his "frank conversation with Buckwheat" (that is, Noah reduced to a Little Rascal), but by the capicola. The cold cuts knock Tony cold.

His first faint was after the Satriale episode. Before the roast beef dinner, young Tony watched his father and mother dance. His father's badinage mixed sex and meat: "You like it with the bone standing in it," he says, ostensibly about Livia's menu. "The lady loves her meat," Johnny-Boy jokes, squeezing Livia's buns. She rejects his *All of Me* dance. Her only good mood was the day of the meat delivery. Tony has since associated raw meat with violence, blood, his first intimations of sexuality, and his responsibility "to bring home the bacon." Tony's cold cuts are Proust's madelaine, his floodgate to memory.

At the same time, Tony remembers that he was fascinated, not repelled, by the violence. His father praised him for watching the attack on Satriale, instead of "running like a little girl." So rather than "getting the belt" for disobeying his father's injunction to wait in the car, little Anthony is praised for stomaching the violence.

The traumas of the father are visited upon the son. Tony encourages AJ's football effort. On AJ's first heroic play, a fumble recovery, he crawls out from under the gang tackle with his vision and hearing slowed, as if he were concussed. His father's cheers seem like animal growls until they focus. When AJ is appointed defensive captain, he faints. He doesn't want the responsibilities of being "made" this way; AJ went into football just to wear the cool jersey. Now his father's support becomes a pressure on him. AJ offers to visit Meadow just to escape Tony's lecture over a television football game.

AJ bristles at Adriana's tease about cheerleaders because frosh football is too marginal to have cheerleaders. Perhaps he doesn't want football to become a way for others to project themselves onto him, whether it's Adriana's sexuality or Tony's own linebacker success. The frightening burden of his success at football may prompt him to reject college because of its smarter "freaks."

Tony's pressure on AJ extends to two surrogate sons. Tony promised Jackie Aprile to look out for his son, Jackie Jr., and to keep him out of crime. Though Tony asks Chris to keep an eye on him as well, Chris exploits Frankie's idea of robbing the Amnesty International benefit concert at Rutgers (the featured performer makes this a Jewel robbery). At their lunch meeting Jackie acts like an alienated son when he arrives late, in unnecessary shades, and overreacts to Tony's advice.

Tony has always treated Chris "like a son," watching and promoting his "nephew" (for example, I, I), though he is actually the son of Carmela's cousin. When Chris is "made" this relationship is formalized. "This Family comes before anything else"—including one's family. Tony is like a father to all his "made" men, to be brought any problems they may have. Ironically, Chris's induction gift is the football gambling business, which exploits the weakness Johnny-Boy taught little Tony to avoid. When the chorus of "Where's the money?" (Dan Hicks and his Hot Licks) attends the end-credits, Chris's predicament—struggling to meet the responsibilities of a "son's" maturing—stands for the entire episode and all its sons, real or virtual.

All these sons chafe under the "roles" their fathers impose on them. At the school football game, the peridontist Romano swears at the referee like a wiseguy. Daughters resist the same pressure, as when Meadow favors the forbidden Noah. She makes a point of telling Carmela she is spending the weekend with him at the Connecticut home of his parents' friends (from NBC yet!).

Carmela is caught between her daughter and her husband. To prevent their confrontation, she discourages Tony from coming to visit Meadow, but defends him. He comes "from a place and a time where he thinks he has your best interests at heart." This statement is fair to both. In a more sterile relationship, Adriana's mother can't lend Chris money because "she's still paying for her hysterectomy."

Janice proves an even more problematic daughter when she campaigns for Livia's record collection. She claims several motives for wanting the old records back. "These old albums, they're a window into her soul," she tells Tony. Then she is making a documentary on the power of popular music in the lives of Livia's generation. In the next episode she tells the Russians "These records are all I have to remember my mother by." But Tony knows Janice wants the records to sell on the Internet. When she takes for hostage Svetlana's $20,000 artificial leg (with the Kenneth Cole calfskin boot), she indirectly draws Tony into her conflict—and into another unwilling encounter with Irina, now engaged to be married. Svetlana demonstrates her assimilation when she dismisses her old leg as "Russian piece of shit" and urges her fiancé to ignore Janice: "Bill, don't waste breath's. This cunt is gonna be sorry she fuck with me."

In the opening scenes, first Chris tells Adriana, then Tony tells Chris, they have seen "too many movies." Adriana fears that Paulie's call to be made may rather be to his murder, as happens in *GoodFellas* and *Donnie Brasco* (Mike Newell, 1997). But the only violence in this visit is Paulie's fashion statement: "Shoot your cuffs," he preps Chris.

Parodying the parent/mentor relationships, Janice's current fiancé is a 19-year-old who "can go all night." Similarly, when the newly made Chris and his sponsor Paulie say they love each other, the next shot is of two strippers kissing as they dance g-string to g-string, another ritual performance of "love."

■ Carmine from New York knows all about Tony's blackouts and his psychiatrist and assures him "There's no stigmata these days." That is, Tony won't be martyred for such modern phenomena.

III, 4: Employee of the Month

Written by Robin Green and Mitchell Burgess. Directed by John Patterson.

Ralph Cifaretto takes over Richie Aprile's garbage business and Jackie Aprile's widow, Rosalie. Ralphie ingratiates himself with her son Jackie Jr. by paying him for helping beat up a debtor. New York boss Johnny Sack moves to a mansion in New Jersey. Svetlana sets two Russian thugs upon Janice to recover her artificial leg. Dr. Melfi is beaten and raped in her office parking tower. When the rapist is released on a technicality Melfi considers unleashing Tony's justice.

The most powerful episode to date centers on the fragile state of our civilization. Dr. Melfi's rape is shot to emphasize her pain and—in the last view—her exposure and helplessness. The legs so elegantly crossed in her sessions with Tony here tighten in pain and shame. She is outraged when the rapist is freed on a technicality—then again when she finds him Employee of the Month.

Despite his name, Jesus Rossi represents another world than Jennifer's. Where the episode emphasizes Richard's careful preparation of a special chicken dinner, Rossi works in one fast-food chain and is arrested in another. Both pale beside the New Vesuvio restaurant where Tony's gang holds their better meetings. But Rossi's savagery connects both worlds.

In the episode's last scene, Melfi fights off the temptation to tell Tony what happened to her. He would deliver a justice that the law failed to provide. "What," Tony asks, "I mean, you wanna say something?" Melfi is sorely tempted to unleash Tony on Jesus (!) Rossi. But she chooses silence, to respect the ideal of law and order. This contrasts to the *omertà* of Tony's world, silence outside/against the law. In a hard close-up the episode ends on her climactic "No."

The central issue is Melfi's wavering faith in legal control, the benchmark of civilization. Here they discuss the "traffic accident" that injured her:

MELFI: You can't control everything that happens.
TONY: But you can get pissed off.
MELFI: And then what? You lose control?

Her rape reveals how fragile our civilization is. The act itself is savage. So is its aftermath. Melfi, Richard (her ex-husband, now back in her life), and their son Jason all lose their faith in justice. They want to take the law into their own hands. This desire increases when the rapist is freed because a misplaced evidence kit violated the chain of custody. On the blind scales of Justice that procedural violation outweighed Melfi's.

The rape shivers Melfi's relationship with Richard. She senses that he blames her for the rape, for ignoring his advice not to go alone at night to the parking lot. In return, she blames him for distracting her on the phone just before the rape: "You and your fuckin' hard-on about my patient [Tony]." And: "You should have seen your face when you heard the fuckin' shitbag who raped me had an Italian name." Richard's self-esteem is so weak that he cannot bear the idea of a countryman's transgression. Because of his anger at the Italian-American stereotype he cannot accept any Italian-American guilt.

Before the rape, the danger in Melfi's dealing with Tony was one of Richard's two preoccupations. Like her therapist, Dr. Kupferberg, Richard urged her to refer him to a behavioral therapist. Richard's second preoccupation is with the media's representation of Italian-Americans, which is a widespread concern about *The Sopranos* itself. For Melfi, Italian-Americans are "an advertisement for The American Experiment. We did great." But Richard is adamant: "Hollywood tries to give these sociopaths the tragic grandeur of Al Pacino." That, of course, Silvio changes to comedy.

The rape provokes vicious impulses in the two educated Italian-Americans who feel slandered by the gangster stereotype. Richard would kill Rossi but "they'd put me in jail, that's how messed up things are." Essentially, the good doctor Richard is now in Tony's camp, lacking only the courage to take the law into his own hands. Melfi's intellectual (well, at least deconstructionist) son Jason slips immediately into savagery: "I'm

gonna kill those motherfuckers"—a colloquialism truer here than normally—"A bunch of animals running wild and they're winning." This is
the Jason who was embarrassed when his mother fumed at the woman
smoking in the restaurant (II, 11).

The psychoanalytic Melfi discovers her desire for Soprano justice in a
dream. When her arm is stuck in an Acme Cola vending machine, whose
operative coin is raw macaroni, Jesus Rossi comes to rape her again. This
time he is attacked by a vicious Rottweiler, which at first threatened Melfi.
As she tells Kupferberg, the breed descended from the Romans' guard dog,
with hulking shoulders and brute power—the image of Tony. The dream
restores the relief and safety that she lost in the rape.

Acknowledging she's been "charmed by a sociopath," Melfi is persuaded to pass Tony on to a behavioral therapist. But after her rape, when
Tony agrees, she blurts out "No." Perhaps her experience and frustration
have given her a visceral understanding of him. Or she may need to stay
connected to his power, for assurance if not deployment.

Accordingly, there is no civility in Melfi's language. "The justice system
is fucked up, Elliot," she tells her therapist. Richard is spending $300 an
hour for a lawyer to investigate the dropped charges "while that Employee
of the Month cocksucker is back on the street and who's going to stop him,
you?" Though she "won't break the social compact," Melfi assures Elliot,
she takes immense "satisfaction in knowing I could have that asshole
squashed like a bug if I wanted." Gangster films provide their audience
with a vicarious appreciation of illegal justice (as Chase observes on the
Season One DVD interview). So we share Melfi's pleasure at that thought—
and probably hope she will overcome her scruples and sic Tony after Rossi.

That temptation swells in the last scene, after she breaks down and is
consoled by Tony. In the episode's last word—"No"—she suppresses it. If
this elegant psychiatrist cannot control her anger then that other great
experiment—civilization—will also have failed. So, rejecting Tony's reflex
of consolation, she urgently detaches herself: "Go. Sit over there. Don't do
this. Go. . . . It's just my knee."

Jennifer Melfi's attack is paralleled by Janice's assault by the Russian
thugs sent to retrieve Svetlana's "pathetic leg" (as Irina correctly mispro-
nounces "prosthetic"). After Jennifer recognizes her freed rapist and spills
her drink, we cut to Janice struggling with the chords for "I can't get no
satisfaction."

Though Janice is far more negative and less innocent than Jennifer and
all she suffers is a few broken ribs and the loss of those record sales, their

cases connect. The Russians' "justice" confirms the danger of the vigilante. The different cases of Jennifer and Janice and our very different estimations of the women and their predicaments complicate any simple view of illegal justice.

Janice is not enhanced when her assault makes her a Born Again Christian, because she is obviously self-unaware and faddist. Before "the man I loved died," she says, "I was functioning at a very high level." Now that she has hit bottom, "it's odd, I feel Born Again in the Lord." Tony lists her previous conversions. Janice's religion is a hollow parody of Jennifer's faith in civilization.

As usual, the comic language replays the serious concerns. Melfi's increasingly violent language conveys the tension between civility and brutishness (or, *Civilization v. Its Real Contents*). More comical is this restaurant exchange:

RALPHIE: I'm the guy who's dating your mom.
JACKIE: 'Dating'?
RALPHIE: Don't get fuckin' filthy about it!

The language in this series may be of unprecedented vulgarity for television, but it often has a poetic wit and it constantly embodies the tension between the free and the forbidden. These wiseguys speak as they live—like unchained maladies.

So, too, the barrage of jokes about Johnny Sack's fat wife are curtailed when he enters. The Fat Woman jokes—funny in a puerile way—would normally confirm the Boys Club atmosphere of the Bada Bing/ Satriale's. In context, however, their brutalism is on the same spectrum as the Russians' assault of Janice and Rossi's rape of Melfi.

The jokes against Ginny Sack are qualitatively different and worse than the "Fat Fuck" sobriquets given Pussy and Bobby. Cruel, superior, and misogynous, the Fat Woman jokes express the disrespect that enables the violence against women. When Johnny interrupts those jokes, their viciousness contrasts to his dignity and warm authority. Our sympathy shifts further when we learn (in III, 8) that Ginny used to be "some hoofer" and now needs therapy for her physical condition.

In any case, the violent context undermines the traditional humor. What in another episode might have seemed harmless bawdry here occurs on the spectrum that leads to Janice's assault and Jennifer's rape. Similarly, Furio's pornographic magazine is quietly contrasted to the broken Melfi's *New*

Yorker. This humor makes a case for rather wider "behavior modification" than just Tony's.

There is no language in the end-credit song this time, Daniel Lanois's "Fisherman's Daughter." After Melfi's "No" has recovered a more honorable code of silence than the gangsters' *omertà,* we get a wordless blues.

The two women's assaults overshadow the activities in Tony's business world. But there are other Employees of the Month. To control the impetuous Ralphie and to maintain order, Tony makes Gigi captain of the Aprile family. Tony's attempts to keep Jackie from the criminal world are thwarted by the kid's laziness (He drops out of Rutgers) and his eagerness to work for Chris and Ralphie. Though Jackie wet his pants as the getaway driver, Chris still endorses him (perhaps because he remembers his similar embarrassment when he was beaten).

For all its seriousness, the episode still ripples with lighter ironies. The FBI hears Tony kiss Chris: "I love you. You're a good boy." The unerringly wrong FBI agents try to identify "Lord Fuckpants," Chris's one-off reference to Jackie. Tony's anxieties about Johnny Sack's ominous moving to Jersey reflect in Silvio's comment about another breakdown of civilized order, the fatal soccer stampede in Zimbabwe: "Unassigned seating, always a problem." The episode introduces Ralphie's infatuation with *Gladiator* (Ridley Scott, 2000): "What we do in life echoes through eternity." However comical, that quote is our last word on Rossi's, Ralphie's, Jackie's, and Janice's action—and on Melfi's silence.

■ The name of Melfi's detective, Piersol, may allude to baseballer Jim Piersall, whose memoir *Fear Strikes Out* was the subject of Tony's school book review (III, 2). The allusion contrasts Melfi's courage to Janice's religiosity in responses to fears.

■ In a comic version of contrasting cultures, Furio tells Ralphie that Pope jokes "don't translate" in Italy. Of course, it is rather a question of faith than of language.

III, 5: Another Toothpick

Written by Terence Winter. Directed by Jack Bender.

Carmela joins Tony's therapy session, with little success. When a black cop gives Tony a speeding ticket, he has him demoted. Carmela's Uncle Febbie dies of cancer. Minor hood Mustang Sally brutishly assaults an Aprile gang member, then calls on his godfather, Bobby Baccala Sr., for help. The old man dies in a car crash after whacking him. Uncle Junior reveals he has stomach cancer. Artie admits he loves Adriana, plans a partnership with Tony, and pushes Charmaine toward divorce.

While the intermingling of weakness and power is a running concern throughout the series, here it moves front and center. In this episode, success and failure are inextricable. Tony, Artie, and Uncle Junior assert their authority—despite their mortal impotence. The paradox is caught in Ralphie's quotation from his beloved *Gladiator:* "In this world or the next, I shall have revenge." We postulate "the next world" because we know our powers and effect are so limited in this one.

The episode's title is what Livia remarked whenever someone died of cancer. As Janice and Tony over wine contemplate Uncle Junior's cancer, she explains that in the face of futility black comedy gives us the illusion of control: "You say the most horrible shit you can think of in the face of tragedy." In that spirit Ralphie jokes about the crony in a coma: "Look at the bright side. He wasn't that smart to begin with." Ralphie is called heartless—by the men who proceed to eat the patient's box of chocolates.

The opening scene in Dr. Melfi's office seems to continue the silence from the previous close, until the pan reveals Carmela's presence. She says she is frustrated with Melfi's inability to help Tony. Feeling targeted, Carmela suggests he carries unresolved guilts. Sticking his "dick into anything with a pulse" could be "a root cause." Tony still transfers blame. When Melfi observes, "You're both very angry," he wheels upon her: "You must've been at the top of your fuckin' class." Later, Janice may sense another source of Tony's guilt when she asks what really happened to Pussy. Tony spurns her invitation to pray with her.

In the story of the cop Wilmore—a man who is bigger than Tony and with more will and moral fiber—Tony's power brings him more guilt. After flashing his Policeman's Benevolent card and offering dinner for the cop and his wife do not cancel Tony's speeding ticket, he gets Assemblyman Zellman to do it. Wilmore is demoted to the Property Room and loses his overtime. Tony has second thoughts when he finds Wilmore working as a junior clerk in a garden statuary store.

Zellman assures him that Wilmore deserves demotion. He is a "rabble rouser" with mental problems (that is, unwillingness to be bribed). Tony may feel some sympathy—or even empathy—for the wound-up trouble-maker. But he feels validated when a black hood steals Meadow's 10-speed bike. Tony rejects Meadow's argument that black crime is an economic and class issue, not racial. When Zellman offers to cancel Wilmore's punishment, Tony decides: "Fuck him. He deserves what he got."

When they next meet at the store Wilmore declines Tony's charity—more firmly than Beansie. Having flexed his power over Wilmore, Tony is reduced by his conscience. In the last shot, as Tony walks away, he shrinks among the garden statues, which are as macho/phallic as the gangsters' cigars but less flattering.

Artie lives out a similar frustration in the face of success. His flourishing restaurant and Tony's offer of a packaged food business cannot assuage his suffering over Adriana. His joy from a profitable night is deflated when she quits her job. His waspish teasing provokes Christopher to threaten him with a fork. Tony shifts from rough anger at Artie's baiting Chris to affectionate sympathy after Artie says he loves Adriana. Consoling him, Tony kisses Artie's bald head, a reminder that the older man's quest is hopeless—even if he does wear an earring. Having pushed Charmaine to leave him, Artie is spurned by Adriana at her "retirement" dinner.

In contrast, 68-year-old Bobby Baccalla Sr., who coughs relentlessly and red from his lung cancer, snatches one last success from the smoking jaws of death. Baccalla is a surprise guest at Febbie's funeral. First, as Mustang Sally's godfather (no film allusion intended), he approves Tony's move against the hood. When Baccalla seems the only person who can get to him he eagerly accepts the contract. It's the feeble old man's last shot at authority. This murder gives him "something to live for." There is more honor in Baccala's taking the job than in the upstart Jackie's and the irreverent Ralphie's offers.

After finishing the messy job, Bobby celebrates by lighting up a cigarette in the kitchen. With America's "Sister Golden Hair" on the car radio, he enjoys another to the phrase "I just can't live without you," despite his machine-gun cough. Stooping for his bloodied atomizer he blacks out and has his fatal crash, to the lyric "just can't make it." The car radio music implacably reflects an old hero's pathetic end—or a pathetic man's heroic end. Old Bobby is at once dignified and pathetic in his last hit. But that's the human condition here: a success and a failure in the same moment. Bobby Sr. knows what Charmaine tries to teach Artie: "Be happy in thine own self."

Uncle Junior is not. His cancer makes him more belligerent than usual. He is uncharacteristically humorless at Febbie's funeral, snapping at innocent observations. He rejects Bobby Jr.'s sadness about his dying father: "All this goddam morbidity." Having promised to spare old Bobby the assignment ("I'm still the boss of this family"), he saves face by telling Bobby Jr. he decided not to tell Tony to cancel it: "Some things are a matter of duty."

When he hears of old Baccala's death Uncle Junior runs amok. He hoped Bobby Sr. would die of cancer, not a car accident, so that the "comes in threes" would exclude Junior. This superstition is also articulated in Janice's Catholicism. Bobby Jr. doesn't understand Uncle Junior until he explains why he won't attend Baccala's funeral: "You selfish fuck, I can't go because I'm sick. I've got cancer." The opening insult to the orphaned Bobby qualifies under Janice's "the most horrible shit you can think of in the face of tragedy."

Or, as Tony describes those old-timers, "the more hard-assed their attitude the more they can suppress their feelings." Uncle Junior tries to keep his cancer secret, but such a fact will out. Tony immediately tells Janice and Junior himself has to tell Bobby Jr. As Uncle Junior and Artie demonstrate, and as Dr. Melfi has been telling Tony, strong feelings will make their own release, often in the violence of action or language.

Two statements emerge from the movie Junior is watching on TV when Bobby Jr. leaves for his father's funeral. The first is the standard Soprano response to a death: "But what can you do?" In the second Frank Sinatra's character rushes off with "Lady, I missed the boat a long time ago." That's the human condition.

On the other hand, as if to remind us there is a sympathetic God out there, Meadow unwittingly takes the FBI's painstakingly bugged lamp away to her college dorm. She's of the Old School, too: the new-fangled halogen gives her a headache.

III, 6: University

Written by Terence Winter and Salvatore Stabile. Directed by Allen Coulter.

Tony is unwillingly drawn into the life of one of the Bing dancers, Tracee. When she is killed by her pimp/lover, Ralphie, though he is "a made guy" the enraged Tony beats him up. Meadow is troubled by her roommate Caitlin's morbid hyper-sensitivity. Noah introduces Meadow to his father, then breaks up with her.

This powerful episode extends the critique of male power and cruelty from III, 4, where Melfi's rape went unpunished. The show intercuts two stories about young women completing their education. Meadow's college experience includes a neurotically obsessive woman, roommate Caitlin, and the hot-and-cold loving of the self-serving Noah. Meanwhile, the 20-year-old pole-dancer Tracee learns the dangerous folly of her romantic naiveté and her hot-and-cold Ralphie, who kills her.

This episode is framed by the pole-dancers' song, "Livin' on a Thin Line" by The Kinks. The ballad states that stories of past wars don't mean much anymore. Heroic sagas are "all the lies we were told." At the end it leaves us "livin' on a thin line," wondering "What are we supposed to do?" In this episode, even the idealists—like Noah Tannenbaum—are severely compromised.

The Kinks's wisdom notwithstanding, Ralphie foolishly plays at the heroic style of *Gladiator*. In the first Friday-night Executive Club party at the Bing, Ralphie enters high on (among other things) that movie's rhetoric: "I have come to reclaim Rome for my people" and the more prophetic "You are all dead men." He attacks doorman Georgie with a pool-cue spear and then a chain, injuring ("It was an accident.") his eye. At the Sopranos' dinner, Ralphie says he would have been an architect if he hadn't had to drop out of high school to raise his siblings. Despite Tony's skeptical smile, Ralph sees himself an empire-builder, after the glory of Rome. He's so committed to *Gladiator* that he ridicules Chris's recommendation, (the far superior) *Spartacus* (Stanley Kubrick, 1960). But all that emperor Ralphie rules is Tracee, his whore, whom he destroys.

To his later regret, Tony rejects Tracee's attempts at friendship. He refuses the date and walnut bread she baked to thank him for suggesting she take her son to a doctor. He spurns her after Ralphie's ruckus interrupts Tony's blowjob and again when she comes naked to show him her—new dental braces (which Silvio has funded instead of the usual breast implants). When she confides her pregnancy Tony recommends she abort, because of Ralphie's unreliability.

But Tracy finds no support in her world. Avuncular Silvio drags her back to work from Ralphie's apartment, where she has been sick, slaps her, and insists, "Until you pay what you owe, that shaved twat of yours belongs to me." Ralphie's laugh at her abuse flows over into Rosalie's dinner for Tony, Silvio and their wives.

At the end Ralphie attacks Tracee for insulting him in front of his friends. First he feeds her romantic fantasy, promising to help her have her baby and to get a little house for them. Her hopes thus raised, he dashes them. When she resists he goes at her viciously. Fired by her taunting—"That makes you feel good? You feel like a man?"—he kills her in a painfully prolonged beating. He walks away with a cold "Look at you now," then tells the gang she fell down and hurt herself.

Tony tells Dr. Melfi and Carmela that he is troubled by the death of "a young man" who worked for him. It was "a work-related deat'." In Tony's Jersey English, Tracee's death is indeed a debt. He missed several opportunities to help her.

Meadow's roommate Caitlin is as helpless as Tracee. Her initial NYC party craze has brought her down. "I have nowhere to go," she apologizes, when she returns to find Noah and Meadow on the bed. Caitlin is freaked out by *Freaks* (Noah is correct: Tod Browning, 1932). Growing up in an Oklahoma small town has not prepared her for people who find amusement in others' pain, or for a bag lady who wears newspaper underwear. "I think I miss my ferrets." As self-destructive as Tracee, Caitlin compulsively plucks out her hair.

Though Noah at first seems sensitive toward Caitlin, he abandons her after her blathering results in his writing a C-essay. Noah lets his lawyer father file a restraint order against her. This erases Meadow's earlier impression that Noah was "sweet. Most guys wouldn't give a shit." He doesn't either. In contrast, Meadow cares enough to take along her Exacto-knife when she leaves Caitlin to go upstairs to Noah.

When Meadow—impressed but not intimidated—meets Noah's high-roller father at a posh restaurant, she translates her father's waste management to "Environmental clean-up." In his dealing with Tracee Tony fails to live up to that. On Noah's social ladder—exemplified by his father's dinner—"Everybody's Jumpin' " (The Dave Brubeck Quartet). When Noah says his father is "in the business" (III, 2), he means show business, as if only that business matters. As an entertainment lawyer he's on the other side from Tony. As in entertainment "the business" subsumes everything from law and PR to the actual production, Tony's "business" subsumes all its variously respectable fronts. Again, the legal and illegal worlds reflect each other.

After Meadow's first lovemaking with Noah she is joyful when she comes home to Carmela and Tony the next morning. Comfortable in her new maturity, Meadow proposes that she and Carmela recapture her youth by going to see the new Eloise movie scheduled for Christmas release. This contrasts to I, 1, where she spurned her mother's invitation to their annual

New York trip, with tea at the Plaza Hotel under Eloise's portrait. Meadow's new sense of experience allows her to return to that innocence. The cut to the Bada Bing pole dancers reminds us she is still far from her father's world.

Meadow is unprepared for the way Noah breaks up with her. As they study together in the library, he simply states that he doesn't want to see her any more, because she's too negative: "You have this underlying cynicism about everything." He then returns to his book. The show does not idealize Meadow's black/Jewish lover. Though Tony is wrong to have opposed the boy, he proves to be as arrogant, exploitative and misogynous as the boys at the Bada Bing. Back home Meadow conceals her upset in the adolescent's belligerent anger ("Isn't there anything to eat in this house?"), at which Tony and Carmela exchange a knowing glance.

By interweaving the stories of Meadow, Caitlin and Tracee, the episode explicitly connects the worlds of the haves and the have-nots, across a range of female sensitivity and vulnerabilty. Tracee's proud new braces pathetically parallel Meadow's cavalier attitude toward her dental appointment. The scene-bridge of Ralphie's callous laughter contrasts Tracee's bondage to Silvio with the Dante/Aprile/Soprano plenty. Carmela's anecdote about an empty milk carton is a complacent parody of poverty. Caitlin's comfortable small-town upbringing and Meadow's affluence are opposite antitheses to Tracee's life of abuse.

The editing confirms these parallels. In successive shots Tracee and Meadow walk to their respective doors. We cut from the bag lady's newspaper undies to Paulie's wad of bills, from Tracee forced to fellate a cop to Caitlin raising her head from a pillow. From Meadow's snuggling in bed with her mother, discussing Noah, we cut to Tracee desperately asking Tony for advice about her pregnancy. After Tracee's murder we cut from the dark ravine behind the Bada Bing to Meadow's sunny campus. The point is that Meadow's world—the haves—draws its advantage, money, and strength from the exploitation in Tracee's world—the have-nots. Tony's "taste" from Ralphie's pimping of Tracee supports Meadow's college.

The episode ends with the Bing's eye-patched doorman Georgie admitting a new student into the Executive Club. Here the registration fee is "$50 plus a blowjob later." Even more chilling, the other dancers know what happened to Tracee but they're cowed to *omertà*, too. They live on a thinner line than the rest of us.

III, 7:   Second Opinion

Written by Lawrence Konner. Directed by Tim Van Patten.

Though Uncle Junior's cancer surgery is successful his surgeon recommends a second operation for malignant residue. After Tony urges him to seek "a second opinion," he opts for chemotherapy instead. Christopher's probation creates tensions with Paulie. Meadow's dean at Columbia takes Carmela to lunch to solicit a donation toward the new Students Center. After meeting alone with Dr. Melfi Carmela has a session with one of Melfi's old teachers. He recommends she leave Tony.

There are several "second opinions" in this episode. Usually that is recommended because even an expert can be wrong. After all, Chris and Paulie both err on their women's shoe sizes. AJ is glad he took his parents' "second opinion" and took the school trip to Washington, D.C.—because the hotel had some cool video games.

Matters of the heart especially invite an additional perspective. Where Meadow thinks that in Noah she lost "a wonderful man because of Dad," we might advise that she was well rid of the self-serving and self-righteous twit—notwithstanding his film scholarship. More discreetly, Meadow declines Carmela's invitation to express her view of her parents' marriage.

The "second opinion" also suggests human inconsistency. Thus Chris can be irate that in his 2 a.m. check, Paulie sniffs Adriana's panties, and yet betray her himself. As Paulie notes his premature adultery, "You're not even married yet, you're dipping into whores already?" Paulie agrees to respect the sanctity of Chris's marriage to Adriana: "As of her wedding day, anything that touches her pussy is off limits." As Tony admits, Paulie "can be a little quirky."

The only literal "second opinion" involves Uncle Junior's medical situation. This is the sense in which Melfi used the term re: her failed starter (I, 6). Tony suggests talking to another doctor before continuing with the surgery-happy Dr. John ("Cut, zip, over and out") Kennedy. Uncle Junior's devotion to that surgeon derives from his worship of the deceased president of the same name. As for the prosecution of Hoffa and his Teamsters, "That was the brother." This episode abounds with such hairline moral distinctions (e.g., the sanctity of marriage, above and below).

Dr. Mehta recommends the chemo, even though it may not avoid further surgery. The consensus board also recommends this, but only after Dr. Kennedy petulantly withdraws: "Mehta? . . . The last thing I need is to operate with that little shit looking over my shoulder." Apparently, you don't have to be a gangster to be profane, high-handed, self-serving, racist and undependable.

Normally "second opinions" are viewed less favorably in Tony's world, because they undermine the clear lines of authority. Tony smashes Angie's car with a baseball bat because, having spent his money on a Cadillac, she complained to Carmela that she needs $1,200 for her poodle's operation. "If you have a problem bring it to me, not Carmela." Similarly, Paulie threatens Chris if he ever again takes "any shit between us" to Tony.

To ease the atmosphere Paulie buys a fish that sings "YMCA" for the Bing office. That's another, unwitting "second opinion." Earlier Tony was so upset by the Bing fish that sang Annie Lennox's "Take Me to the River" that he smashed it on Georgie, still showing his wounds from Ralphie's equally irrational assault. Tony associates the song with Pussy, who now sings with the fishes instead of to the Feds. Ralphie's violence in the previous episode is disturbingly echoed in Tony's attack on Georgie and in Chris's attack on Adriana (when she recalls fellating Penn—of Penn and Teller—"the big one"—in an Atlantic City washroom). The context provides a "second opinion" on all these characters.

Sometimes Tony is enhanced by a "second opinion." When Carmela's mother bad mouths him after a disrupted Sunday dinner, Carmela reminds her parents of the behind-the-scenes help he has given them: "I earn it, you two get a free pass." Her mother's constant criticism of Tony again recalls *GoodFellas*, where the hero's wife (Lorraine Bracco, as it happens, pre-Melfi) is similarly torn between her unreliable husband and her critical mother.

Despite Uncle Junior's adoration, Dr. Kennedy does not answer Junior's phone calls until Tony and Furio confront him on the golf course, offer him a titanium club, and threateningly back him into the water trap: "Show that man the respect he deserves. Answer his phone calls." Dr. Kennedy drops in on Uncle Junior's treatment, compliments his doctor, and leaves his home number to call if he ever needs him (echoing Tony's earlier promise of help). In dealing with Dr. Kennedy, Tony's repellent criminal ways are attractively effective.

The most dramatic "second opinion" comes from the therapist whom Melfi recommends to Carmela. The white-bearded Dr. Krakower is a moral traditionalist, in complete contrast to the non-judgmental Melfi. Her airy modern office contrasts to the book-lined room in his home, with a glowing fireplace and a Freud-like (if not Freudian) clutter of personal objects and mementos. Melfi's therapist, Dr. Kupferberg, also leans toward the suspect modern, with large abstract paintings behind him and her (II, 9). Where Melfi recommends self-help books, Krakower prescribes Dostoyevsky's *Crime and Punishment*. In contrast to Melfi's intermittent marriage to Richard, this doctor has been married for 31 years. His Jewish respect for the sanctity of marriage matches Carmela's (not to mention Tony's, Christopher's and Paulie's) Catholic.

After Melfi's liberalism, her teacher's advice sweeps through like an Old Testament prophet's rage: "A depressed criminal, prone to anger, serially unfaithful, is that your definition of 'a good man'?" He implicitly criticizes Melfi's tolerance: "Many patients want to be excused for their current predicament because of events that occurred in their childhood. That's what psychiatry has become in America. Visit any shopping mall or ethnic pride parade to witness the results." Tony's whores "are probably the least of his misdeeds."

Dr. Krakower advises Carmela to follow her initial impulse "and consider leaving" Tony. Otherwise she will never feel good about herself or escape the guilt and shame of being his "enabler," if not his "accomplice." When she cites Father Phil's advice to "Work with him to make him a better man," the Old Shrink cogently replies: "How's that going?" Sensible virtue can also be pragmatic. Dr. Krakower's conclusion is devastating: "I'm not charging you because I won't take blood money. You shouldn't either. One thing you can't say—that you haven't been told." It is not that Melfi is wrong. The traditionalist—genuinely of the Old School—is more substantial. He speaks with moral heft.

When Junior is irked by Dr. Kennedy's neglect, Bobby consoles him: "What are you going to do? These doctors—it's not like on TV." As it happens, we see them on TV, albeit in a show that's not like what's usually on TV, not just for including Junior's barf but for the complexity and ambivalence of its moral vision.

At the heart of this episode is the antithesis of the two Dr. K's. Kennedy is the ultra-modern doctor of science, hustling stock deals between his brisk surgeries and his leisurely golf, who is self-serving and corrupt even when he falls back on principle. Krakower is the old-fashioned moralist, modest, selfless, who stands on the literature of spiritual awareness and moral responsibility.

At the end of the episode Tony finds Carmela curled asleep on the sofa in daylight. Having retreated from divorce, she has asserted herself against him in another way, by committing to a $50,000 donation to Columbia, when Tony approved only five. Dean Ross—a second-generation Italian-American, a bobbed Rossetti, also from New Jersey—and his "Development" project Tony has dismissed as "those Morningside Heights gangsters." At first Tony won't pay: "I know too much about extortion." But when Tony finds Carmela depressed he submits to her shakedown, for Meadow's "protection" at Columbia. Carmela will continue to take the "blood money." If Columbia University courts it, why shouldn't she?

When she and Tony walk away in the last shot, Carmela is cocooned in her heart-covered blanket. It is a parody of feeling warmed by love. In the foreground, two candlesticks form a profane altar that honors the blood money—and now and then puts it to respectable use. In another secular parallel to lost idealism, the song over the credits—Nils Lofgren's "Black Books"—reminisces about tender moments, a lost love gone because of "too many different needs to satisfy." "She wants new shoulders to cry on, New back seats to lie on," and "She always gets her way." The song plays over Carmela's troubled solitude when she waits outside Meadow's room, then at the end. There are second opinions on Carmela, too. One has her a corrupted idealist, the other a virtuous pragmatic. But, as David Chase remarks of her hospital scene with Tony in I, i, Carmela "made a deal with the devil" (Season One DVD, disc four).

When Tony coerces Dr. Kennedy to accept the titanium golf club, the doctor backs down from his principled refusal of a gift: "Well, I could use a little extra distance." "Who couldn't?" Tony agrees. This episode is about keeping one's distance from corruption (for example, Tony). Angie, Meadow, Dean Ross, Uncle Junior, Chris and Adriana, Carmela and her parents, and now Dr. Kennedy—all profit from Tony's corruption. Only Dr. Krakower keeps a morally proper distance—which is utterly to reject him and his money. When Carmela paraphrases his advice as defining her border and keeping "a certain distance," he corrects her. That mealy-mouth advice she got from her priest. Dr. Krakower requires the total rejection of Tony and his money—however charming and helpful they might respectively be. When Dr. Kennedy accepts Tony's gift he is caught in his water trap.

III, 8:   He Is Risen

Written by Todd Kessler. Directed by Allen Coulter.

After Ralphie snubs Tony, Tony has Carmela cancel their Thanksgiving invitation to Rosalie and Ralphie. Johnny Sack persuades Ralphie to apologize. When the stressed captain Gigi has a fatal heart attack on the toilet, Tony makes Ralphie captain. Meanwhile, Meadow and Jackie Aprile Jr. start courting when Jackie gives her Ecstasy (the drug). Tony starts an affair with one of Melfi's patients, a Mercedes-Benz salesperson named Gloria.

As the title suggests, this episode originally ran on Easter Sunday. At Tony's Thanksgiving dinner, when Janice's new boyfriend, Aaron, snaps out of his narcolepsy to meet Jackie, Aaron's instinctive greeting is "Have you heard the good news? He is risen." Aaron himself periodically rises, only to sink back into sleep. This line provides the episode's unifying metaphor.

There are a variety of "rises" here, of which only Aaron's is Easterly. The most bathetic is Jackie's romancing of Meadow. On their first night together his "rise" ("I can't stop now") is thwarted when Meadow passes out from excessive tequila and the prophylactically named Ecstasy. At the end, after Meadow crashes his car, she asks to go to his place. As in his Uncle Richie's courtship of Janice, Jackie's interest in Meadow is shaded by his opportunity to rise in her father's gang. Tony's power also requires Jackie treat Meadow with extra care and respect, but the boy falls short.

Rosalie, Janice, and (more reservedly) Carmela are eager for this union. It would serve Tony's undertaking to care for his old boss's son. But despite their parents' encouragement, the teenagers are attracted to each other. Jackie's casual attitude toward both college and integrity prove him more interested in the Family than in the family connection. This "rise" begins his downfall. Jackie's interest in men's fashion design is like Chris's earlier dreams of Hollywood. Jackie doesn't want to do anything but "to be Hugo Boss."

The most obvious "rise" is the advent of Rosalie Aprile's new live-in boyfriend. Ralphie's tap on the construction industry gives him a new prominence—and a dangerous self-importance. As a "made" colleague, he is properly angered that Tony slapped him in public—"Rules are rules. Otherwise, what—fuckin' anarchy"—even though he was wrong to murder his whore, Tracee. Ralphie is equally at odds with Tony in mentoring Jackie, offering to provide him with Ecstasy and in a later episode giving him a gun.

In Tony's charge—"He showed disrespect for the Bing"—he places the club ahead of Tracee, suppressing his rueful sentiment. The same order is found in Ralphie's apology: "I disrespected the Bing—and the girl." Even Johnny Sack shares this misogyny: "But she was a whore, Tony." It is to Tony's credit that he feels so troubled about Tracee's death. When he and Ralphie finally meet the song behind them is "Ghost Riders in the Sky," as if Tracee were a spectral presence.

For most of the episode Ralphie chafes against Tony, even asking Johnny Sack about switching families. In their reconciliation, Ralphie is awkward and Tony rigid. His authority cannot let Ralphie go unpunished. But because Ralphie is such a good earner, Tony decides—despite having refused to do so—to promote him to captain. This resolution is prompted by Tony's reading of Sun Tzu's *The Art of War*. Tony finds this medieval Oriental text better on strategy than the "Prince Machiavelli," whose *Cliff's Notes* he has crammed.

In his own resurrection Tony is moved to express his loving concern to Meadow, when her approach with the cake reminds him of the murdered Tracee. Tony sees the parallel between the two women that was implied by the narrative organization of episode III, 6. More broadly, Tony is now so comfortable in his sessions with Dr. Melfi that he chats up one of her patients, Gloria Trillo, when Melfi has double-booked them.

The Mercedes saleswoman is beautiful, apparently poised, witty, strong, and independent, so it is no surprise to see Tony interested in her. Both fib about why they see Melfi. Tony claims to be trying to stop smoking (perhaps a fair metaphor for the Hell-bent), while the more innocent Gloria claims to be criminal: "Serial murderer—I murdered seven relationships." In a pointed coincidence, Uncle Junior remembers her father as a stonemason who had seven daughters. Though Gloria presumably referred to her romantic life, the number confirms the inescapability of family influence.

The episode follows Tony's developing interest in Gloria from their meeting to their consummation. In contrast to the series' opening shot, in this one Tony sits comfortably (though formally) beside the woman on Melfi's waiting room couch. He seems to stand shyly in the background, almost boyish, when Melfi leads Gloria into her office and closes the door on Tony, who has watched them depart. When Carmela mentions the

Meadow-Jackie possibility, Tony is distracted by the Mercedes commercial on television. Not only does Carmela encourage him to buy one, the ad's "Here's how you'll get your thrills" anticipates Uncle Junior's advice: "Take what pleasures you can."

Tony's test-drive with/of Gloria concludes with the camera drawing back discreetly from the tryst, showing Tony's boat (the ever-phallic *Stugots*) on the left and Gloria's Mercedes on the right, parked face-to-face like lovers. The image is of complementary transports of delight, shadowed by betrayal and truancy. This naval encounter and Ralphie's new captaincy share the pretense of submission in the closing song, Kasey Chambers's "The Captain": "You be the captain, I'll be no one."

Finally, Melfi seems on the rise as well, recovering from her rape and its aftermath. She calmly declines Tony's offer to walk her to her car after their after-hours appointment, even though—as she tells her therapist, Elliot— "I almost fell in his arms crying." She complains to Elliot about her whining, unreasonable patient, Gloria, and Melfi's sense that the therapist needs the help she is giving others. Elliot properly praises her strength of will through her terrible trauma.

One brief scene establishes the normalization of the gangsters' life. The black Reverend James arrives to receive his parish's share of the truckload of turkeys Christopher has hijacked. Hesh arrives, concerned about the stories about Ralphie's disrespect for Tony. The tangle of professional and personal betrayals is played out against the background of Thanksgiving, both as an appreciation of life's blessing and as a family event.

Finally, there are two lighter forms of resurrection. One is the running gag about leftover turkey sandwiches—starting at Tony's Thanksgiving dinner itself. The other is the urban resurrection that our heroes are planning to exploit, the huge New Jersey mall construction project. At the center of the Esplanade is the Newark Museum of Science and Trucking, which neatly combines the public and the private interests afoot.

■ Perhaps the only major character in this episode who does not "rise" is the stressed, constipated Gigi Cestore, who dies on the toilet. In the next scene Uncle Junior works up a contrary despair: "I don't give a shit anymore. . . . Everything goes through me." *The Sopranos* abounds with such paronomastic irony.

III, 9: The Telltale Moozadell

Written by Michael Imperioli. Directed by Daniel Attias.

Carmela enjoys her family's birthday gifts. Christopher makes Adriana manager of the club that Rocco lost on football bets. AJ is punished for being part of a group that vandalized the school swimming pool. Jackie advances his position with Meadow but incurs Tony's paternal ire. Tony and Gloria arouse Dr. Melfi's suspicions.

The two dominant metaphors in this episode are gifts and fucking oneself. They may be related. The mix is even present in the film Tony is watching on TV: *It's a Gift* (1934) is the W. C. Fields classic about domestic afflictions.

With regard to the former, Carmela's birthday gifts are a sapphire ring from Tony, a DVD of *The Matrix* from AJ ("Right up her alley," Tony sarcastically observes), and from Meadow a daylong session at a Soho spa, purchased along with a session for Meadow on Carmela's credit card. Tony brings Gloria a present but impresses her more when he meets her at the zoo. Tony gives Jackie money (strings definitely attached) to buy dessert on his dinner date with Meadow. Tony even tips Dr. Melfi, overriding her refusal, when he pays his monthly bill.

Christopher "gives" Adriana The Lollipop Club, but only to run it; he and Furio remain the silent partners, with a secondary role left the owner/loser, Rocco. Jackie "gives" a friend's friend the illusion that he has secured his Ecstasy sales at that club in return for a kickback. The time Jackie lavishes on the Sopranos—cleaning out their garage, coaching AJ in defensive football—is equally self-serving, to impress Meadow and her parents. Courting Jackie's favor, Ralphie gives him a .38 pistol.

All these "gifts" are motivated by self-service. Though some gifts (AJ's, Meadow's, Jackie's) are more obviously selfish than others, all the gifts serve the giver's interests at least as much as the recipient's. AJ transparently rationalizes when he says he didn't wrap Carmela's gift because "it's wasteful to the environment." That's a falser front than Tony's Waste Management.

The second metaphor is introduced when Paulie, watching a nature TV show with Tony, remarks that because a snake combines both sexes, snakes reproduce spontaneously. That's why untrustworthy people are called snakes: "How can you trust a guy who can literally go fuck themselves?" This truth overrides even the Bible: "Snakes were fuckin' themselves long before Adam and Eve showed up." At the zoo, Gloria and Tony have sex in the snake house.

What joins these metaphors is the idea that people who serve themselves end up screwing themselves. Rocco loses his club because he bet over his head, not with it. Jackie starts on a very slippery slope when he courts Tony's interest by dating Meadow but fails his promises. He averts Tony's discovery at the Bing, but is caught at the casino. Worse, Jackie starts acting like a Godfather (film allusion intended) when, with minion Dino behind him to end the meeting, he agrees to ask his "associate," Christopher, to allow his friend's Ecstasy sales in the club.

When Jackie tells Tony he got an A in his literature paper, he omits that it was the essay Meadow gave him on Edgar Allan Poe. "I never should have taken 'The Literature of Obsession' " course, he tells her. In fact, he needs to learn from that course, to gain perspective on his own obsessions. So the shortcut of Meadow's gift is not in his best interests. When Tony and Jackie hug and kiss at their first parting, they look like twins in their matching black leather bomber jackets. But Jackie aspires to become like Tony, not what Tony wants for his daughter. Jackie lacks the character to grow out of the "gifts" of his family background (the advantages of which Ralphie spoke in III, 6).

The burgeoning romance between Gloria and Tony also serves both metaphors. That is, it is both a gift and self-destructive. Both lovers are so exhilarated that Dr. Melfi senses they are lying to her. Tony seems suspicious when he quotes Gloria's philosophy (another dubious "gift"): "Buddha preached joyful participation in the sorrows of the world." His second-hand Buddhism too easily justifies the neurotic lovers' self-indulgence. Tony does not cite culture well. He hears *Aida* as I EAT HER?

Gloria is especially vulnerable, having tried to commit suicide when her last relationship ended. Now she turns self-righteous when Melfi mentions hearing a man's voice when Gloria cancelled her appointment (That was *Stugots* Tony): "I don't pay you to be under your surveillance." In a similarly defensive response, Tony snaps "What the fuck does she know?" at Jeannie Cuzamano's name for Mercedes-Benz sportscars: "Midlife-Crisis-Mobiles." The adulterer doth protest too much, methinks, especially having just told Carmela he didn't buy a Mercedes because he felt like a douche bag in it.

Rosalie's romance with Ralphie also seems a mixed blessing. At lunch Carmela encourages Rosalie to "hold on to" Ralphie, as if he were not the murderous sociopath who promises her son Ecstasy and provides a .38. The gangster wives see the irony in their marriages surviving that of hardworking, responsible Artie Bucco. But Carmela's explanation—"You can push a man only so far"—undermines her own pretense, that she stays with Tony to make him a better person. In one shot she looks past his kiss to her new sapphire ring. Later Tony looks past Gloria's kiss to see if anyone sees them. In both cases the commitment of the kiss is compromised.

The school's relaxed response to AJ's delinquency is another example of a dangerous gift. After Tony has taken a hard line with his son—"Your football career—down the drain!"—the school suspends his punishment. This scene comes right after Jackie assures his troubled friend that "Chris and me are associates. You got nothing to worry about." The parallel defines the school as also self-serving. The coach contends: "It would be against [AJ's] best interest—and the team's—to sever his relationship" with the football team.

The teacher's "The Wall of Pride: What kind of animals . . ." recalls Carmela's "What kind of animal smokes marijuana at his own confirmation?" (II, 7). After a lawsuit ended detentions, the school may echo the parents' indignation but leaves all punishment to them. The teacher concludes with a hollow threat: AJ will be expelled if he commits just one more violation of the school code. Unless, presumably, the freshman football team still needs him. The school does AJ no favor by declining to take a hard stance. That gift screws him.

In all this flawed humanity, Aaron cites the Lord as the reason he will not drink alcohol. But when Tony cites Jesus's wine Janice responds: "He was Jesus, Tone. You can't make comparisons." The cocaine residue Tony brushes off her nose suggests Janice has accepted her human fallibility and admires the half-dead Aaron's proximity to God. The characters in this episode fall far short of Jesus—and use human imperfection to justify self-indulgence.

■ This episode features Carmela's favorite song, Andrea Bocelli's "*Con Te Partiro,*" at her birthday party. It is also heard in II, 1, and 4.

III, 10:   To Save Us All from Satan's Power

Written by Robin Green and Mitchell Burgess. Directed by Jack Bender.

Under the rush and tensions of approaching Christmas, Tony remembers some gang meetings around Christmas, 1995, when Pussy's mysterious behavior seems to have augured his betrayal. The beautified, free Charmaine continues to work at Artie's restaurant and tells Tony she does not want the gang there. Jackie courts Meadow even after Tony beats him up. Meadow has a disconcerting Christmas gift for Tony.

Like Scrooge in that other seasonal classic, Dickens's *A Christmas Carol*, Tony is haunted by the spirit of Christmas past. In particular—1995, when O. J. Simpson's civil suit dominated the TV news, Tony had hair, and Big Pussy went to Boca to set up a sit-down to reconcile Uncle Junior and Boss Jackie Aprile, whose truck Junior had hijacked. The latter detail casts new light on the Season One episodes when Chris and Brendan robbed trucks under Junior's protection, and he appealed to Boss Jackie for justice.

The memories drip irony. In the first flashback, Jackie tells Pussy "You need money, come to me." Tony urges Pussy not to sell heroin: "Too risky." "I always wanted a house by the ocean," Pussy muses, "Maybe in another life." Pussy missed the sit-down, suspiciously, and that—Tony now realizes—was when the FBI "flipped" him. When Pussy arrived in the Santa suit for the children's party, he was already wearing a wire for the FBI. That's why he tried to talk business and angrily broke the jukebox when he was interrupted. With unknowing prescience, Silvio greeted him with his imitation of Pacino identifying his treacherous brother in *The Godfather Part II*: "It was you, Fredo."

Memories of Pussy give Silvio a nightmare about stolen cheese in the Bing and the dead rat—Pussy—on the floor beneath the sequined costumes. The latter image was set up in the previous episode, when Silvio complained about the problems of running a strip club beyond all the glitz and the glamour.

Of course, they don't make Santas like they used to. In Pussy's absence, Bobby Baccala is coerced into playing Santa, despite protesting "I can't. I'm shy." Bobby's suspicion that one little boy is on his second visit provokes the kid's "Fuck you, Santa." Bobby can't "Ho ho ho." At episode end, the gang agrees that Pussy was a great Santa. But as Paulie concludes (in non-Yule imagery), "I loved that cocksucker like a brother and he fucked me in the ass. . . . The world don't run on love. He was a rat bastard. . . . In the end, fuck Santa Claus." A Santa can smile, and smile, and be a traitor. But so can a husband, as Tony, Silvio, and Paulie compare what they gave their *goomahs* for Christmas.

In more devotional preparation for Christmas, Janice and her Born Again Aaron work on what he calls their "great motherjumping lyric" about Jesus's stain-cleaning blood. "Like Ajax?" Janice wonders. Even their sacred reeks of the profane, especially in Aaron's "motherjumping." Eschewing wine, they drink a jug of grape juice. Janice insists she is sincere in her new faith. Though she and Aaron do not sleep together any more, Christianity is "the fastest-growing marketing sector in the music business today." The episode includes traditional Christmas music as well, for example, Alvin and The Chipmunks' "Christmas Don't Be Late," The Drifters's "White Christmas," and Eartha Kitt's "Santa Baby."

In this comedy of the unholy, in which the O. J. Simpson trial defines the time, Janice is moved to genuine emotion when the television news reports her Russian assailant found severely beaten under Santa's sleigh in a store window display. She guesses who put him there. Waking Aaron from the salad, she announces: "What's missing from the song is the brother concept." Aaron rises to a cliché: "You mean, 'He ain't heavy'?" Janice cries: "Sometimes we don't see our loved ones." Tony's assault on the Russian raises Janice briefly into Yuletide joy.

Of course, Tony's violence was not completely in the Christmas spirit of brotherly love for Janice. Primarily, he had to preserve his own authority. Had he let the assault on his sister pass, he would have lost major face. He did what he had to do.

When Charmaine accuses Tony of making Artie "a friggin' mess," Tony sweeps Chris and Silvio off to a new club, where he finds Jackie under a lapdancer. In the men's room Tony beats him up for his looseness and hypocrisy—and finds his gun. "You bottomed out," he says, leaving him crumpled on the floor from a kneed groin. When Jackie brings the Sopranos the Apriles' Christmas gifts, Tony privately admits he hasn't decided what to do with him yet: "You bullshit me and you betray my daughter." The next episode disproves Jackie's dedication on the locket he gives Meadow: "I will always be true."

Carmela understandably doubts Tony's claim that when he was out all night he was "the monogamy poster boy." With Gloria holidaying in Morocco, he is almost faithful. But now Carmela—haunted by Tony's high school romance—thinks Charmaine is beautifying herself for him. When Tony gives Carmela the $50,000 sapphire bracelet to match her necklace and earrings, she glows with love regained.

To Tony's grateful surprise, Meadow also beams at him—"It's Christmas"—and innocently presents her gift that she wants to see on his desk. The wall-mounted fish turns to sing at him accusingly: "Take me to the river, Drop me in the water. . . ." Despite this symbolic resurrection of Pussy, Tony musters a grateful smile and a kiss for his daughter. Even from his house in the ocean Pussy does not stay silent.

In different ways, all the characters fulfill Melfi's observation. "The pressures we put ourselves under" at Christmas make her call the time "Stressmess." After all, the gang's annual Christmas party for the neighborhood children began in a cognate hypocrisy. Johnny-Boy launched it to ease the resentment when the beloved old Satriale killed himself after Johnny-Boy took over his store. The basic Christmas tradition here is the false front of community. The end credits have a more hopeful song: "Jesus told me, Everything is going to be alright." But then, He never had to live through a family/Family Christmas.

▪ In a secular parallel to Janice's stain-removal song, Tony uses the Russian gangster boss to launder $250,000 of personal money in this episode and $200,000 in the next. Clearly, this series is post–Cold War as well as postmodernist.

III, 11: Pine Barrens

Written by Terence Winter (story by Tim Van Patten and Terence Winter). Directed by Steve Buscemi.

Gloria storms off *The Stugots* after Tony admits fibbing about Irina's phone call. Paulie and Christopher, collecting Silvio's gambling debt from the Russian hood Valery, end up beating him to presumed death. In the frozen wastes of Pine Barrens, South Jersey, they bungle his premature burial and he escapes. They almost freeze to death before Tony and Bobby rescue them. Meadow discovers Jackie's shallowness and infidelity.

This black comedy demystifies the Family. Each of the three plots exposes the illusions of honor and effectiveness both in family and Family life. Here everyone is, in Irina's term, "broken up."

The failed execution of Valery and his chase through the snowy forest are a homage to the Coens' *Miller's Crossing* (1990) and *Fargo* (1996). Our heroes' bungling undercuts the gangsters' pretense to effectiveness. Paulie goes from ordering the "satin finish" on his nails to shivering in the shelter of an abandoned septic tank cleaner's truck, eating frozen packets of catsup and relish, and hoarding his Tic-Tacs. Chris is concussed and Paulie freezing with a shoe lost in the snow. They threaten to kill each other, Chris pulling his gun to break Paulie's stranglehold. Their squabbling and mutual suspicion and Paulie's indignation at having to collect a debt for the sick Silvio deflate their vaunted fraternity. But in the end, Christopher supports Paulie's story.

The arrogance and xenophobia in Paulie's treatment of Valery—with his sneering jokes at Russian technology, overcrowding, rubles, the Cuban missile threat—are destroyed by the indomitable victim's escape. Valery chews his way through the duct tape, overcomes the two armed gunsels, and escapes even after he is shot, apparently in the head. Though he's only wearing what Paulie calls "pajamas" Valery is more comfortable in the frigid wild than his jacketed assailants: "I wash my balls in ice water. This is warm!" The comedy of Bobby Bacala's hunting uniform parallels the epic survival skills of the underdressed Valery.

Paulie's inadequacy is reflected in his confusion. On his crackling cell-phone Tony tells him Valery was a commando in the Russian Ministry of the Interior and he killed sixteen Chechins. This Paulie reports to Chris as an interior decorator who killed sixteen Czechoslovakians. As Chris has been haunted by his killing of the Czech Emil, the mistake adds to the nightmarishness of his experience.

Their problem begins when Paulie smashes Valery's universal remote control. For the rest of the episode Paulie struggles to regain control over Valery. He ultimately needs Tony to rescue him from the wilds. Their inconsistent cell-phone connection dramatizes the problems of their remote control, as Tony is continually called away from his family and from Gloria.

Paulie acknowledges he "fucked up," but he clearly resents Tony's criticism. He ends frozen, disheveled, humiliated, and ominously sullen. The question is whether the Russian boss Stava will prove more loyal to Valery, who is "like a brother" to him and who saved his life or, preferring his profitable arrangement with Tony, will excuse his friend's abuse. But Tony makes it clear that Paulie will bear full responsibility for any consequences of Valery's assault and escape.

Meanwhile, Meadow loses her romantic delusions about Jackie. He can contribute only three-letter words to their Scrabble game—"poo," "ass," "the"—and he thinks "oblique" is Spanish. Having told Tony he flunked out of Rutgers, he still lets Meadow think he's at school, though—in defense of his vocabulary—"not an English major." Even after she catches him lying to her and with another woman, Meadow resists her friends' conclusion that he's a "drip" and a jerk: "It's all my fault. I shouldn't have pressured him."

That young couple promised the one oasis of idealism and virtue in the Sopranos' world. But instead of following his dead father's character, Jackie emulates his Uncle Richie, the creep who sought advancement by marrying into the Sopranos. So Jackie complains to his "date" not that he lost his love but that he alienated "Tony Soprano's daughter." Jackie might have transcended the Soprano/Aprile ethos through the idealistic Meadow, but he lacks the moral will.

In their session with Melfi, Tony and Carmela reveal a new openness and harmony. But this marital peace is another illusion because—as Tony admits—it is based on his illicit happiness with Gloria. "As much as I love my wife, being with Gloria makes me happier than all your Prozac and your therapy bullshit combined." His adultery makes him a better husband and a better father, he avows. As in the other two plots, the illusion of harmony and loyalty is punctured by the characters' dishonesty and self-indulgence.

Even the Gloria relationship is brittle. In two scenes she attacks him for his unreliability: "If I wanted to be treated like shit I'd get married." The Moroccan gown she gives him creates an illusion he is at home in her apartment. That ends when he braves her barrage of steak and crockery to rescue Chris and Paulie.

Tony's last session with Melfi is introduced with a close-up of her waiting room statue, the Woman that unsettled Tony in the pilot episode's first shot. Tony tells Melfi that Gloria puzzles him: "Why does everything have to be so hard?" Melfi suggests that Tony is drawn to women like Irina and Gloria—depressive, unstable, impossible to please—because they are like his mother. In a phrase, for whatever fields our heroes are pining, they are barons of the barren.

And whatever happened to Comrade Valery? We don't know. One of this show's virtues is that it leaves some loose ends untied.

- Director Steve Buscemi is an extremely effective actor in such films as *Miller's Crossing, Billy Bathgate, Barton Fink, Reservoir Dogs, Hudsucker Proxy, Pulp Fiction, Dead Man, Fargo, Kansas City, The Big Lebowski,* and *Ghost World.* He directed the films *What Happened to Pete, Trees Lounge,* and *Animal Factory,* as well as episodes of *Oz* and *Homicide.*

III, 12: *Amour Fou*

Written by Frank Renzulli. Directed by Tim Van Patten.

Fearing she has ovarian cancer or is pregnant, Carmela wants to straighten out her life. She seeks counsel from a priest doing a Ph.D. in Psychology. Tony flees Gloria's tantrums, returns, then breaks off for good when he learns she introduced herself to Carmela. Taking his cue from Ralphie's nostalgia and his courage from crack, Jackie jumpstarts his career by robbing a card game. One player is killed, Furio wounded, and Jackie identified. Tony knows what his Captain Ralphie will selfishly need to do about Jackie.

"*L'amour fou*" is how Dr. Melfi identifies the Tony-Gloria affair, with its intensity and wildness—"crazy love, all-consuming"—after Tony has ended it the first time. But the term applies more broadly across this episode. It covers both the intense emotion in Jusepe di Rebera's painting, "The Mystical Marriage of St. Catherine," and Carmela's weeping at the sight of it: "She's so at peace. Beautiful. Innocent. Gorgeous little baby. Come on, let's go eat." At the other extreme, it applies to Jackie's overriding determination to be "made."

In contrast stands the stability of a loving marriage. Dr. Melfi is certain that Tony would never leave Carmela. "Despite your mothering," Carmela was his one good choice in all his relationships with women. And "In spite of everything, you're a very conventional man." Gloria's insulting Carmela— for her homemaking and jewelry—drives Tony to his first violence against her. Her threat to tell Carmela and Meadow of their affair makes him want to kill her. To ensure that she won't, Tony sends Patsy Parisi on a test-drive with Gloria. On a country road Patsy pulls a gun and warns that if she approaches Tony or his family again he will kill her: "My face is the last face you'll see. Not Tony's. It won't be cinematic." Thus Patsy inures Gloria against romantic thoughts of Tony killing her (as she begged him to, under his throttle).

For all his passion, Tony does prove himself the "hard, cold captain of industry type." Though he and Gloria drive each other into rage as well as ardor, in the crunch Tony proves cool. He stops short of killing Gloria when he first wants to. In dispatching Patsy he both defuses the Fatal Romance and measures his response. He shows the same strength when he refuses to let Christopher whack Jackie after the kid robbed and shot at him and wounded Furio. Though Chris charges him with hypocrisy in protecting Jackie, Tony insists he will make his own decision, not accept Chris's. Besides, "Every person you whack, you risk exposure." In an angry clutch that recalls his last scene with Gloria, Tony demands Chris's respect more than his love.

When Ralphie, as expected, comes to see Tony about the missing Jackie, Tony delivers a clinic in management style. As Ralphie is living with Jackie's mother and is nakedly ambitious, and as Jackie is still called Jackie Jr. long after the gang boss's death, Tony is in a very sensitive situation. It's further complicated by Tony's excessive response to Ralphie's murder of Tracee and by Tony having promised Jackie Sr. to look out for his son. Ralphie's strategy is to take the lead in defining the seriousness of Jackie's transgression, then concluding, as if reluctantly: "I want to give the kid a pass." Rather than argue, Tony advises Ralphie to go with his instincts.

However, as Tony elaborates his support for whatever Ralphie, as Captain, decides to do, he plants the seeds that will change Ralphie's mind. Tony is confident Ralphie will be able to handle what Chris and Furio would think of that "pass"—and if not, maybe they do not matter. "Who cares what shit they say, they don't have the balls to say to your face?" True, "The kid disrespected you," but "They don't have to live with your commitments." No one can say it was Ralphie's fault: "You took this kid under your wing. You schooled him the best you could." Then Tony returns Ralphie's .38 that he took from Jackie around Christmas.

By the time Ralphie steps into the clear bright day—the neon Satriale pig-head grinning over his shoulder, as in Chris's murder of Emil—he knows that his own reputation requires him to whack his lover's son.

The Tony Soprano Management Manual must be in the works somewhere.

Ralphie is a bad manager. First, he gives his young charges an unfocused directive: "Three fifty gets you a hello. Watching your back's gonna require a little more initiative." He encourages their foolhardiness with Jackie's father's example: "He wanted it. So he stepped up and took it." Ralphie brags about his own youth, when he, Tony, Silvio, and Jackie Aprile were all small-scale hoods, until Jackie proved his balls—"big as an Irish broad's ass"—by robbing a wheel's card game. Only a case of the clap kept Ralphie from joining that historic escapade. He ends his lecture with an insulting directive—"Rinse your plates before putting them in the dishwasher so they won't clog"—that fires Jackie to prove his manhood at Ralphie's expense. Jackie suggests Ralphie is a latent homosexual, both to bolster his own confidence and to assuage his feelings about his mother's lover. As the Dr. Fried commercial stresses, the entire episode is based on anxiety about potency. The boys want to be men.

Jackie Jr.'s attempt to match his father's "balls" fails. His robbery plays out as a comedy of impotence. His and Dino's first resolve is derailed by Sharon Stone's famous pubic flash in *Basic Instinct* (Paul Verhoeven, 1992) on TV. They're pussies after all. In the event, Furio is wounded so high in the leg as to threaten his manhood. For his safe treatment, Tony calls Dr. Fried, his private(s) doctor, away from taping a commercial for his treatment of erectile dysfunction. Conversely, when Tony sets Ralphie to deal with Jackie, instead of letting Chris assume the risk, Tony prefers method over macho.

As Tony has learned, Gloria and Ralphie are dangerous because they don't play by the rules. Tony initially misread Gloria as strong, independent, not the basket case Melfi knew and tried to counsel. The darkness he saw was in Gloria's eyes—like a Spanish princess in "one of those paintings by Goyim" (that is, *Gentiles,* for *Goya*)—not in the "bottomless black hole" that makes her like Livia. Melfi later defines both women by the "selfishness, incessant self-regard" that "passed for love." Both women kept Tony off-balance by their unpredictable, shifting demands, compelling him always "to try to please her, to try to win her love."

Though she doesn't have the most dramatic scenes in this episode, Carmela and her values may be its primary focus. The opening scene starts with a close-up on her purse and Tony's gift, her green sapphire ring, then broadens to show her striding among the sculptures at the Metropolitan. This recalls the sculpture frame in the waiting room outside her first solo visit to Melfi. Appearing large when the focus is on her wealth/style/baggage, she is reduced by the cultural and religious context. In the museum, she is defined as vulnerable, physically by her non-menstrual spotting and emotionally when a painting moves her to tears. Later she cries at a dog food commercial that waxes lyrical about the animal's protectiveness. Its brand name, Pedigree, may point to her arriviste life.

Where Dr. Krakower advised she leave Tony, the black priest here insists: "You made a sacred vow. Divorce is out of the question." She should define an area of comfort and self-respect in her marriage and to live within that, foregoing "those things that are without it"—the archaism may be moral as well as linguistic. "Learn to live on what the good part earns" may be a moral compromise but given Tony's laundering system that distinction is impracticable. The priest's glib pragmatism is essentially what the lunching women conclude: Hilary Clinton is "a role model for us all" because she spun all her husband's "negative shit" into gold.

Dean Martin's "Return to me. . . . Hurry home to my heart" plays over several scenes of domestic reconciliation. We hear it early, then again when Rosalie agonizes for news about Jackie, then when Tony returns home, where Carmela recasts her escape in terms of selling real estate and bakes lemon snaps for the church sale. We last hear it when Patsy Parisi lugs the groceries to his car, pausing to assure his wife on his cellular. He drives away, another killer presented as a warm-hearted and supportive husband.

For all her craziness, Gloria is pathetically alone. She feels bereft at banishment from her sister's children. She is bitterly envious of Carmela's children and husband. Gloria is doubly hurt when Tony comes to her office to break up with her and her colleague wants to switch shifts so he can take his kid to the Raffi concert. Patsy and Tony both enjoy the family life she craves but cannot achieve.

Those men's domestic scenes contrast to Gloria's black and testily driven solitude and to Jackie's failure to have through Meadow escaped his origins. Gloria is right when she says Tony has "a fuckin' dream life compared to mine"—but she denies her responsibility for it. The end-credits song—The Lost Boys' "Affection"—speaks for all the episode's lovers and leavers: "Gimme some affection, Why is it so hard? . . . Don't trust no stranger. You should know better." That is the "favorite" song Gloria turns up on the radio during a frolic with Tony. It haunts her at the end.

III, 13: Army of One

Written by David Chase and Lawrence Konner. Directed by John Patterson.

Ralphie finally has Jackie killed, renewing Meadow's doubts about her family. AJ and a friend are expelled for cheating on their geometry mid-term. Affected by Jackie's death, Carmela is finally persuaded to send AJ to a military school, but his panic attack saves him. Uncle

Junior is freed from house arrest. Paulie's discontent with Anthony grows when he loses his arbitration with Ralphie. The FBI assigns an undercover agent to befriend Adriana.

The third season's conclusion focuses on the tension between genetic compulsion and individual responsibility. What latitude does a person have in which to change?

The title refers to the individual strength that the military school aims to develop through its collective enterprise: "Here the higher good is the good of the corps," not the individual student's. The public school system confuses children with "too many options." In his interview with AJ the Major offers "a blueprint for total self-discipline that will take you through your whole life." He tells the parents that the regimentation is less of a factor than the mentoring in small classes and the faculty's involvement in the students' dorm life.

Paradoxically, the military school's values and methods closely parallel the gang's. Even the Major stretches his discipline, when he smokes during his interview with Tony and Carmela—albeit at an open window. There is some truth to Carmela's concern that a military school would "train him to become a professional killer." As Jackie Jr. proves, AJ could learn that at home.

Tony blames AJ's panic attack on "that putrid, rotten, fuckin' Soprano gene." Dr. Melfi disagrees: "It's a slight tic in his fight/flight response. . . . When you blame your gene you're blaming yourself." Tony admits no responsibility for Jackie's whack, but says he failed as a guide. Tony says he failed him, but "what the fuck are you gonna do, well, today?"

Any tragic dimension in young Jackie's death is deflated by Uncle Junior's recollection: "The kid was always a dumb fuck" who almost drowned in three inches of water at the penguin pond. Jackie can't learn chess from the little black girl whose father is hiding him. As the latter suggests: "You shoulda played that out. That's the only way you're gonna learn." Compared to the little black girl in the projects, Jackie is a failure less by his situation than by his will. His obviously bright host underscores Jackie's wasted advantage.

In another example of someone transcending her origin, the FBI casts a close-cropped mousey clerk as the brassy big-haired moll who will inveigle herself into Adriana's confidence. If that transformation seems implausible, remember what Woody Allen did with the waif Mia Farrow in *Broadway Danny Rose* (1984).

Meadow breaks down at Jackie's death because he is the first mortality her age she has known. His bell tolls for her. When she doubts that Jackie was killed dealing drugs, Carmela rejects her pointed suspicion. Meadow like so many others seeks to blame "bogeymen with Italian names." Meadow reacts differently when Jackie's sister cites the stupidity of his criminal ambition. She has a clearer sense of their families' power than Meadow's naïve insistence that their families only occasionally dealt with the Mafia. The Family's hollow valor is undercut by the windy rhetoric Ralphie hears over the Super Bowl coverage.

Meadow is torn. With Carmela, she acknowledges Jackie's lack of parental guidance but she denies her parents' "excuse to get intrusive and controlling" in AJ's and her life. When, after Jackie's burial, Uncle Junior enraptures the restaurant crowd with his song about "an ungrateful heart," Meadow drinks too much, starts to throw bread-balls at him, and then runs away from Tony. "This is such bullshit," she cries, and narrowly escapes the traffic. Meadow is clearly uncertain about her own and her family's identity. She can't hold to her earlier resolve—Tony's advice in II, 13: "You have to max out the good times with the people you love."

As for AJ, Tony tells Melfi the boy "would never make it" in his business. Typically, AJ's flustered excuse for cheating on the test is that the other boy peed first and that made AJ need to, too. Both boys are dumb enough to score a suspicious 96 percent on the test of which they stole a preview, then fall for the old DNA identification bluff. The teacher offers their Witness Protection Program: "If you cooperate now it will be easier later." AJ would probably be well served by the military school, with its 5:30 A.M. to 10 P.M. schedule and no television. He might learn more plausible alibis.

Tony is toughening toward all his "sons." He walks away from Chris's apology and reaffirmation of his love. He rejects Jackie's call: "Talk to your stepfather. Let him help you." His anger toward AJ is only briefly relieved by affection and compliments, such as how good he looks in his military uniform. As in the previous episode, the Dr. Fried commercial reflects on Tony's attempt to make AJ a man—though the uniform makes AJ "feel like a total jerk-off."

More ominously, Tony alienates Paulie. Partly to reward Ralphie for having offed Jackie, Tony settles Paulie's $50,000 claim against Ralphie for $12,000. Paulie is further embittered because now he can not leave his mother in Green Grove. When Paulie's mother uses the Livia line—"My son lets me live in a place like this"—it is out of gratitude: "He's such a good boy." She does better by her gangster son than by the doctor.

Uncle Junior's song at the reception warms the conclusion. It shows his resolve "to stop and smell the roses" (a felicitous variant on Tony's "stop and smell the gorilla shit" in III, 9). The scene is satisfying in part because it surfaces our extra-textual knowledge that the actor, Dominic Chianese, is an accomplished lounge singer. Also, it provides a different kind of summary canvas than the earlier two seasons' conclusions: close-ups of the individuals responding pensive and moved to Uncle Junior's earnest singing. In contrast to Janice's self-promoting funeral music disc, Uncle Junior personifies the Old Country values and sentiments here. He provokes tears from Bobby, Patsy, and Johnny Sack, and prompts Artie to hold Charmaine even as he casts a baleful eye on Adriana kissing Chris. Meadow's and AJ's silliness only confirms Uncle Junior's dignity.

At the end other singers and three other songs are overlaid, as if to broaden the cultural context in which we see but don't hear Uncle Junior sing. By this abstraction we are pushed out of the scene. In the last shot we are above and behind Tony, Carmela, and AJ. After all its complex identification, the season ends by detaching us from the family and returning us to a perspective of objective judgment.

The third season plants some possible seeds for the fourth. In the central family, Meadow has lost her moorings. How will she define her identity? So, too, AJ, for as Tony asks Melfi, "We can't send him to that place. How're we gonna save this kid?"

Among the Family tensions, Ralphie has Janice snuggling up to him when he jokes at the funeral reception, boding to blossom into another Richie. Worse, Paulie turns away from Tony, complaining to Johnny Sack and committing to Carmine. He told Uncle Junior "Tony fundamentally doesn't respect the elderly." Then, of course, where's Valery? Christopher, too, has been distanced from Tony and his indiscreet Adriana exposed to the FBI. As the Super Bowl Game reduces the crowd at Jackie's funeral, it is clear that the old center does not hold. Or as Patsy Parisi (III, 12) tells the sick Gloria in transit: "It's over, *kapeesh?*"

Conclusion

In the beginning are the credits.

The same montage opens every episode in the first three seasons of *The Sopranos*. Its familiarity breeds comfort. The same song, the same images— the same intro provides the assurance of meeting an old friend. As we relax into the familiar title sequence, we're set up for the episode's surprises.

In addition, that ritual sequence has its own "content," its own meaning as it reflects the shows it prefaces. It collects meaning from the three seasons' experience. Basically, the visuals tell the same story as the title montage of our other great television-family series, *The Simpsons:* Good old Dad drives home from work. But where the cartoon series intercuts Homer's trip with his family's activities, here the focus is on Tony's drive. All we see is him and what he sees. Also, Tony drives from New York City to New Jersey, from the familiar crime-film setting into this show's unique territory. But the montage is not a literal route. It would take a "huge circle to get to all those places," director Henry Bronchtein remarks in his commentary on the Season II DVD (disc 3).

The first shot is up to the lights of the Lincoln Tunnel ceiling. Metaphorically, we emerge from a depth, a darkness that has been lit. From our experience of the series, that light represents the exposure of the Id or the suppressed impulses of our outlaw spirit. Literally and figuratively, the tunnel brings our hero from the underworld. The tunnel's artificial light sanitizes even its Freudian depth and makes it feel safe.

After we're directed to the New Jersey Turnpike we see Tony at the toll station, paying for his ticket to ride. In context, this shows him following the rules, paying his toll dutifully. He may take a bit of dangerous liberty— using both hands to light his cigar while driving—but so far our hero breaks no rules. According to director Allen Coulter's commentary on the Season II DVD (disc 4), Tony was intentionally veiled in a thick burst of cigar smoke and the cigar was intended to suggest "the prow on a ship" leading him home.

Most of the montage is what Tony sees. He looks down at his pinky-ringed hand on the steering wheel—and sees that it is good. He looks at the city reflected in a passing hubcap—and sees that it is good. What he sees outside his car-window must also strike him as good: a series of industrial sites, with long bridges across the abysses, smokestacks, familiar business logos, a statue of a giant worker, a Pizzaland store. Amid these emblems of business and industry there are quick glimpses of the Statue of Liberty and a church. From Tony's perspective this is an assuring survey of his kingdom, the world of blue-collar capitalism.

Especially as he passes his Satriale's Pork Store, where so much of his business is conducted—meetings, butchering, cold storage—and the site of his most shaping (that is, traumatic) boyhood experience. This shot disturbs the comfort of that montage; it connotes Tony's psychological vulnerability. That's where Tony saw his father chop off the debtor's finger and where his own panic attacks began.

This negative shot invites other questions about the montage contents. For example, where is the natural world? All we see is the man-made: factories, icons, bridges. The only animal we see is the fake pig atop Satriale's—a parody of animal life. Without vegetation and natural comfort Tony's industrial empire seems a wasteland. We only see other people in one quick shot, four young men walking abreast. Whether to work or from work or without work, they are a feeble balance against this non-human characterization of Tony's world. (Bronchtein remarks that shots of the principal characters were dropped from the montage.)

The human presence is implied when Tony passes through a series of residential neighborhoods. But we still don't see any people—just rows of uniform, modest houses, of diminishing class and comfort. They start with some traditional old-money homes and conclude with small, cramped bungalows. From them we cut to Tony's neighborhood, North Caldwell, with trees—and space—and the manorial scale of the new-money flash. It's a jolt to pass from the shabby bungalows to Tony's mansion. Aptly, Tony drives *up* to his home, as he leaves behind the drab, cramped, industrial world. Driving home from work, Tony takes us from the wasteland to the pocket of luxury that wasteland supports.

Although the meaning of those visuals may be subtle, the soundtrack has a clear and explicit impact. A3—a.k.a. Alabama 3—is a British-pop group given new prominence by the show's signature adoption of their song, "Woke up This Morning." We get the first five verses at the start of each episode.

The lyrics fit Tony so well they could have come from his horoscope. He wakes up each morning effectively to live by the gun—even when others do his whacking. Tony was born under a bad sign (given Livia, Johnny-Boy, Uncle Junior) and he has a blue moon in his eyes—both that rascally gleam and the kind of good luck that a gangster maybe gets once in a blue moon. So he is looking good and feeling fine—and about to delve into his shame.

If his Papa did tell him about right and wrong he got the direction signs wrong. The Sopranos' value system seems a "world turned upside down." And as Tony's business does "turn shit green" (Massive's criterion for music in I, 10), when garbage provides his fortune, Tony has "that shotgun shine." As gangsters go, Tony is rather high caliber—though not a big bore.

As well as the lyrics, the voices set the tone. With A3 the Blues indeed walk us into their town. Their voices are low, rasping, "beat" in the 1950s sense of life-weary, like a trio of Tom Waitses. As they cling to the bass line, even their buoyant imagery hangs low.

The song ends as abruptly as the low-rent neighborhood. The last sound we hear is precisely ambiguous. It could be the phonograph needle ripped off in mid-note—where the pertinent *Public Enemy* ends with a record spinning after the song is over. Or it could be that other kind of forty-five—with a silencer. That's the gun in the show's brilliant logo, where the letter R—or the verb "are," to be—is replaced by a pistol. For the Sopranos, "Guns R Us." If Carmela *is* Tony's life, so are guns.

■   ■   ■

Though an extended TV series can deepen characterization and develop searching, shifting relationships, the industry has preferred to keep the formula secure, the plots simple, the characters shallow. In that respect, television has not changed much since Parnell Roberts quit the successful *Bonanza* series in protest against its static characterization (after which the show thrived and Roberts disappeared).

Occasionally, a series episode may rise to provoke a larger theme. Lucy, overwhelmed by the chocolate packing machine, articulates to the Chaplinesque satire of modern man overwhelmed by modernity. The death of Chuckles the Clown raised *The Mary Tyler Moore Show* to a circumspect anatomy of the function of comedy and of our paradoxical emotions, when an absurd death provokes laughter and its poignancy frees tears. Sometimes a show may prove of prophetic form, like the self-referentiality of Ernie Kovacs, Sid Caesar, and *The Burns and Allen Show*.

But what is rare—perhaps unprecedented—is a series that springs from such a rounded and profound conception of its characters and experience that a single episode apprehends multiple views and themes. Here are

characters so full that their behavior can be shocking, completely unpredictable, and yet completely consistent with the character as subtly established—like the Zen Janice's murder of Richie. The character ambivalence
that *The Sopranos* brought television compares to the complexities that
Shakespeare added to the simple dramatic structure of Lyly. *The Sopranos*
may be a phenomenally successful television series. But—to twist Robert
Burns—art is art for all that. For all its broad popularity, *The Sopranos* is
a work of art for the ages.

Because of the show's strong central vision, there are innumerable links
between the episodes. For example, in III, 3, when AJ is appointed defensive
captain of his freshman football team, he faints. At the time it seems funny,
especially since he only joined the team to wear the cool jersey and rode
the bench for most of his first game, before he was blessed with a fumble
recovery. But an implicit irony lurks behind the joke: His father has been
fainting from panic attacks. But the incident stays a joke. The episode is
recalled 10 weeks later. Only when AJ faints at the prospect of military
school are the Sopranos informed about his football faint. Then they are
properly angry that the school did not tell them. The school again put its
(and their football team's) interests ahead of the student's and his family's.
For the viewer, the III, 3, incident is not fully defined until III, 13.

In its every specific, *The Sopranos* turns conventional materials to ex-
pressive use. As we have often noted, the music comments on the action
and themes. The series follows on the Scorsese gangster films' period pop
soundtrack and Coppola's incorporation of Italian songs and opera. The
key music—the opening and end-credit numbers—either encapsulates or
ironically reflects on its themes. It builds on *GoodFellas*, which opens with
Tony Bennett's "Rags to Riches" and concludes with Sid Vicious's deviant
"My Way."

The show pays lip service to institutional religion, but deflates it. The
Christian church in particular is characterized as weak, especially when its
most respectable officer—the black priest in III, 12—is blatantly insensitive
to Carmela's moral needs. Carmela's Father Phil and Paulie's "Protector"
Father Felix are weak, secular, and of suspect dedication. The strongest
religious spokesman is the Jewish psychiatrist, Dr. Krakower—with his Old
Testament values and intellect—though he is balanced by Dr. Sam Reis, the
ludicrous Jewish therapist who counsels Melfi's family.

That brings us to the question of the show's negative stereotyping of
Italian-Americans. Does it? No more than it stereotypes black leaders as
hustlers (for example, the Reverend James, Massive Genius) as often as

solid citizens (Officer Wilmore, Jackie's chess-playing hosts). Or "the desert people," a.k.a. the Jews, as sneaky grubs, such as Jackie Jr.'s Ecstasy salesman, Dov Ginsberg, who leaves when his Reserve Unit is called up in Israel (III, 8). Even the Orthodox, Talmud–spouting Teittlemans squabble over the matching seediness of their marriage and motel. And all those—effective—Jewish lawyers. Even the warm and wise Hesh may have exploited his black singers.

As *The Sopranos* takes satiric aim at the moral ambivalence of our times, no ethnic group is sacrosanct. Certainly not the WASP-ish authorities in the high school, military school, or the professions (for example, Dr. Kennedy). In each community the series depicts, one can identify a moral ideal—Dr. Krakower, the senior Rev. James, Dr. Melfi—and the myriad pretenders whose rationalization and respectability make them dangerous. The series is a satiric representation of contemporary sin and folly—regardless of race, religion, color, and creed.

Penultimately, a word about the language. It is often delightfully rascally. If we are critical of Tony's treatment of Noah Tannenbaum, there's a guilty pleasure in his imaginative insults. Noah's mistreatment of Caitlin and Meadow proves that this series does not allow us easy moral judgments. Everything and everyone is ambivalent. So Noah's unfortunate behavior is paralleled by the exuberance of Tony's improper language for him: Oreo, the Hasidic Homie, Buckwheat.

Nor is the wall-to-wall profanity gratuitous. It provides an authenticity that any Bowdlerizing would destroy. The profanity provides an energy and insouciance that reflect the self-assertiveness of its characters' outlaw lives. They talk as they live, beyond the norm—and often the pale. From Jason's "motherfuckers" (after his mother's rape) to the somnambulant Aaron's sanctimonious "motherjumpin,' " the profanity plays sometimes poetic characterization and wit. Here Jason is honest and passionate, Aaron an opportunistic deadhead, and their language exposes them. The profanity tends to speak truth, unvarnished. Tony properly warns Junior that Carmela may cut him "another asshole" (II, 13), but Nils's euphemism—"I tore her a new one" (I, 1)—is a limp lie, because he didn't really excoriate the restaurant hostess, nor get her to seat him.

Finally: What about Tony? What are we to make of a show that warms us toward a fat, middle-aged man whose character falls off the scales of the heroic? He lies, he is unfaithful, he is insensitive and brutish toward his children, and he breaks most laws for what is a disgustingly excessive living. Oh, and he kills people.

First, this is not an amoral show. Portraying an immoral society should alert our moral vigilance. Its every sympathetic transgression is a moral test for the viewer. We have to struggle to upright our moral balance against the hero's sympathetic pull. In shading its moral spectrum so finely the show provides a rigorous exercise for our relativist age.

But *The Sopranos* goes even further. It humanizes the Other—what people don't acknowledge in themselves. We may prefer to think that the mobsters are—like Fitzgerald's rich—not like the rest of us. They readily do what we recoil from the idea of doing, what our every reflex of education and self-respect compel us to abjure. Or they do what we wish we had the *stugots* to do. In either case, they are still human. They are us.

The show's refusal to demonize its villains may perhaps be its moral benchmark. We can even empathize with the vile Richie Aprile for his touching sentimentality and the dignity of his Old School values. The scatterbrain Janice has a wolverine's compulsion to survive, in a world that is at once too sordid for her aspiration and too full of crackpot temptations to allow her rational growth. Even for the vicious Livia we can muster sympathy for her terror at being neglected, alone, hated, the very fate that her selfishness feeds.

And so to Tony. The man struggles to do his best, to meet his responsibilities to his family and to the Family, to keep his home and business wheels oiled and spinning and rewarding. He may not have our code but he has his. Tony is the best of men and the worst of men. He reminds us that whatever enemies we have, however threatening, if our antagonist is a human we have more in common than we have to fear. Indeed, what we may most fear is that disturbing part of ourselves that we project on an enemy. In restoring humanity to its villains lies perhaps the greatest spin of the show's dramatic irony and its greatest service to the viewer, both in self-knowledge and compassion.

With its rich style and the substance that constantly serves, *The Sopranos* is the rare television show that rewards multiple viewings. Other series have been enjoyable in rerun—*The Honeymooners, I Love Lucy, Dragnet, Alfred Hitchcock Presents, The Fugitive, The Prisoner, Star Trek, Seinfeld*—but that is usually to reexperience a familiar pleasure or to catch a missed episode. Re-viewing *The Sopranos* provides different rewards. It reveals new meanings, new connections, new ironies, new depths, or delights on each viewing. Happily, as it appeared when VHS was ensconced and DVD emerging, viewers can buy their own set, to backtrack or to replay to reconsider its riches. Perhaps this potential for re-viewing, for "reading" a television series over and over, like a Dickens novel, encouraged the producers' ambition to make this show so dense and to amplify the cross-references as the seasons proceeded.

What effect will *The Sopranos* have on North American television? The jury will be out on that for quite a while. The most obvious effects will probably be a loosening of the language, perhaps an increase in frontal female nudity, and an increase both in continuing series and in gangster programs. But that is small gnocchi. The big difference that this series will make—if we are lucky—is that the networks might realize there is a significant audience out there that craves adult drama, with sophisticated themes and treatment, with rounded, surprising characters and—above all—with moral complexity. They want to be provoked, not numbed. If that proves to be the effect of *The Sopranos*, then all those fictitious corpses and whacked television conventions will have died for a noble cause.

Appendix

Godfather to *The Sopranos*

Of the various influences that have fed into *The Sopranos*, the most important is Francis Ford Coppola's monumental *The Godfather* trilogy (1972, 1974, 1990). Though David Chase exalts *GoodFellas* for its comedy, brutality, and realism (Season One DVD, disc four), the classical and operatic *The Godfather* was more popular among mobsters. *The Godfather* influence on *The Sopranos* is so pervasive that one writer, Stephen Holden, suggests that it is this series, "more than the wobbly, histrionic" *The Godfather Part III*, that is "the real sequel" (p. xvi) to the great first two films.

That the films were a remarkable achievement was immediately apparent. The first won three Oscars for Best Picture, Actor (Marlon Brando), and Adapted Screenplay (Coppola and source novelist Mario Puzo). *The Godfather Part II*—unprecedented for a sequel—won six Oscars, including Best Picture, Director, Screenplay, Supporting Actor (Robert De Niro), Musical Score (Nino Rota), and Art Direction (Dean Tavoularis, Angelo Graham, George Nelson). Coppola wanted to title the third film *The Death of Michael Corleone* but the studio insisted on the formula, *The Godfather Part III*. Though the third was considered a disappointment, it has grown into an emotional capstone to this epic trilogy. In 1981, the first two films were re-cut for a marathon television presentation, with their scenes rearranged into chronological order, as *Godfather: The Complete Epic, 1902–1958*, with 15 minutes of additional footage.

Coppola's *The Godfather* both revived and revised the gangster-film genre. Its dominant value was not the overweening individualism of the classic film but the corporate model that saw the Family as family and validated its criminal activities by principles such as family identity and fealty. It also played the criminal story as opera, with sweeping emotions, opulent settings, and a new emotional intensity. Coppola's trilogy proposed a nexus of crime, capitalism, and the family. That passed through Martin Scorsese's gangster classics—*Mean Streets* (1973), *GoodFellas* (1990), *Casino* (1995)—on to *The Sopranos*.

Coppola's influence on *The Sopranos* ranges from the passing to the profound. Holden notes the shared "crosscutting between scenes of extreme violence and domestic warmth, and interspersing the narrative with semi-hallucinatory flashbacks" (p. xvi). Clearly Coppola proved a major source for the vocabulary: *omertà, consiglière*, "sleeping with the fishes," "going to the mattresses," the men kissing each other in ritual greeting, the family/Family tension, the homage paid the Godfather, the politicians' and religious figures' collaboration with the criminals, the persecution by the Feds, the Families' rivalry under the power of New York, and so on.

In I, 4, Uncle Junior jokes about "the Chinese godfather" who makes an offer they could not understand, riffing off another famous phrase. The "offer you can't refuse" is quoted by—unfaithful—non-Italians: Hauser in I, 9 and Amy in II, 7. *The Sopranos* builds upon the detailed knowledge we have from Coppola. The Mob website Meadow shows AJ (I, 4) offers "The Sleeping with the Fishes Report." When Ralphie teaches Jackie how to cook spaghetti (III, 9), Chase upholds Coppola's inclusion of a good recipe in each film.

The Godfather influence operates in two general ways. One is the dramatic irony when the series parallels the earlier films. Sometimes it is incidental, like the family photographs formally taken in the first and third films and in II, 7. Richie's shame at his son's ballroom dancing career is an aptly cut-rate version of Michael Corleone's opposition to his son Tony's opera career. Tony's recovery from his assassination attempt parallels Vito's in the first and Michael's in the third. Carmela's irregular confession to Father Phil in I, 5 follows the reluctance and pain of Michael Corleone's irregular confession to the Pope in *The Godfather Part III*. Both begin with "It's been so long" and end in weeping.

More significantly, the I, 3 intercutting of Uncle Junior's assault on Christopher and Brendan with Meadow's choir performance of "All through the Night" parallels the climax of the first *Godfather* film, where the church organ unites the the baptism of Michael's godchild and the orchestrated assassination of the Corleones' rivals. The second and third *Godfather* films end by similarly intercutting a variety of fatal plots. In the Soprano version, Tony's paternal pride in Meadow's singing recalls the *Godfather* films, for the baby baptised in the first was Coppola's daughter Sofia. She plays Michael Corleone's daughter in the third, where they enjoy his son Tony's operatic success. The peacefulness of Meadow's "All through the Night" echoes the baptism music from *The Godfather* and contrasts to the violence of the third's *Cavalleria Rusticana* (ironically, meaning "rustic chivalry"). That's apt, given that Tony is uninvolved in Uncle Junior's vendetta. The opera ending of II, 7 similarly bridges Pussy's betrayal and Christopher's re-dedication to Tony.

The Sopranos' business trip to Sicily in II, 4 recalls Michael's trip to hide there in *The Godfather*, the family's flashback in the second and the aged Michael's return in the third, where he is hailed as *Commendatóre*. Indeed, the entire De Niro prequel in *The Godfather Part II* lies behind Tony's boyhood flashbacks in I, 7. The wedding in I, 8 recalls the opening scene of *The Godfather*, complete with a "Johnny Fontane" type singer. *Tony* (and hence son Anthony Jr.) Soprano may even be named in homage to Michael Corleone's son, Anthony. For that matter, the name of the increasingly troubled Catholic Carmela may derive from Father Carmelo, the priest briefly introduced at Anthony's communion dinner in *The Godfather Part II*, where the religious aspect is shaded by secular deal-making.

The *Godfather* context is especially pointed in II, 9, when the Hell-bent Paulie complains to his priest that 23 years of generous donations to the church did not buy him "immunity" from Hell. If Father Felix falls short of the Old School priest (for example, Bing Crosby, Barry Fitzgerald, Ward Bond), he is completely undercut when he responds—"You should've come to me first and none of this would've happened." This is almost verbatim what Vito Corleone (Brando) tells the undertaker Bonasera who comes for a favor to the Godfather-daughter's wedding in the first scene of *The Godfather*. Perhaps innocuous in itself, the echo recasts the priest as a godfather figure, precisely the protection-seller that Paulie is—and that Paulie requires the church to be. This allusion operates on the writer's level of irony, not the character's. Paulie's worldly, cynical, smoking priest seems to have stepped out of the corrupt, conniving Vatican of *The Godfather Part III*, which supports the *Sopranos*'s clerical satire and its sense that our respectable institutions mirror Mafia methods and values.

In the second form of *Godfatherly* influence, the characters cite the trilogy. In I, 4, the film is so dominant it does not have to be named. "In One" Pussy says, explaining the "Moe Green special" as a reference to the Bugsy Siegel figure in the first *Godfather*. Silvio corrects him with Talmudic fastidiousness: Moe Green was shot in the mouth because he squealed. "The eye is how Francis framed the shot. For the shock value." But Silvio is wrong—or his need for poetic justice overrides his perception. The shot is in the eye, as we see and as Hyman Roth (Lee Strasberg) confirms in *The Godfather Part II*.

In I, 10, both the white-bread Italian doctor and his friends ("How real was *The Godfather*?") and the black music hustler praise the films to ingratiate themselves with Tony and Chris respectively. In I, 1, Carmela tells Father Phil that Tony's favorite *Godfather* film is the second, where Vito returns to Sicily. Tony confirms this in II, 4, citing the sound of the crickets in Don Ciccio's courtyard. The scene is not as peaceful as he remembers it, however. But in his nostalgia for the Old School he sentimentalizes it.

Tony's choice is even more pointed. For that film has two scenes in Don Ciccio's courtyard. In the first, young Vito's mother is killed when she comes to beg Don Ciccio to spare her last son's life. Don Ciccio has ordered both sons killed so they won't avenge his murder of their father. In the second, the adult Vito (Robert De Niro) returns, receives the old Don's blessing, then kills him, now avenging his mother's, father's and older brother's murders. (Don Ciccio takes little pleasure in being proved right.) By choosing the second scene, Tony denies the one in which the hero's mother is killed. This coheres with his suppression first of his hatred of Livia, to the point of wishing her dead, then of her plot to kill him. Tony emphasizes the quiet crickets subconsciously to evade his mother's violence.

His choice also gives Tony the vicarious satisfaction of a hero satisfying his family's honor. This leads to Tony's second point of profound *Godfather II* influence. Despite Michael Corleone's assurance from his mother that "You can never lose your family," the thrust of the second film is indeed Michael's loss of his family and his familial comfort, trust, and honor. He loses his mother, wife, and children, is alienated from his sister and has his last remaining brother murdered. The joyful family flashback that concludes the film taunts Michael with what his advancement has cost him.

For whatever conscious reasons Tony dislikes the third film, one subconscious reason must be its depiction of Michael's pain at having lost his family. Not until his confession does he confront this behavior and its costs. He spends the third film trying to recover his children but dies bereft and alone. The trilogy supports Tony's grief at the loss of his ducks and his fear of losing his family.

Some characters' self-conception is based on those films. Hence, Silvio's recurrent impersonation of *Godfather III* Pacino: "Just when I thought I was out, they pull me back in." Ironically, this pretense at "getting out" demonstrates the character's deliberate immersion in the *Godfather* world. Silvio's party trick is part of his characterization. There is a powerful dramatic irony when he does "I know it was you, Fredo" for the traitor Pussy. If Tony needs any justification for lying to his wife about his love or business life, he finds ample precedent in Pacino's Michael.

In the same spirit of homage, Silvio's Bada Bing Club takes its name from the verbal riffs of Santino (James Caan) in *The Godfather*. Paulie's car horn plays the *Godfather* theme (I, 11). A variation is heard as background music at the restaurant to which Tony successively takes Irina and Carmela (I, 1). When Jackie Aprile Jr. sets up as a lower-level godfather, he has his own *consiglière* stand behind him, like Robert Duval behind Brando. At Jackie Sr.'s funeral Uncle Junior pretends to the dignity of Brando's and Pacino's Godfather. In I, 7 Anthony Junior tells Tony that Jackie's funeral confirmed his suspicions of his father's criminal life because the guests and the photographing Feds reminded him of *The Godfather*.

When Livia dies (III, 2) the undertaker Cozzerelli dutifully—though unnecessarily—promises: "I will use all my powers, all my skills." This repeats Don Corleone's requirement of Bonasera, the undertaker in *The Godfather*, for the mutilated Santino: "I want you to use all your powers and all your skills. I don't want his mother to see him this way." In the event, the unmutilated Livia is left in a closed casket, adorned with her bridal photo, but Cozzerelli lives up to his (Coppola) role. The actor, Ralph Lucarelli, resembles Salvatore Corsitto, who played Bonasera (more or less the perfect name for an undertaker: loosely, "Good night" indeed.).

When Tony tries to soften Uncle Junior's leadership style by citing Octavius Caesar, he draws on Frank Pentangeli's comparison to the Roman Empire *(The Godfather Part II),* especially to encourage a traitor's suicide. The assassins model their attempt on Tony—gunning him down outside his newsagent's—after the grocery-stand attack on Vito Corleone.

Surprisingly, Christopher is inaccurate when dumping a body in the Meadowlands: "Louis Brasi sleeps with the fishes." Pussy corrects him: "Luca Brasi. Luca, Christopher." Compounding the irony, Pussy will suffer the very fate he correctly cites here. The equally bulky Luca Brasi in *The Godfather* strategically pretends to switch to another Family but ends up "sleeping with the fishes." The difference is that Pussy's "flip" to the Feds is real. To Tony's conscience Pussy continues to sing as a fish.

As a result of these parallels and echoes we can often read *The Sopranos* against the context of the *Godfather* trilogy. The TV families flaunt the luxury of their homes, but none has the Old World character of the Corleones' estate. As the Sopranos' décor pales in comparison, they fall far short of their models. Where Brando's and Pacino's Don Corleone meet their colleagues and the people courting their help in a plush paneled den, even on their modern Nevada estate, Tony and his cronies meet in seedy little rooms, backstage at the Bada Bing or at ice-cream tables outside Satriole's pork store. The Corleones' life seems a Paradise Lost, to which the contemporary family/Family can aspire but not achieve.

Similarly, *The Sopranos* depicts an organization dedicated solely to its own benefit. In at least the first two *Godfather* films the Godfather provides valuable social services to the tight, helpless immigrant community. The current gangsters may value those films for they provide a value and dignity that they no longer have. After the generosity of the Brando and De Niro characters, however, Pacino's Michael turns from service to self-interest. Under Michael Corleone the Family turns from serving the underdog to promoting its own corporate interests. Even their munificent donations are self-serving.

The Sopranos extends Michael Corleone's corruption. The current gangsters don't help people unless there's something in it for them (for example AJ's Science grade boost if his teacher's car is recovered). Brando's Corleone would have settled the Teittlemans' problem (I, 3) amiably, for possible reciprocation in the future, but Tony immediately requires a continuing partnership in the motel. Tony's donations are as calculating as Michael's—and much cheaper. On the other hand, where in *The Godfather Part II* Michael hardens into a mask of unfeeling efficiency, *The Sopranos* depicts Tony's progressive humanizing, his softening and growth in self-awareness, along the lines of *The Godfather Part III* though without—so far—the father's emotional death on the murder of his daughter.

Some *Sopranos* characters may be read as variations on Coppola's. For example, Hesh recalls Robert Duval's Outsider *consiglière* and counters the more treacherous Jewish figure, Hyman Roth of *The Godfather Part II*. He also evokes the parallel world of Jewish criminals in Sergeo Leone's *Once upon a Time in America* (1984). Christopher may fancy himself another Michael but his unpredictability and temper make him like the doomed Santino. Both are shot while in their car.

So, too, the women. Livia dramatically contrasts to Vito Corleone's wife (jazz singer Morgana King), who is peripheral to the business but a figure of compelling strength, dignity, and warmth in the family, and to Michael's sister, Connie, who across the three films grows from spoiled princess into a tragic queen. Vito's wife actually prompts him to help his neighbors, establishing the base of his respect. Though Connie may ultimately grow beyond Carmela, the latter has more strength, character, and effect than the more marginal wives of the Corleone sons. No door closes on her as Michael's does on Kay (Diane Keaton). *The Sopranos* seems to redress Coppola's patriarchy by providing two such strong women, one positive, one dramatically negative.

When Carmela breaks down in I, 5, guilty for letting Tony's "evil" into her house and around her children, she presents an alternative to Kay

Corleone, who aborted a baby because she felt her marriage and Michael were "evil." Where Kay leaves Michael, marginalizing herself in her children's lives, Carmela stays to help Tony become "a good man."

In I, 5, Meadow tells Tony that her friends prefer Scorsese's *Casino* over Coppola's *Godfather*, for the abiding grace of Sharon Stone and the 1970s fashions. That may reflect the New Woman's strength of character—or each generation's need to deny its parents' values. So Meadow's shallow preference proves *The Godfather* avatar of traditional values and ideals of conduct. So, too, when Chris violates Tony's grief at Boss Jackie Aprile's death by urging war against Uncle Junior (I, 4), he confirms his insensitivity and wrong-headedness by citing *Scarface* (Brian de Palma's 1983 remake). That's the wrong Pacino movie. As we have noted, Jackie's funeral restores the dignity—and FBI surveillance—of *The Godfather*.

Similarly, Ralphie's obsession with *Gladiator* is yet one more way he proves himself outside the tradition and disrespectful. In his most Gladiatorial episode (III, 6), he hurts Georgie and kills Tracee. Also in that episode, Noah Tannenbaum takes Meadow to see *Dementia 13* (1963), Coppola's first film, and uses that film as evidence that they should distance themselves from her hypersensitive roommate Caitlin. In III, 5 Gigi agrees to "control" Mustang Sally "with extreme fuckin' prejudice," paraphrasing Coppola's *Apocalypse Now* (1979; *Redux* 2001). In these cases, the characters lack the wisdom and character that the "right" Coppola film would have provided.

Throughout *The Sopranos* the aesthetic and moral benchmark is the *Godfather* trilogy. The last words of the traitor Sal Tessio (Abe Vigoda) in *The Godfather Part II* echo through the series: "It was never personal, just business." And for all the show's satire, cynicism, violence, profanity, corruption, and despair, through the exuberant liberty of *The Sopranos,* echo the first words of the first *Godfather*, the undertaker Bonasera's "I believe in America."

Cast

Irina	Oksana Babiy
Svetlana	Alla Kliouka
Gloria	Annabella Sciorra
Lilliana Wasilius	Katalin Pota
Jackie Aprile	Michael Rispoli
Rosalie Aprile	Sharon Angela
Richie Aprile	David Proval
Jackie Aprile Jr.	Jason Carbone
Ralph Cifaretto	Joe Pantoliano
Father Phil	Paul Schulze
Neil Mink	David Margulies
Attorney Melvoin	Richard Portnow
Assemblyman Zellman	Peter Riegert
Newscaster/Anchor	Annika Pergament
Larry Boy Barese	Tony Darrow
Raymond Curto	George Loros
Jimmy Altieri	Joe Badalucco Jr.
Johnny "Sack" Sacrimoni	Vincent Curatola
Georgie	Frank Santorelli
Bobby "Baccala" Baccalieri	Stephen R. Schirripa
Mikey Palmice	Al Sapienza
Gigi Cestone	John Fiore
Vito Spatafore	Joseph Gannascoli
Patsy Parisi	Dan Grimaldi
Albert Barese	Richard Maldone
Chucky Signore	Sal Ruffino
Vin Makazian	John Heard
Dave Scatino	Robert Patrick
Dr. Bruce Cusamano	Robert Lupone
Jean Cusamano	Saundra Santiago
Skip Lipari	Louis Lombardi
Agent Harris	Matt Servitto
Agent Grasso	Frank Pando
Frank Cubitoso	Frank Pellegrino
District Attorney	John Doman

Hunter Scangarelo	Michele DeCesare
Caitlin Rucker	Ari Graynor
Noah Tannenbaum	Patrick Tully
Brendan Filone	Anthony DeSando
Matt Bevilaqua	Lillo Brancato Jr.
Sean Gismonte	Chris Tardio

SEASON ONE

Featured Performers

I,1

MRI technician	Alton Clintoni
Nils Borglund	Phil Coccioletti
Sandrine	Elaine del Valle
Restaurant owner	Giuseppe Delipiano
Nursing home director	Justine Miceli
Beppy	Joe Pucillo
Father Phil	Michael Santoro
Emil Kolar	Bruce Smolanoff
Irina	Siberia Federico

I, 2

Bonnie Di Caprio	Johann Carlo
Perrilyn	Debrah Ellen Waller
Jerome	Mike Epis
Arnaz	Yancey Arias
U.S. Attorney Braun	Tibor Feldman
Talk show host	Harvey Levin
Vincent Rizzo	Steven Randazzo
Counter person	Kate Anthony
Martin Scorsese	Anthony Caso
Joe	Victor Colicchio
Fanny	Marcia Maufrecht
Nude dancer	Desiree Kehoe
Bouncer	Michael Parr
Antjuan	Sharif Rashed
Truck driver #1	Charles Santy
Mr. Miller	David Schulman

Truck driver #2   Manny Silverio
Special K   J. D. Williams

I, 3
Shlomo Teittleman   Chuck Low
Ariel   Ned Eisenberg
Hillel   Sig Libowitz
Russian man   Sasha Nesterov
"Nurse"   Bernadette Penotti
Russian man   Slava Schoot
Woman at party   Angelica Torn
Trucker   Joseph Tudisco
Miss Marris   Jennifer Wiltsie

I, 4
Kid #2   John Arocho
Lewis Pantowski   Michael Buscemi
Jeremy Piacosta   T. J. Coluca
Salesperson   Guillermo Dias
Kid #3   Daniel Hilt
Teacher   Ray Michael Karl
Stripper   Theresa Lynn
Yo Yo Mendez   Shawn McLean

George Piacosta   Sal Petraccione
Kid #1   James Spector
Woman   Corinne Stella
Lance   Anthony Tavaglione

I, 5
Fabian Petrullio (a.k.a. Fred Peters)   Tony Ray Ross
Peters' wife   Lisa Arning
Bartender   Ross Gibby
Admissions Dean   Mark Kamine
Gas station attendant   Michael Manetta
Bowdoin Student   Keith Nobbs
Lon LeDoyenne   Luke Reilly
Lucinda   Sarah Thompson
Peters' daughter   Olivia Brynn Zaro

I, 6
Batman   Freddy Bastone
Old man   William Conn

Waiter	Maurizio Conn
Old woman	Sylvia Kauders
Mr. Capri	Salem Ludwig
Mechanic	Prianga Pieris
Sammy Grigio	Salvatore Piro
Rusty Irish	Christopher Quinn
Card player	Dave Salerno
Guy on bridge	Donn Swaby
Eggie	Sonny Zito

I, 7

Johnny Boy Soprano	Joseph Siravo,
Young Junior Soprano	Rocco Sisto
Young Livia	Laila Robins
Contractor	Paul Albe
Pearl	Shirl Bernheim
Young Janice	Madeline Blue
Young Tony	Bobby Borriello
Rideland kid	Michael Jordan
Rideland kid #2	Scott Owen Cumberbatch
Father Hagy	Anthony Fusco
Byron Barber	Rob Grippa
Rideland cop	Jason Hauser
Jared	Greg Perrelli
Wiseguy	Nick Raio
Guy	Steve Santosusso
Mr. Meskimmin	Tim Williams

I, 8

Dr. Sam Reis	Sam Coppola
Bakery counter boy	Brian Geraghty
Comedian	Ed Crasnick
Bakery customer	Joseph Gannasoli
Aida Melfi	Barbara Haas
Jeffrey Wernick	Timothy Nolen
Bandleaders	Barbara Lavalle, Robert Anthony Lavalle
Bride	Brooke Marie Procida
Joseph Melfi	Bill Richardone
Emil Kolar	Bruce Smolan

I, 9

| Bobbi Sanfillipo | Robyn Peterson |
| Coach Don Hauser | Kevin O'Rourke |

Ally Vandermeer	Cara Jedell
Deena Hauser	Candace Bailey
Heather Dante	Jaclyn John
Bebe	Donna Marie Recco
Moldonado	Steve "Inky" Ferguson
Receptionist	Nell Balaban
FBI man	Moises Belizario
Taylor	Mary Ellen Cravens
Waitress	Elaine Del Valle
Delivery boy	Brian Guzman
Capman	Mark Hartman
Waiter	Patrick Husted
Becky	Marisa Jedell
Shelley Hauser	Joyce Lynn O'Connor
Contractor	John Nacco
Soccer referee	Bill Winkler

I, 10

Massive Genius	Bokeem Woodbine
Orange J	Bryan Hicks
Richie Santini	Nick Fowler
Vito	Gregg Wattenberg
Bass player	Chris Gibson
Drummer	Ned Stroh
Squid	Bray Poor
Jack Krim	Jim Demarse
Randy Wagner	James Weston
Eric	Phil Coccioletti
Rita	Terumi Matthews
Mullethead	Dan Morse
Wendy Krim	Alexandra Neil
Manager	Ken Prymus
Gallegos	Jessy Terrero
Barb Wagner	Elizabeth Ann Townsend
Police officer	Cedric Turner

I, 11

Debbie	Karen Sillas
Kevin Bonpensiero	Giancarlo "John" Giunta
Dr. Mop'n'Glo	Doug Barron
Girl	Veronica Bero
Traffic cop	Britt Burr

Bonnie DiCaprio	Johann Carlo
Feds	Ramsey Faragallah, Matthew
	Lawler, Chance Kelly
Male anchor	Bobby Rivers
JoJo Palmice	Michele Santopietro
Detectives	Tim Kirkpatrick, Peter Bretz

I, 12

Isabella	Maria Grazia Cucinotta
John Clayborn	John Eddins
Rasheen Ray	Touche
Nurse	Karleen Germain
Boy	Johnathan Mondel
Vendor	Jack O'Connell
Newscaster	Denise Richardson
Doctor	Bittu Walia
Donnie Paduana	David Wike

I, 13

U.S. attorney	John Apreo
Janitor	George Bass
Police officer	Gene Canfield
EMT	Frank Dellarosa
Jeremy Herrera	Santiago Dorylas
Russian woman	Militza Ivanova
JoJo Palmice	Michele Santopietro
Ms. Giaculo	Candy Trabucco

SEASON TWO

II, 1

Barbara Giglione	Nicole Burdette
Manager	John Billeci
Proctor	Darrell Carey
Ernest Wu	Dan Chen
Dr. D'Alessio	Robert Cicchini
Caller #2	Mark Fish
Samantha Martin	Karen Giordano
Peter McClure	Bryan Greenberg
Philly Parisi	Dan Grimaldi
Caller #3	Philipp Kaner

Sylvia — Katrina Lantz
Caller #1 — Wayne W. Pretlow
Kevin — Kevin Sussman
Lee — Robert Thomas
Tom Giglione — Ed Vassallo
Tom Amberson — Terence Patrick Winter

II, 2

Rev. James Sr. — Bill Cobbs
Rev. James Jr. — Gregalan Williams
Jack Massarone — Robert Desiderio
Protesters — Michael Broughton, Derrick Simmons, Jay Lynch, David Lomax, Ron Van Clief, Herb Kerr
Truck driver — James Collins
Arlene Riley — Catherine Dent
Therapist — Elizabeth Flax
Judge Greenspan — Sam Gray
Doctor — Timothy Huang
Duty nurse — Tertia Lynch
Ralph Georgio — John Mariano
Old guy — Tony Rigo
Surgical nurse — Laurine Towler
Nurse's aide — Kellie Turner
Funeral guest — Beatrice Winde

II, 3

Dr. Schreck — Matthew Sussman
Beansie Gaeta — Paul Herman
Beansie's mother — Antonette Schwartberg
Gia Gaeta — Donna Smythe
Miriam — Diana Agostini
Yoga instructor — Getchie Argetsinger
Nancy — Leslie Beatty
Comedian — Ed Crasnick
Nurse — Catrina Ganey
Partygoer — Marc Freeman Hamm
Joint copper — Linda Mann
Policeman — Joe Pacheo
Joey — Charles Sammarco
Big Frank — Mike "Scuch" Squicciarini
Hospital patient — Deirdre Sullivan
Pizza kid — Craig Wojcik

II, 4

Annalisa	Sofia Milos
Zi Vittorio	Vittorio Duse
Jimmie Bones	Mike Memphis
Partner	Jay Lynch
Nurse	Emme Shaw
Raffaelle	Ciro Maggio
Sontag family	Danton Stone, Melissa Weil, Jason Fuchs, Jessica Peters
Antonio	Gano Grills
Waiter	Anthony Allesandro
Host	Frank Caero
Manager	Ricardo Zeno
Mother	Pina Cutolo
Kid	Fausto Amato
Camillo	Raffaelle Giulivo
Nino	Antonio Lubrano
Pino	Guido Palliggiano
Prostitute	Alida Tarallo
Kid	Alex Toma
Tanno	Giuseppe Zeno
Hotel manager	Ricardo Zinna

II, 5

Dahlia	Linda Emond
Dominic	Stephen Payne
Rosie	Lydia Gaston
Russian man	Sasha Nesterov
Russian woman	Elena Antonenko
Cynthia	Oni Faida Lampley
Acting student	Scott Lucy
Omar	Ajau Naida
Mitch	Robert Prescott
Brenda	Phyllis Somerville

II, 6

Barbara Giglione	Nicole Burdette
Eric Scatino	John Hensley
Christine Scatino	Maureen Redanty
Fishman	Felix Solis
Sunshine	Paul Mazursky
Frank Sinatra Jr.	Himself
Dr. Fried	Lewis Stadlen

College rep	Adam Alexi-Malle
Gudren	Angela Covington
Mrs. Gaetano	Barbara Gulan
Hooker	LaTayna Hall
Hillel	Sig Libowitz
Cop	P. J. Brown
Priest	David McCann
Dealer	Carmine Sirico
Tim Giglione	Ed Vassallo

II, 7

Jon Favreau	Himself
Sandra Bernhard	Herself
Janeane Garofalo	Herself
Amy	Alicia Witt
Security guard	Arthur Barnes
Hotel clerk	Stephen Bienskie
Assistant director	John Devlin
Gregory Moltisanti	Dominic Fumusa
UTA receptionist	Andersen Gabrych
Hotel manager	Bryan Matzkow
Michele Foreman	Andrea Maulella
Bellman	Jason Minter
Matt Bonpensiero	Steve Porcelli
Stace	Elizabeth Reaser
Blaine Richardson	Asa Somers

II, 8

Joan Cusamano (and Jean)	Saundra Santiago
Bryan Spatafore	Vinnie Orofino
Therapist	Susan Blackwell
Secretary	Joseph Carino
Donny K.	Raymond Franza
Liz La Cerva	Patty McCormack
Stasiu	Marek Przystup
Gaetano Giarizzo	Stelio Savante
Gia Gaeta	Donna Smythe

II, 9

Jimmy	Brian Auguiar
Doctor	Seth Barrish
Detectives	Michael Cannis, James Sioutis

Daniel King	Tom Cappadona
Joanne Moltisanti	Nancy Cassaro
Quickie G	Scottie Epstein
Kevin Culler	John Christopher Jones
Father Felix	Peter McRobbie
Michelle	Judy Reyes
Felicia Anne	Lisa Valens
Nurses	Gameela Wright, Denise Burse

II, 10

Christine Scatino	Marisa Redanty
Beansie Gaeta	Paul Herman
Frank Cippolina	Mike Squicciarini
Vic Musto	Joe Penny
Detective Giardina	Vince Viverito
Larry Arthur	Chuck Montgomery
Carole Arthur	Molly Regan
Detective Ramos	Antone Pagan
Ramone	Adrian Martinez
Fran	Olga Merediz
Karen	Janice Dardaris
Mother	Susan Campanero
Boy	Mitch Holleman

II, 11

Catherine	Mary Louise Wilson
Dr. Schreck	Matthew Sussman
Dick Barone	Joe Lisi
Helen Barone	Patricia Marand
Connie	Jennifer Albano
Bobby	Vito Antuofurmo Sr.
Tracy	Sabine Singh
Maître d'	James Biberi
Woman smoker	Ilene Kristen
Man	George Xhilone
Agent Marquez	Gary Perez
Michael McLuhan	Ron Lee Jones
Sanitation worker	Louis Petraglia
Siraj	Remy K. Selma
Nurses	Janet Bushor, Lesli Deniston
Orderly	Robert McKay
ER Doctor	Amy Hart Redford

Dr Baumgartner	Roy Thinnes
Tom Amberson	Terry Winter
Guests	Frank Adonis, Alan Levine, Paul Borghese, Russ Brunelli
Chuckie	Gary Lamadore

II, 12

Victor Musto	Joe Penny
Dick Barone	Joe Lisi
Richie Aprile Jr.	Andy Blankenbuehler
Ramone	Adrian Martinez

II, 13

Annalisa	Sofia Milos
Barbara Giglione	Nicole Burdette
Quintina	Barbara Andres
Flight attendant	David Anzuelo
Meadow's friend	Kathleen Fasolino
Airport guard	Ray Garvey
Vice Principal	David Healy
Hillel	Sig Libowitz
Sundeep	Ajay Mehta
Indian man	Jay Palit

SEASON THREE

III, 1

Agent Marquez	Gary Perez
Agent Tancredi	Neal Jones
Agent Jongsma	Jay Christanson
Agent Malatesta	Colleen Werthmann
Agent Theophilus	Dennis Gagomiros
Brigid	Erica Leerhsen
Jason	Etan Maiti
Rob	Matthew Breiner
Xavier	Tommy Savas
Colin	Ian Group
Egon Kosma	Mark Karafin
SET	Anthony Indelicato, Murphy Guyer
Judge Lapper	Jesse Doran

Coach Goodwin — David Mogentale
SET Lineman — Brian Smyj
FBI agent — David Raymond Wagner
Ed Restuccia — Robert Bogue
Stasiu — Albert Makhstier
Son — Anthony Dimaria

III, 2

Reverend James — Gregalan Williams
Barbara Giglione — Nicole Burdette
Cozzerelli — Ralph Lucarelli
Father Felix — Peter McRobbie
Mr. Zachary — Tim Gallin
Fanny — Marcia Haufrecht
Bobby Zanone — Vito Antuofurmo Sr.
Young man — Dimitri de Fresco
2 to 5/7 to 9 — Marie Donato
Tom Giglione — Ed Vassallo
FBI techs — Gary Evans, Carlos Lopez
FBI agent — Michael Strano
Donny K. — Raymond Franza

III, 3

Johnny-Boy Soprano — Joseph Siravo
Junior Soprano — Rocco Sisto
Young Livia — Laila Robins
Dino Zerilli — Andrew Davoli
Benny Fazio — Max Casella
Carmine Lupertazzi — Tony Lip
Security guard — Peter Byrne
Punked out co-ed — Megan Curry
Pizza customers — Steve Grillo, Jessica Ripton
Roy DelGuercio — Kevin Janicelli
Male student — Mario Lavanderia
Bill Owens — Steve Mellor
Coach Goodwin — David Mogentale
Football dad — Peter Napoliello
George Piocosta — Sal Petraccione
Operators — Frank Savino, Paul Reggio
Junkie — Johnny Spanish
Warren Dupree — Brian Anthony Wilson
Francis Satriale — Lou Bonacki

Young Tony — Marka Damiano II
Young Janice — Juliet Fox
Young Barbara — Elxis McLaren

III, 4

Arouk Abboubi — Shaun Toub
Ginny Sack — Denise Borino
FBI techs — Gary Evans, Glenn Kessler
Edwina Fowley — Traci Godfrey
Clerk — Zabryna Guevara
ER doctor — Steven Kunken
Detective Piersol — Jill Marie Lawrence
Jesus Rossi — Mario Polit
News reporter — Bobby Rivers
Igor Parnasky — Igor Zhivotovsky

III, 5

Officer Wilmore — Charles S. Dutton
Bobby "Baccala" Sr. — Burt Young
Mustang Sally — Brian Tarantina
Bryan Spatafore — Vinnie Orofino
2 to 5/7 to 9 — Marie Donato
FBI techs — Gary Evans, Glenn Kesler
Tina — Vanessa Ferlito
Receptionist — Sheila Gibbs
Carlos — Michael Martochio
Woman — Sheelagh Tellerday
Petey — Michael Variano
Manager — Erik Weiner
Eugene Pontecorvo — Robert Funaro

III, 6

Tracee — Ariel Kelly
Georgie — Frank Santorelli
Len Tannenbaum — Michael Garfield
Waiter — Daniel Booth
Homeless woman — Yvette Mercedes
Police officer — Richard Verdino
Mandee — Michette Ardente
Debbie — Kelly Kole
Strippers — Luiza Liccini, Marie Athanasiou
Jeff — Kenneth Franquiz

III, 7

Dr. John Kennedy	Sam McMurray
Dean Ross	Frank Wood
Dr. Krakower	Sully Boyar
Dr. Laurens	Ilene Landress
Dr. Mehta	Ismail Bashey
Paxton	Peter Davies
FBI man	John Fiske
Chooch	John Freudiger
Miles	Lorenzo Gregorio
RN Collins	Tony Hale
Dr. Enloe	Zachary Knower
Anesthesiologist	James Shanklin

III, 8

Dino Zerilli	Andrew Davoli
Aaron Arkaway	Turk Pipkin
Rev. James	Gregalan Williams
Little Paulie Germani	Carl Capotorto
Benny Fazio	Max Casella
Donny K	Raymond Franza
Caterina Cella	Annie Assante
Ginny Sack	Denise Borino
Epsilon Zet	Kieran Campion
Joe	William DaRuffa
Dov Ginsberg	Michael Hogan
Lisa Cestone	Margo Singaliese
Tracee	Ariel Kiley
Eugene Pontecorvo	Robert Funaro
Frat boys	Kieran Campion, R. J. Reed

III, 9

Dino Zerilli	Andrew Davoli
Benny Fazio	Max Casella
Carlo Renzi	Louis Crugnali
Aaron Arkaway	Turk Pipkin
Little Joe	Joe Bacino
Guiseppe	Frank Bongiorno
Cops	Charles Trucillo, David Warshofsky
Matush	Emad Tarabay
Principal Cincotta	Daniel Oreskes

Egon Kosma	Mark Karafin
Father Nicolai	Bill Kocis
Rob	Matthew Breiner
Colin	Ian Group
Girl	Cyndi Ramirez
Xavier	Tommy Savas
Rocco DeTrolleo	Richard Petrocelli
Club kid	Gregory Russell Cook
Bouncer	Jay Boryea
Janitor	David Ross
Miami Relatives	Scout: Ashen Keilyn, Nigel Rawles, Rimas Remeza, David Weintraub

III, 10

Stava Malevsky	Frank Ciornei
Valery	Vitali Baganov
Dancer	Jana Januskova
Agron	Alik Sakharov
Igor Parnasky	Igor Zhivotovsky
Aaron Arkaway	Turk Pipkin
Beppy	Joe Pucillo
Kevin Bonpensiero	Dominic Charles Carboni
Young Jackie Jr.	Matt Cerbone
Mother	Domenica Galati
Little boy	Tyler Gubizio
Little girl	Loulou Katz
Debbie	Kelly Madison Kole
Second dancer	Rosie Chavolino
Cop	Larry Clark
Store employee	Capathia Jenkins
EMT	Diego Lopez
Dino Zerilli	Andrew Davoli
Man	Barry Shurchin
Waitress	Sian Heder
Donna	Randi Newton
Cook	Tony Rhune

III, 11

Valery	Vitali Baganov
Stava Malevsky	Frank Ciornei
Nurse	Crystal Fox

Rita	Dayna Gizzo
Ambujam	Deepa Purohit
Ilana	Anya Shetler

III, 12

Dino Zerilli	Andrew Davoli
Father Obosi	Isaac De Bankole
Sunshine	Paul Mazursky
Dr. Fried	Lewis Stadlen
Carlo Renzi	Louis Crugnali
Matush	Emad Tarabay
Dr. Rotelli	Victor Truro
P.A.	Joanie Ellen
Woman in car	Anna Mastrionni
Martin	Michael Lee Patterson
Service manager	Stephen Peabody
Roy Del Guerico	Kevin Janicelli
Cholos	Anthony Zayas, Freddy Martinez, Cesar Deleon
Card players	Paul Cicero, Jack Lotz

III, 13

Major Zwingli	Tobin Bell
Agent Deborah Cicerone	Fairuza Balk
FBI agent	Norman Maxwell
Detective Filemon Francis	Marc Damon Johnson
Ginny Sack	Denise Borino
Mackenzie Trucillo	Danielle Cautela
Kelli Aprile	Melissa Marsala
Marie	Patricia Mauceri
Nucci	Francis Esemplaire
Cadet Delaunay	Ryan Homchick
Egon Kosma	Mark Karafin
Principal Cincotta	Daniel Oreskes
Mrs. Giaculo	Candy Trabucco
Father L'Oiseau	Dick Latessa
Ray Ray	Michael Kenneth Williams
Saleswoman	Monique Lola Berkley
Leena	Lekel Russell
Little Bruce	Geoff Wigdor
2 to 5/7 to 9	Marie Donato

Wiseguy	Phil Larocco
Cozzarelli	Ralph Lucarelli
Junior's friend	Dino Palermo
Dr. Fried	Lewis Stadlen
Eugene Pontecorvo	Robert Funaro

Bibliography

Holden, Stephen, ed. *The New York Times on "The Sopranos,"* ibooks. New York, 2001.

Rucker, Allen. *The Sopranos: A Family History.* Channel 4 Books. Macmillan, London, 2000; Updated New American Library, 2001.

Video and DVD sets of the first two seasons are available from video outlets everywhere and from the HBO website.

Select Web Sites

www.hbo.com/sopranos
www.hbo.com/sopranos/wernick
www.hbo.com/sopranos/community
www.hbo.com/sopranos/community/cookbook
www.hbo.com/store
www3.simpatico.ca.silver_tongue_devil/thesopranos.html
www.mobstory.com
www.sopranoland.com
www.NJ.com/sopranos
www.angelfire.com/ga2/sopranos
www.Clubs.gist.com/tvclubs (Recommended for episode summaries, cast lists, music)
www.members.tripod.com/hbo/sopranos
www.geocities.com/Hollywood/Boulevard/8076/sring.html
www.imar.com/promote/index.jsp?medid=18&aci=927 (For a three-hour Sopranos tour of New Jersey)

Of Interest from Continuum

Donald Bogle

Toms, Coons, Mulattoes, Mammies, and Bucks
An Interpretive History of Blacks in American Films
Fourth Edition

"Mr. Bogle continues to be our most noted black-cinema historian."
– SPIKE LEE

482 pages $22.95 paperback

Peter Bondanella

Italian Cinema
From Neorealism to the Present
Third Edition

"Extremely interesting and stimulating." – BERNARDO BERTOLUCCI

560 pages $26.95 paperback

Will Brooker

Batman Unmasked
Analyzing a Cultural Icon

"Brooker cuts through the mumbo jumbo to deliver incisive analysis and very sharp reporting." – *Entertainment Weekly*

"Brooker offers a deliciously subversive commentary on America."
– *Albuquerque Journal*

368 pages $19.95 paperback

Emanuel Levy

Oscar Fever
The History and Politics of the Academy Awards

"Levy appears to know everything worth knowing about the Oscars."
– *Washington Post Book World*

384 pages $19.95 paperback

Robert Emmet Long
Broadway, the Golden Years
Jerome Robbins and the Great Choreographer-Directors

"A marvelously entertaining and exuberant history." – *Publishers Weekly*

312 pages $35.00 hardcover

Alison McMahan

Alice Guy Blaché
Cinematic Visionary

The life story of the world's first woman filmmaker.

368 pages $35.00 hardcover

Available at your bookstore or from Continuum International
www.continuumbooks.com 1–800-561–7704